BODY & SOUL

Caitlin Press Inc.
8100 Alderwood Road, Halfmoon Bay, BC VON 1Y1
www.caitlin-press.com

Text design by Shed Simas / Onça Design
Front cover design by Vici Johnstone
Cover art by Carolina Echeverria, carolinaecheverria.ca
Printed in Canada

Caitlin Press Inc. acknowledges financial support from the Government of Canada and the Canada Council for the Arts, and the Province of British Columbia through the British Columbia Arts Council and the Book Publisher's Tax Credit.

Library and Archives Canada Cataloguing in Publication

Body & soul : stories for skeptics and seekers / edited by Susan Scott.

ISBN 978-1-987915-93-8 (softcover)

1. Spirituality. I. Scott, Susan, editor II. Title: Body and soul.

BL624.B63 2019   204   C2018-905968-0

Body & Soul

STORIES FOR SKEPTICS AND SEEKERS

Edited by Susan Scott

Contents

Wake Up: A Foreword

ALISON PICK

Despite the dark nights of December, despite Times Square, despite the colourful streamers and flutes of champagne, September always feels like the New Year to me. As a child, September meant going back to school, and going back to school meant new writing supplies. Fat red pencils, three-ring binders, Hilroy notebooks in the various pastel shades of the rainbow were my celebration. Later, a pot of ink and a fancy fountain pen. The time to start a new story and the earthy, concrete tools required to do so.

My birthday also falls in the first week of September. This meant it was often forgotten by my classmates. The teacher, who was just getting her bearings after the summer that seemed to have lasted—am I wrong?—for years, forgot too. Still, despite being passed by in terms of attention, I knew in my heart that the New Year, *my* New Year, was beginning.

Was it the first week of school I found out I was half Jewish? It was grade six, I think, and Jordan Ross, who I had a crippling crush on, had heard a rumour from Stephen Richardson, who had heard it from his mother, Annette. Annette recognized Pick as a common Czech Jewish surname, in the same way Smith or Jones is common among WASPs. *No*, I said to Jordan, and then to Stephen, and then to anyone who would listen. No, my father wasn't Jewish. I had been raised Christian, with the trauma of the Holocaust in my family paved over like an ancient burial ground. I knew, without ever having been told, to deny what felt like an accusation. But somewhere deep in my body a sound had begun, quiet at first but increasing in urgency. Perhaps it was the sound of the shofar, the great curled ram's horn that blasts us open each Jewish New Year. Wake up! it calls.

The shofar is blown on Rosh Hashanah, as the summer is ending and the edges of the leaves are crimping red. All through the Days of Awe, until Yom Kippur eight days later, we are asked to take stock. To ask forgiveness—of God, of each other and of ourselves—and to think about how we will make the New Year different. To get out our fat red pencils and our gummy pink erasers and begin to draft the story of the weeks and months to come.

September, the Jewish New Year, the month I was born, has also always been the birthday of my books. Publication has many joys, but it also signals an end—the end of the process of writing itself. The end of those early morning hours, rising in darkness, at my desk at 5:00 a.m. in the winter night, with a candle, taking dictation. I experience writing as a deep kind of listening. I ask frequently for guidance. I write by hand in a notebook, each entry concluded with the Hebrew word *Amein*. I am aware, of course, that others might find this strange, but I am ridiculously, unrelentingly grateful for the hours of quiet concentration that feel so close to prayer. Letting go of them is always hard, and this year I find myself especially reluctant. Just a few months ago I was engaged in the act of creation. Now, my book is out in the world. It is supposed to feel good, but it feels awful. Vulnerable. I hate the ego roller coaster of waiting for reviews to come in. And the book, which I love, which I gave my whole life to, has not landed on any of the prize short lists. It has not been seen by the big rolling eye of the world. It has not been Chosen.

I feel shame. I feel sadness. I feel, again, like my birthday has been passed by in the classroom. The world is full of mystery, however. Did I tell you what happened with Annette, the person—the Czech Jew—who first saw me for who I really am? A DNA test revealed that she is a distant relative. A far cousin of my father's. Wake up! calls the shofar. Now, thirty years after being called out, I am a practising Jew. I spend the High Holidays with Annette and her family, which includes my own family. My book has failed, by some measures at least, but I see how, on every level, my New Year is beginning.

For a writer, of course, real solace comes from the act of writing itself. Poet Mary Oliver describes this revelation this way: "I saw the difference between doing nothing, and doing a little, and the redemptive act of true effort. Reading, then writing, then desiring to write well, shaped in me the most joyful of circumstances—a passion for work."

What kind of effort? *Redemptive* effort. In our deepest work—the kind that, if we are lucky, sometimes feels like prayer—we are redeemed, not from sin but from the terrible wheel of the ego. We are released into a sacred world that feels lavish and abundant and filled with mystery.

It is *this* world that shines through in the essays in this marvellous collection. They are thoughtful, gorgeous, honest, sometimes irreverent. The authors have birthed them into their own Septembers. Their shofars are sounding. Wake up! And to you, the lucky reader: Wake up! There are fat red pencils. There are blank notebooks. There are invitations to begin again, like so many balloons floating up through the dark sky on the first night of the New Year.

Introduction

Body & Soul opens with a Sikh who leaves her native England to travel the world in search of the missing piece that will make her whole. The collection closes with a rookie birder's epiphany on the wind-lashed shore of Lake Ontario. These accounts bookend deeply personal stories that turn on longing and belonging, on fear, grief, wonder, revelation, doubt, sex, gender, power, love and calls to action. These voices from the margins—writers and poets who identify variously as immigrants, as racialized, as LGBTQ, as rooted in communities that fall outside the mainstream—have agreed to take a risk and make something deeply private, public. They have committed to the question: How to divulge intimate experiences (good, bad or ugly) with spirituality, faith, tradition, ceremony, practice or religion?

That "how" is important because that list comes with a lot of baggage.

The word "spirituality," for instance, is commonplace now to signal the search for meaning—what some call the sacred—beyond the confines of a faith or organized religion. Trouble is, that's a selective reading of the words. We can look to definitions for some guidance, but the scholars' definitions seldom satisfy practitioners, and vice versa.

Try it: choose one word from that list, and see how it colours a life story—yours, mine, a passing stranger's. Where does that word place a person? Which world view is implied? Whose cultural heritage is being honoured, and whose diminished or erased? Now try this: ask yourself who will understand the words you choose the exact same way as you.

We all make assumptions that exclude unwittingly. Not everyone is steeped in the Quran or the Kabbalah, or has a clue why Eve made history when she bit into that apple. Which among us knows the deep history of this land, let alone its sacred stories coast to coast to coast? This selective knowledge makes it hard to talk about the fullness of a life. Where there is no common language or heritage—or where there is a mash-up—it's not clear how much others will even understand.

So, let's ask this question outright: are there creative ways to talk about the fullness of our lives without sermonizing, sentimentalizing or finger pointing?

Yes, I think there are.

Body & Soul is an attempt at creating an open, inclusive space for readers who are unfamiliar with everything from chi kung and Hindu pilgrimage to icons and ayahuasca—but even fans of spiritual memoir will find fresh combinations here, from clowns + mosques + mothering to uterus + shaman.

Welcome, skeptics and seekers. This book is for you.

As an educator, I urge risk taking. Without risks, there is no transformation. I urge people to document their experience in ways that balance the embodied, day-to-day with the wild, philosophical, transcendent. As the nonfiction editor at *The New Quarterly* (TNQ), I look for works steeped in empathy and candour, works that can't be written off as flaky. In workshops, I urge people to push the limits of creative nonfiction, then release their stories to the world. I do this not just because these intimate stories deserve a hearing but because we in the West stand at a critical juncture—society facing fresh assaults on multiculturalism, the humanities, public discourse, on democracy itself. The stakes could not be higher if we want an open, just society. If we do, then we need to grapple not just with abstract issues but with people's needs—with the burdens people carry. That means taking seriously the histories, myths, rituals, practices, conventions and traditions that people are trying to preserve, critique, merge, flee or reinvent.

We can do this. There are ways.

In an era of deep dividedness, we can begin a dialogue by exchanging stories like those gathered here—earthy, generous, transgressive stories that make way for other stories.

Think of this book as a starting point. As permission to claim your own experience and to do so without fear of being silenced, corrected or, God forbid, converted.

And if you don't feel the need to speak, may these stories grant you space to question and observe, to look and listen, to support others who are speaking up. "Be a lamp," Rumi says, "or a lifeboat, or a ladder."

If we can grant one another space, learning from one another without judgment, we'll have opened new vistas of truth and understanding. We'll have come home to ourselves, to something greater than ourselves. To some place deeply human.

Susan Scott
Waterloo, Ontario
December 2018

Unfinished Journey

JAGTAR KAUR ATWAL

I was born a Sikh at the local hospital in Derby, England. I was that girl who hated going to the gurdwara. Once a month I'd tell Mum I was on my period, even if it didn't fall on a Sunday, and I'd get to stay at home. When I had to go, I'd sit on the patterned rugs surrounded by strangers, watching the Granthi with his long white beard and yellow turban reading from the Sri Guru Granth Sahib and pretending I understood what he was reading. I sat cross-legged behind Mum so she couldn't see me, with my elbow resting on my knee and hand cradling my head as my finger followed the curly red and gold patterns on the rug. I'd bite my lip or pinch my thigh to stop myself from crying for being forced to do one more thing I didn't want to do.

During the morning assembly at school I was introduced to another kind of religion. My classmates and I would shuffle through the double doors into the grey auditorium, where two teachers standing at the doors handed out plain white booklets before we quietly took our seats. The headmistress would ask us to stand and turn to the Lord's Prayer. The rustling of crisp white pages echoed around the room as we followed her lead and began to recite the prayer in unison. Our morning sessions ended with singing "Kum Ba Ya" and "Morning Has Broken."

I visited many Christian churches not to find God but because of my love for old buildings and the history that lingered in the bricks. I'd close my eyes and lay my hand on the cold stones and try to go back hundreds of years and imagine labourers laying the stones. The older I got, the less I attended Sikh services. In the last twelve years, I've been to the gurdwara twice. Once for my dad's funeral in Derby and the other time, on Christmas Eve, when I travelled to India with Mum and visited the Golden Temple in the city of Amritsar, Punjab.

The temple was a five-hour drive from our ancestral home in Goriyar, Punjab, from bumpy, dusty roads to freshly laid motorways. We'd pass men pulling their cows, cars driving in the wrong direction and monkeys sitting by the edge hoping to be fed by strangers. My senses were overloaded in Amritsar, a busy city that seemed chaotic to my Western eyes. I'd press my palms against my ears to soften the noise of blasting horns and close my eyes to shield them from the crowded streets.

Relief came when I could see the golden globes of the temple against the deep blue sky. This gurdwara is the holiest shrine for Sikhs, with thousands of visitors every day, and the temple with the largest free kitchen in the world. The temple itself is surrounded by a deep moat, where men, women and children bathe in the water for purification and where catfish mouths break the surface of the water to grab food before diving back into the darkness.

I never told my family about my turn to Christianity, although here it didn't matter which god I believed in because in Sikhism all are welcomed into the gurdwara in the belief that there are many ways to heaven. I suppose I didn't tell Mum because I wasn't sure how she would react. I told myself it didn't matter if the family didn't know.

. . .

I wasn't looking for Jesus when he turned up in my life after I became friends with Katie. She and I met at the local gym in 2009. We worked out together and shared our life experiences, and one day she told me she was a Christian. She talked a lot about Jesus and sin and how He was the only way to Heaven. I already felt like I was in Hell. I needed a friend who could love me uncon- ditionally and guide me through my life. In my thirties I'd travelled the world looking for the missing piece—the piece that would make me feel whole. After a year of traipsing by foot, car, van, chicken bus, train, plane, horse, elephant, camel, boat and canoe, I returned home with a battered backpack, photographs and memories. What did I have to lose, trying church? Maybe it was Jesus who could fill the emptiness.

My first visit to the church service wasn't what I had expected. Instead of a choir swaying to hymns, there were guitars and drums with a lead singer belting out Christian tunes as if they were pop songs. There were cushy theatre chairs with drink holders, so not the stiff wooden pews I had pictured.

After a couple of months of this, I decided to talk to Katie about a part of me I found difficult to share. I decided to tell her I was gay. I knew she'd shrug her shoulders and say, "So what," and that I'd be embarrassed for making a big deal about it, so I aimed for one evening when we were working out.

I stopped to rest from training, to watch the flat screen hanging from the ceiling. Oprah was interviewing two gay men when Katie also stopped to watch. "It's a sin," she said. "God didn't make Adam and Steve. It's disgusting."

I turned away to pretend to start my workout before she saw my cheeks turn red.

My friendship with Katie fizzled out, but I still went to church. It was a place where I'd made friends. Every Sunday I'd wait for them at the grey, round table with my coffee, the floor-to-ceiling windows spreading light in the foyer, and I'd watch while a handful of black and brown faces stood smiling, dressed in their smart church clothes.

The preacher told jokes during sermons. When I first saw the preacher, I half expected him to be behind the pulpit, shouting out sermons with frantic urgency, like the evangelicals on television with their cheesy white smiles and expensive suits paid for by donations. This preacher walked around the stage in faded jeans, shirt hanging out, his hair down past his shoulders. Sometimes he'd flick it like a girl.

The first time I heard the preacher talk about homosexuality, I sat in my comfy seat shrinking, my stomach turning like a Ferris wheel and my heart beating loudly in my ears. I couldn't be gay and Christian. I would have to choose. If I wanted to be saved, then I had to overcome my desire to have a relationship with another woman. I was so desperate to belong and feel normal that I decided I would be faithful to God even if it meant having to lie to myself and pretend I was straight to all my Christian friends.

I got busy changing my life.

I didn't want to be reminded about being gay so I stopped participating in softball, a lesbian league, and left my Toronto gay friends behind. I moved out of the city to the suburbs and rented a room from my straight Christian married friend.

. . .

In June 2012 the headaches started. It was as if my head was in a metal vise and someone was turning the handle, slowly. I couldn't sleep. I spent most nights crying from the pain. Loud noises and bright lights would make me dizzy, and I'd want to throw up.

The doctor would tell me *It's stress* and my Christian friends would tell me *Pray to God for guidance*. I started surfing the Web for a painless way to die and listing the things I needed to do, making a will, cleaning house, giving away my books, sending my house deeds to my sister. On and on it went. The fear and pain drove me finally to a therapist, a small woman with curly hair. She reminded me of Brian May from Queen.

"What brings you here?" she asked.

"I can't stop thinking about suicide."

My therapist recommended meditation. I'd roll my eyes and say, "Just in case you missed it, I rolled my eyes." She laughed, but it didn't stop her from suggesting meditation every session.

I had meditated twice in my life. The first time, in my twenties, my work colleague, Raj, dragged me to a Buddhist meeting. We walked into a crowded hall and all I wanted to do was shake Raj off and leave the room, but he pulled me along as he hugged his friends. We sat on high-back chairs with padded seats. A bell rang and silence fell, and as the strangers began to sit, it was as if the thirty or so people had up and left the room. In harmony the group began to chant *Nam myoho renge kyo* over and over and over again. I kept my mouth closed and looked around at closed eyes and moving lips.

I was pissed at Raj for bringing me, and I was scared of what felt like a cult.

But the vibrations of the chanting captured me. I shut out the bright light and began to chant with the others. The blood in my veins moved slowly. I couldn't feel the hard spindles against my back or the cushion under my bum.

The air cradled me as I floated above the chair.

The second time I meditated was in my thirties, when I was travelling around the world. In Central America I ended up in San Marcos La Laguna, Guatemala, a small village at the base of a mountain and a boat ride away from the main town, Panajachel. I was staying at the outskirts of the village at a spiritual retreat. I slept in a simple hut made from stone, with just a bed, and at night I could see the stars through a square cut in the wall. I stayed there for four weeks, exploring the forest of thick vegetation, the trails stamped into the ground by bare feet. Sometimes I just sat on the docks, feet cooling in the lake.

I met Natalie, a reiki master, a Polish woman in her thirties with black hair and green eyes, who lived by the lake, high up on the mountain. Her cabin had a wraparound porch and stripey hammock. Natalie became my teacher as I studied reiki.

Before the second stage of reiki I had to first go through a ritual. The day of my initiation, it had been raining hard all morning, the courtyard empty, yet by the afternoon there was little sign that it had rained. The leaves were dry but the soil still moist and the classroom muggy. I sat with the reiki group on the floor, legs crossed, our wrists resting on our knees, palms facing the heavens. Natalie walked around us, on the old creaky floorboards. Her soothing voice was hypnotizing, with every word she seemed far away as she described an imaginary forest. She led us to the outskirts of this forest in our minds. "Walk into the forest," she said, and the grass beneath my bare feet tickled my soles. Then she said, "You've reached the centre, look around for your key." I saw a dark rusty key sitting against the fresh green grass. "Pick it up," she said.

In my mind's eye I watched myself touch the key, and as I held the key I felt pressure on the top of my head spreading until it covered my crown, and as it did my crown began to peel, like a flower opening in the morning. A pillar of light rushed in and travelled inside my body, the heat warming my palms.

.   .   .

The night of April 19, 2013, I could hear nurses walking up and down the corridor, their rubber soles squeaking on the linoleum floor. They were whispering. My bedroom door slightly open, the corridor light shone on the large wall clock. I lay in the hospital bed facing the clock, watching the second hand glide over the numbers. It was after midnight, seven hours before I would be wheeled into surgery to have a piece of skull removed.

I didn't think of God that night. I hadn't thought of God in a loving way in a long time. I had begun to believe religion was just another way of controlling people, making us believe we couldn't do anything without him. I was never going to be good enough as long as I was gay and I'd grown tired of punishing myself, pretending to be straight.

In the hospital bed, my brain infected with lesions, I lay curled up like a baby in its mother's womb. I watched the clock, hypnotized by the second hand.

I call what happened next my awakening.

A thought drifted into my mind like a feather falling gently. It said, "You're searching for you."

I sobbed into the pillow. That night I let go of everything my body had been holding on to. I cried in relief. I knew my search for belonging had finally come to an end.

. . .

At home, I recovered from surgery but my mind wouldn't rest. I couldn't stop thinking about my awakening in the hospital bed and I didn't know where to start. I thought of my therapist's words, and decided maybe meditation would calm me. I began to practise on a regular basis. One afternoon I leaned my head against the cream sofa and pressed my back against the soft pillows. I let my arms fall to the side and as I closed my eyes, the noise of the traffic died away. A purple cloud appeared out of the darkness. In my mind, I watched the cloud shifting and changing shapes as a warm glow settled between my breasts.

My eyes flickered open and stung as they adjusted to the light. I pulled my head forward and watched my reflection on the black television screen, as a sensation circled below my belly button. I heard my inner voice whisper, *Shame and unworthiness.*

My body slowly trembled as I began to understand what my inner voice was telling me. My whole life had been filled with shame and unworthiness, everything I had touched, every thought, every action, every word had been based on shame and unworthiness.

I was in shock.

I cried when I lay in bed.

I cried when I had a shower.

I cried when I ate.

I cried at work.

I cried in the car.
I grieved for "me" for a year.

.   .   .

I don't believe in a god that lives in the sky. I'm learning to believe in me rather than a deity. I believe in closing my eyes and searching inward. I believe that we are all connected. I believe in feeling free so we can grow, evolve and learn to welcome all good things that come.

In a Canoe, Chasing My Métis Grandmother

CARLEIGH BAKER

1.

My Grandma Carrière's family comes from Manitoba, near St. Boniface, the traditional territory of Anishinaabeg, Cree, Oji-Cree, Dakota and Dene peoples and the homeland of the Métis Nation. This is Treaty One territory. My Métis family is from an area referred to by the European settlers as the Red River colony. Many of the Carrières moved to British Columbia when my grandma was a girl. I was born and raised on the unceded territory of the Stó:lō people. I now live as a guest on the traditional, ancestral, unceded territories of the Musqueam, Squamish and Tsleil-Waututh peoples.

Positionality is important, so let's get something out of the way right now. I didn't grow up with knowledge of my Métis ancestry. This is not going to be a story about how I magically connected with my indigeneity, because that magic doesn't exist. I was, and still am, an outsider. Because both my mother's settler (Icelandic) and father's (Cree-Métis) families were marked by alcoholism, abuse and occasionally violence, my parents made the difficult decision to separate from family. It didn't happen all at once; my childhood was a series of negotiations, reconciliations and breaks with extended family members in various states of mental health. When things were going well, I had grandmothers. Most of the time, my mother, father, sister and I were like a family on a deserted island, trying to write a new history. I didn't question this. When you're a kid, you just assume that everyone's family is like yours.

How do we know who we are without a firm grasp of where we came from? I know this isn't a particularly original question, but it's still a biggie, a question that launched a thousand transformative journeys and mid-life crises. Not every family has a well-documented family tree, a history passed on from generation to generation, beyond, say, the odd bloodline celebrity. *Oh yeah, I'm related to Queen Victoria, Jesse James, Genghis Khan.* That's the part people talk about over drinks at a party. Probably because the family we know is usually too complicated for small talk.

At my Grandma Carrière's funeral a few years ago, I met my Métis extended family for the first time. They were warm and welcoming, but I learned that, living away from St. Boniface, many of them felt separated from their Métis background as well. My dad's cousin, Roxanne, had completed the family genealogy and she talked about it with him. The work she'd done later allowed my dad and me to apply for citizenship with the BC Métis Nation. Most of the relatives I was meeting for the first time seemed to identify more with their French Catholic upbringing. When my dad spilled Grandma Carrière's ashes into the Alouette River, the river he'd learned to swim in, we sang "Amazing Grace," for lack of anything better. I started researching my background and found that although I have Métis blood, this means little without a healthy, reciprocal relationship with the Métis community. Feeling ashamed about how little knowledge I had, I was too intimidated to seek out the local Métis organizations. So, I launched my (clumsy) campaign to forge a connection with the land instead. People can (and will) reject you, but it seemed to me that the land would probably be willing to accept me.

For some reason, I didn't go to St. Boniface. I told you, it's a clumsy campaign. Instead, I went north.

Rookie mistake.

To be fair, a really good-sounding opportunity had presented itself: an opportunity to spend twenty-one days canoeing the Peel River Watershed in the Yukon and Northwest Territories. Not the land my family comes from. I crossed my fingers and hoped that any land would do. I did a lot of push-ups and planks. I bought a lot of fleece clothing. After a flatwater certification course, twelve of us set out on the Ogilvie River. We launched six loaded canoes from the side of the Dempster Highway, north of Whitehorse. The team included artists, scientists, even a documentary film crew. We'll get to that later.

While on the canoe trip, I planned to take notes for a memoir about spirituality, identity and stories. I imagined my Grandma Carrière as a mythic character—someone who could guide me through the difficult times and teach me about myself while I paddled. I should also mention that I hadn't been in a canoe since I was ten years old, around the age when, after years of dancing around it, we finally made a fairly pronounced break from said grandma.

This is the part of the story when you probably assume that either calamity or hilarity ensued. You're right on both counts. My Grandma Carrière was not an Indigenous "wise woman" who might have provided a settler fantasy guide into the remote wilderness. Nope. My grandmother wanted no part of her Métis identity, and her heavy drinking ensured most of the family wasn't speaking to her anyway. I'm not sure why exactly, but most of the extended family wasn't speaking to my dad, either. She collected porcelain dog figurines and rattan furniture and dressed like a Florida pensioner: blue-rinse perm and polyester pantsuit. She denied her Cree background to anyone who wasn't family and used a French accent only when she was drunk, then she would swan around like Édith Piaf. Three or more dachshunds were usually at her side, until she was too old to take care of pets. My dad chose to cut her out of our lives for most of my childhood, but I know he still sent her chrysanthemums on her birthdays. By the time I was an adult, I resented her absence so much, I didn't want to get to know her. But after she died, I changed my mind. I wanted more than her, though. I wanted roots.

The thing is, no matter you badly how you want it, it is very hard to plug yourself into a culture you weren't raised in. And to do it without a supportive community is nearly impossible. All I knew for sure was that I was so tired of being an island.

2.

Imagine you and I are sitting somewhere noisy, like a downtown chophouse and oyster bar, hunched over the warm glow of our iPhones, and I'm telling you this story:

CARLEIGH BAKER

The Bible had it wrong, darkness wasn't a problem *in the beginning*. There was actually too much light. Carleigh was in a canoe on the Peel River. It was September. The sun was high in the sky and piercing, but offered little warmth.

Carleigh reached into her bag to pull out her sunglasses. Her arm went shoulder deep into the bag as she grasped for their familiar feel, between the rain jacket and the writing journals. She found them, but when she pulled her hand out of the bag she felt them snap between her fingers.

With a grimace, Carleigh opened her hand slowly. The sunglasses—cheap, mirrored cop shades she bought for the journey to Burning Man seven years ago—were still mostly intact, but one of the arms was broken. The sun glinted off them and made her see spots.

She put the one-armed glasses on her face, hoping she might be able to coax them into place between her toque and the scarf pulled high over her cheeks. She crunched up her nose and lowered her eyebrows. It didn't work.

Carleigh turned around and showed the glasses to Jordon, who was in the back of the canoe.

"Look at my glasses," she said, then regretted it. Jordon must have his own worries and concerns for the day, she thought. She shouldn't bug him.

"What about them?" Jordon said, squinting.

"Nothing, never mind." Carleigh hid the sunglasses in the pocket of her PFD.

· · ·

Maybe at this point in my story, your phone will buzz and you'll take a quick look. Maybe you'll take a quick drink of your vodka soda. Maybe we'll talk about how cute the waiter is. When you think about my story, you might see a handful of busted sunglasses in your mind's eye. But what I saw on that afternoon was the future—fifteen or so days squinting into the sun for seven hours a day. A tiny discomfort rendered massive when added to the discomfort I already felt. It was too much. I thought about my grandmother, whispered a few words to her. "This sucks, Grandma C. Please help me deal."

When I have your attention again, I'll go back to the story.

· · ·

The canoe bounced and pulled a little as Carleigh and Jordon bumped against a rock.

"Hey," Jordon said, "remember to keep an eye out for trees and rocks. I can't always see what's coming from back here."

"Okay," Carleigh said. But she had trouble thinking of anything but the sunglasses, and how uncomfortable she was, and soon she started feeling very sorry for herself. Fat tears formed in her eyes and blinded her. She was still feeling sorry for herself when the canoe hit a partially submerged rock and veered sideways into rough water. She and Jordon were nearly pinned.

"I'm sorry!" She called to Jordon, who swung himself around to lean into the angle of the canoe and adjust his technique.

"Paddle hard," Jordon said, and Carleigh blinked the tears out of her eyes and paddled hard. They righted themselves and paddled to shore.

Carleigh apologized again to Jordon. She apologized to all her team, who were a little freaked out. They decided on a lunch break.

"What happened?" Jordon asked. He was upset, but could see Carleigh felt terrible.

"Look," she said to everyone, even though she felt like a jerk. "Look at my sunglasses, they're broken." They all had their own lists of agonies to consider. But they looked anyway.

"Shit, I can fix those," Jordon said to her. "Gimme fifteen minutes." He went to his tool kit and took some glue and a small rubber sleeve and wrapped it around the arm of the glasses. Then he tied some string from one arm to the other so the glasses could sit around Carleigh's neck when she didn't have them on.

Carleigh took the new and improved sunglasses from Jordon and thanked him. She walked down to the river's edge and sat. The sun was lower on the horizon and level with her eyes, so she put on her sunglasses. When she did, Grandma C. appeared in the space between Carleigh's eyes and the lenses.

"You're lucky I was there," Grandma C. said.

"What do you mean?" Carleigh said. "I asked you for help and I nearly got pinned on a rock."

"Exactly," Grandma C. said. "I put that rock there to remind you why you're here."

"Really?"

"No, dummy," Grandma C. said. "I can't put rocks where rocks don't already exist. I can point out what a great lesson that rock had for you."

"To pay attention?"

"And to ask for help when you need it," Grandma C. said. "But not from me. There are people here who want to help you. Their lives depend on you. Your lives depend on each other."

Carleigh hadn't thought of that.

.   .   .

This is a clumsy story, but it's my story. It's the only story I'm fully qualified to tell. There are some good teachings in there: the importance of community, asking for help, trying to honour ancestors even when they've been problematic figures in your life. Because I'm a storyteller, I know how to put those things in a narrative, but I haven't learned how to live them yet. There's a lot I don't know.

3.

Though it's a commonly used word, there is no "Indigenous" culture. There are instead the unique cultures of hundreds of Indigenous nations and peoples. So, with this in mind, I tentatively offer you this rumination on community, storytelling and culture, inspired by some of my research. I remind you to keep my positionality in mind as you read. Books don't replace experience, but that's where I started my education. One such book is E. Richard Atleo's *Tsawalk: A Nuu-chah-nulth Worldview*.

The Nuu-chah-nulth people come from the west coast of Vancouver Island and their culture should not be considered interchangeable with the cultures of those who call the Peel River Watershed home: the Tetlit Gwich'in, Vuntut Gwitchin, Na-Cho Nyak Dun and Tr'ondëk Hwëch'in, among others. However, in *Tsawalk*, Atleo works to establish what he calls an Indigenous world view—a belief in the interconnectedness of all things. Humans are inextricably linked to nature, and to each other, for better or for worse. I feel like this shared world view makes Atleo's discussion of Nuu-chah-nulth storytelling applicable here.

. . .

Spoiler alert: when it comes to the nature of existence, Western society may not have all the answers. Atleo feels that current Western ideology, with its extreme emphasis on rationality, tends to separate itself from human characteristics such as emotion and spirituality. No big surprises there. He believes that this fragmentation in Western thought, this resistance to focusing on the interrelationships and connections between the mind and the spirit, may be a limitation and not a strength. He quotes Richard Tarnas in calling it a "psychic lobotomy." I like that.

So why would we, as beings striving for a deeper understanding of ourselves and our environment, purposely lobotomize ourselves?

Understand that Atleo is not calling out the Age of Reason. If anything, he's offering reason a helping hand. As he says, "the theory [of Tsawalk] suggests that while the human mind is necessary for human cognition and for accessing and acquiring information, it can also be a conduit for spiritual information that can complement or complete or further illuminate our understanding of existence."

So really, *Tsawalk* is high-fiving reason. But it's also saying, "Hey, have a seat, reason. Sit back, and let me blow your mind."

But back to my story, which is neither in the language of the Nuu-chah-nulth, nor the Tetlit Gwich'in, nor the people in my family: Cree, French, Icelandic. It's a Carleigh special. It's mostly fiction, though I really did break my sunglasses and Jordon really did fix them. While I'm sure it was exciting, you might have found my story a little lacking in context. There's a reason for that.

In Nuu-chah-nulth storytelling tradition, stories would have been shared and passed down through families living on the same land for generations—it wasn't necessary to provide information to listeners about a story's location. So when I told you I was on the Peel, you'd know right away that it originates at the confluence of the Ogilvie and Blackstone Rivers, in the northern Yukon. You'd know that September is a crazy time to be there without adequate preparation. These days, you'd also know that it's one of the largest and one of the last protected watersheds in the world, now under threat of expanded gas and mining exploration.

. . .

When my buddy Calder asked me to paddle the Peel for his film project, I didn't think twice. As a guide and outdoor enthusiast, he's taken many long canoe trips. Being an artsy as well as an outdoorsy guy, he had something a little different in mind than your usual enviro-doc. Calder invited five other artists and me, with varying degrees of tripping experience, to paddle the Peel with him. Five hundred kilometres. Twenty-one days. Pretty intense.

While travelling and making the film, Calder told me to keep in mind the theme of Canadian identity and what it means to live in a country with wilderness that most people never get to see. He called the project an exploration of art, science and Canadian identity. I liked the sound of that, considering my own identity dilemma.

On the river, my grandmother was little help. Maybe because I didn't know how to let her help. My upbringing had convinced me that I was an island, and that counting on other people was for wusses. Alcoholics will always let you down; this was an important lesson of my youth.

Toward the end of the trip, I met Alice Vittrekwa. Her family has always lived in the Peel Watershed. She and her husband hosted all twelve of us at her family's fishing camp. After they had fed us and shared some of the history of the place and made room for twelve sleeping bags in a wood stove–heated cabin, she and I got to talking. Our conversation eventually turned to my grandmother. When I told Alice about the alcoholism, she pursed her lips.

"It's not your fault," she said.

She didn't expand on that—what she thought I might be blaming myself for. Not getting to know my grandmother while she was alive? Not being able to forgive her? Trying to posthumously rewrite her into somebody she wasn't? Or all of the above? This was an unexpected moment of shared language. The language of Al-Anon. I nodded at Alice. I don't know, maybe it was the vulnerability I felt after so many days outdoors, maybe it was the glow of the campfire in her eyes, but I believed her.

4.

Another thing that is implied in Nuu-chah-nulth storytelling is the idea that community is a natural phenomenon. Although an individual may identify a need or formulate a plan on his own, the community will work together to meet that need. So in Atleo's telling of a Nuu-chah-nulth story, if Son of Raven identifies the need for light, he may hatch a plan on his own, but it's a given that the community will support his quest. Get it? I'm not sure that I get it, yet. Settlers like individuality, self-made men. Or, in a colonial context, men who profit from the land and resources of others.

On the trip, something wonderful happened with my fellow travellers. We learned to count on each other. As days went by on the river, our group developed shared themes and stories, even if they were about how hard it is to zip up a tent when your fingers are frozen, or that day I accidentally got sand in the pasta salad. Throughout the day I'd gather up moments and make them into crude poetic offerings that I'd read around the fire every few nights. So when I referenced a beach covered in fossil-pocked rocks, or the laughably cliché rainbow that showed itself at the moment I asked the universe for a sign that I was meant to be there, people knew exactly what I was talking about. We were building our own community, if only for a short and highly concentrated period. With no electricity, no laptops, no cellphones, we remained pretty plugged into each other. Anger or frustration made waves we all felt to some degree. When the science assistant went rogue for a day, having had enough of being told what to do, some of us kept his breakfast warm for three hours in case he came back. Others grumbled.

Here's a little piece I wrote about that. This time, let's imagine I'm telling you the story over a fire, at Jericho Beach. To our right is the city. In front of us, across the water, are the clear-cut hills, housing developments creeping toward the peaks. To our left, a peekaboo view of unobstructed ocean.

. . .

This evening, I am an explorer on another planet. A planet where I paddle a canoe on mercury, and the thick, heavy atmosphere burns liquid nitrogen. Where the wings of startled birds make a hovercraft whoopwhoopwhoop as they pass, and that's the only sound until they land again. Gaetan and I are way out ahead of the group, but the bow position and his gift of amicable silence let me pretend I'm alone here, and I'm not afraid. Dip my paddle in and pull.

CARLEIGH BAKER

Gaetan is pretty quiet tonight, which suits me fine. Today he was at the bottom of our social hierarchy. The outcast. These things always happen in groups, somebody pisses somebody else off and everybody gets in on it.

Yesterday Gaetan had had enough of group dynamics: waking when we're told, eating when we're told, keeping within earshot in case there's a grizzly. So he separated himself. We didn't see him all day. He missed the pancake breakfast, though we kept some warm for him as long as we could. He missed the evening fire, when we all talk about one thing we're thankful for. He was probably thankful for some time to himself. But people don't like it when you deviate from the pattern, disturb the groupthink.

Yesterday, I ran laps up and down the beach by myself, but I stayed within earshot. When the pancakes were ready, I ran a few more laps. I don't like being told what to do, either. But I've come to count on the group, since it's comfortable. At the evening fire, I said I was thankful for a day to myself. I'd spent it writing in my journal, a hundred paces down the beach. Sang a little to the canyon walls, but I didn't see my face in the rock.

This morning, when Gaetan asked me to paddle with him, I gladly agreed. Although we're paddling the biggest canoe today, the one with all the heavy gear, we're both strong. It wasn't long before we were way out in front. He talked a little about feeling like he didn't fit in, and I told him I understood.

Early in the trip the Peel was narrow and frothy, now it's wide and sluggish. Soon we'll slow down, rejoin the group to find camp for the night. But in the meantime, Gaetan and I dip and pull through mercury. Tonight, we're not afraid of anything.

. . .

I was lucky to have the opportunity to learn a little more about what it's like to be part of a community like this—even the rough parts—but nothing about this experience was inherently "Indigenous." I could write another whole essay on this. For one thing, any one of us had the opportunity to leave at any time, and that's just what we did after the trip was over, while the Tetlit Gwich'in, Vuntut Gwitchin, Na-Cho Nyak Dun and Tr'ondëk Hwëch'in peoples, who have lived on the land for hundreds of years, are now fighting the threat of gas and mining interests in their territory. We were tourists, and privileged ones at that.

Remember my quest to win acceptance from the land? I now believe that idea was based on an ingrained settler mindset that the land owes me something. Same goes for my history. Instead of honouring my history, I tried to rewrite it. I don't want to be an island, but it's not my Grandma Carrière or a romanticized lure of my Indigenous or Icelandic ancestry that holds life's answers for me.

If anything, I'd say my life's best lessons are going to come from responsibility. The desire to learn about where I came from and who I belong to, and the understanding that none of this history excuses me from my role as a settler on stolen Indigenous land. The desire to contribute and answer to a community, to my family, to my loved ones and to the land, not the other way around. An appreciation of those who are willing to hold me accountable, because that is a sign of acceptance, no matter how much it stings. Those things take a ton of work. Settler habits die hard.

The Madonna in the Linen Closet

SHARON BALA

Sinthu says she wants to make a stop at temple.

Do you mind? she asks, hauling my suitcase into the trunk. I haven't had a chance to go all week.

Sinthu's car is green and shaped like a breadbox. She climbs into the right-hand side and I take shotgun on the left, assuring her it's not a problem. The temple in Southall was built a few years ago, a group effort by the local Hindu community, and my uncle—Sinthu's father—was a key organizer. I'm curious to see the place he helped create.

Sinthu merges into traffic and we leave Heathrow behind, her little green breadbox zipping past motorcycles and transport trucks, squeezing between other cars. She drives in that blithe London way, negotiating roundabouts on instinct, changing lanes with polite insistence.

The temple sits at the end of a quiet residential street. Inside the air is smoky, heady with camphor, and dimly lit. The gods look out from framed portraits or alcoved statues.

Sinthu wanders away and I am left to my own devices. All around me people intone under their breath, hands in prayer over their chests or raised to the middle of their foreheads. Some kneel on the carpet and bow. I stand in front of a goddess, in a small cluster of others, unsure of what to do with my hands. I am a foreigner here, awkward in this place of worship.

This religion is not mine and I do not subscribe to its tenets. Vishnu, Parvati, a single god with 108 names, that our souls move from one life to the next, good karma and bad coming along for the ride. We are all one, Hinduism says, a single being, divine. And I find this idea impossible, preposterous. How can all seven billion souls be united, let alone divine, when all we do is fight about our differences?

It is 2012 and the war in Syria is entering its second year. There is political turmoil in the Maldives, chaos in Egypt, a coup in Mali. Tomorrow Charles Taylor will be found guilty of crimes against humanity. Child soldiers. Rape. Murder. We are the very opposite of holy.

Still, I am happy to be here. A kind of magic is at work in this temple. The incense, garlands of plastic flowers, all the people who have gathered here for worship on a random Friday morning. The quiet murmur of chanting, the meditative hum of prayer. I close my eyes and feel a rare, genuine contentment.

I have experienced this feeling before: at a monastery outside Lisbon, a pure white place of such incredible architecture it felt like being inside a fondant-iced wedding cake. Nothing extraordinary happened on that day but the sun shone in the jewel-blue sky and a cool breeze blew and I thought to myself: this is one of the happiest days of my life.

So perhaps there is nothing special about this west London temple and my enchantment is merely a trick of the imagination. Mantras in a foreign tongue, the exotic, the unknown. All of it transportive and uplifting but no different than gawking at the intricate arabesques of a Nasrid Palace in Granada, a forty-six-foot-tall dazzlingly white statue of Lord Buddha in Sri Lanka, feeling small and insignificant at the precipice of a cliff overlooking the Atlantic Ocean. Maybe this sense of awe is just the magic all tourists feel. Out of our element and awestruck by novelty.

After ten minutes Sinthu comes to find me. A thumbprint of red powder is smeared at her throat. Ready to go?

·   ·   ·

My ancestors were temple builders. This was in Point Pedro, the northernmost tip of Sri Lanka, in the early twentieth century, before independence, when the British were still acting like they owned the place and Christian missionaries were dangling the carrot of education to convert the populace.

My great-grandmother, the story goes, came from wealth. For her dowry, she brought a chest of gold coins into the marriage. It was meant to be the family nest egg but unbeknownst to her, my great-grandfather was siphoning funds to build a temple. Miraculously, the temple still stands, untouched after twenty-six years of civil war. And among all the gods and goddesses that decorate its elaborate multicoloured tower stands a statue of my great-grandfather, bare-chested and pious, hands together in prayer. But when my great-grandmother discovered the ransacked chest and realized they were destitute, she went mad. My father chuckles when he relays this story. The unspoken moral: religion leads to insanity.

. . .

My mother used to keep a Virgin Mary in the linen closet. She was six inches tall, made of plastic with a blue twist-off crown, and filled with holy water from a trip we'd made to Lourdes the year I turned four. Mary was trotted out before important exams and in times of illness when a drop would be dabbed on our foreheads.

Growing up, there was a line in our family. On one side my staunchly atheist father, on the other my mother in her Sunday best with the linen-closet-Madonna and my sister and me following her lead. For a while we were garden-variety Catholics, but around the time I was eleven or twelve my mom, disenchanted with the rote mass and an absentee god, broke ties with Rome and all the saints and switched her allegiance to the Baptist Church. Virgin Mary stayed in the closet after that. There is only one way to be evangelical and that is full on. Wednesday evening Bible studies. Billy Graham at the Sky Dome. John 3:16. Full on.

My adolescent religion was earnest and uncompromising. The world was divided into believers and non-believers and the latter were going to hell. I remember once having a debate with a more sensible friend on the question of Mahatma Gandhi. Was he burning?

The person I was in those years, my certainties, the black and white con-victions, all of it seems quaint and faintly embarrassing now. Like a mild form of lunacy. My own schism came, predictably, with age. This is neither a new nor a unique story. *When I was a child, I spoke as a child, I understood as a child, I thought as a child. But when I became a man, I put away childish things.*

The definitive break came in my early twenties, when my mother asked a favour. There was upheaval in the church and half the membership had taken against the pastor. I don't remember why. I never understood the controversy or I didn't listen when my mother explained or afterward the ugly episode was scrubbed from memory. Either way, the details are gone.

Some kind of impeachment vote was to be held and since I was still technically a church member, I was entitled to a ballot. Will you come home? Mom asked. Pastor needs all the support he can get. I did not want to go. I was twenty-two and believed in marriage equality and evolution. This was no longer my circus; these were not my monkeys. But, as with most requests our mothers make of us, it was easier to oblige.

Going back to the church I had grown up in felt surreal. It was a weeknight and all the usual, comfortable trappings of Sunday morning—the choir, the piano, heads bowed in prayer—were absent. In their place was a frisson of tension, a tight wariness in every face. The sanctuary was packed, the air crackling for a fight.

I recall nothing of what was said, the complaints that were made, the arguments put forth. What I recall clearly was the animosity, the angry grumble that simmered among half the congregation every time the other side had their say. In this sanctuary, where we had once sung and prayed in harmony, consoled and celebrated each other, people now yelled over each other, hurled accusations. No one was immune; long-time members, church elders, deacons, even the pastor, all slung their mud. There is nothing so ugly as members of a family turning on each other.

In the midst of this commotion, which—despite my distance from the church, my presence there as an undercover agnostic—made me unaccountably sad, I wondered: What the hell happened? Have these people lost their minds?

.   .   .

My mother remains serious about her faith. Her Bible is scribbled with marginalia and underscored passages. The Bible is God's Word and she is a dedicated student. It reminds me of a Muslim friend who fasts during Ramadan and has a special clock that wakes her up at sunrise to pray. There is something admirable about this level of discipline. But it also makes me uncomfortable.

SHARON BALA

Religion is surrender. You must give up your doubts, your questions, and submit to the intangible, to faith. There is no room anymore in my life for this level of unconditional belief, no space for religion or its siblings: church or spirituality. But there is sometimes religion in my fiction. And this too makes me uncomfortable.

Four years after my visit to that London temple, I try to reproduce it in a scene. Not the drive over or the specific place of worship. What I want to recapture is the feeling of stillness and peace, the dust motes swirling in the hazy air. What did the disparate prayers sound like? A cacophony? A low murmur? Was there a gong?

I find the Ganesha chant on YouTube. It is, frankly, stunning, the range and melody of the singer's voice. He intones for a full ten minutes. *Om Gam Ganapataye Namaha*. The chant means something like: We bow to you, Ganesha. A single incantation repeated over and over. There's something wondrous here. The man who chants is solely focused, all of his being fixed on this single mantra. This is what I'm striving for when I write, deep attention, laser concentration. The three final Aums, drawn out and resonant, make the hairs on my arms stand at attention. I have no opinion on chakras—maybe they are real, maybe not—but in moments like these I can understand belief. For two days I listen to this mantra on repeat as I write, muddling my way through the first draft of a scene. The windows are open and I can only imagine what the neighbours must think.

A few years ago, while working on a different story, I became immersed in prayer flags and thangkas and had a different mantra on repeat, a Buddhist monk chanting *Om mani padme hung*. I was incorporating these elements into a story that wasn't about religion at all but about two sisters and postpartum depression and the political situation in Tibet. Religion was in the background, to add colour and texture, in service to the plot.

I have a name for what I do. Religious touristing: dropping in to a religion, immersing myself in some small aspect, picking up a few souvenirs and then walking away. I'm conflicted about my actions—cannibalizing someone else's belief system, appropriating what is useful, approximating the experience of a spiritual practice others take seriously. Is this right?

Writers are magpies. We are forever pocketing every gem that comes into our orbit. A friend's embarrassing anecdote, a funny thing someone's five-year-old did, a witticism overheard in line at the post office. Everything is filed away for later, the building blocks of our stories. Ask a writer's ex and they will tell you nothing is sacred. Should someone's mosque or pantheon be different?

And there is another aspect of my unease. What does it say about me that I gravitate back to religion, that it shows up time and again in my work? A familiar query is often posed to authors: How much of this is autobiographical? That is the wrong question. Autobiography is more subtle. Invariably, our work is stuffed full of our fixations, the obsessions we can't shake loose. We circle back to them, over and over. What is it about religion that preoccupies, that brings me back into its orbit, though I chucked it all in long ago? There is some unfinished business here.

. . .

Several years ago I bought my first car. I was transplanting my life from Toronto to St. John's and hired movers to ship it over to the island. The first moving company drove the car off the lot and rammed it straight into a light pole. I had non-refundable plane tickets and was forced to wrangle the details from afar, negotiating payments, firing the first company, hiring another. My parents checked in on the repairs and sent progress reports. Later, they oversaw the car's transfer to the new movers. When my little blue Honda arrived on the east coast a couple of months later, battle weary (by now it had lost its back window and had a dent on the roof) but still exuding that new-car smell, I found an unexpected passenger in a cupholder: a tiny Jesus stretched out on a cross. My mother had planted him there, a rider sent along to secure safe passage.

Mother and Child

DORA DUECK

That day, the end of May and her twenty-sixth birthday, she came over and we had waffles with white sauce and strawberries, and the meal was delicious and the conversation warm and pleasant, but I've forgotten other details that writers seek for their narratives such as the weather and the table setting and bits of dialogue and gestures or if we lit a candle for lunch. She asked for a story time later, I do remember that, and the fact that she fiddled at the computer with her stories until we sat down to eat, instead of hanging about the kitchen as she usually did when she visited us.

I don't recall the details of the next hour either, only the broad feel of it, the three of us seated in the living room, she in the chair in the corner, her father opposite, and me in the loveseat kitty-corner to them both, and it was the feel of Andrei Rublev's *Trinity*, the most famous of all Russian icons, which I purchased as a souvenir reproduction on a small block of wood while on a tour to Moscow and St. Petersburg. Also called *The Hospitality of Abraham*, the icon portrays three angels who showed up at the old patriarch's home to tell him that he and his wife would have a son. The angels symbolize the Holy Trinity. I love the fresco-like blue green brown tones of the piece, its muted but palpable unity, the understanding that seems to ripple within the circle of figures even though the scene is utterly still. Each head tips downward and toward the other in a powerful humility.

In my memory, our being together that afternoon had the same solemnity, the same leaning in. We parents listened as our daughter told us her stories— fragments, really, of her childhood and youth—and how they formed an arc to an identity we'd not known about or expected.

Queer, she called it. Though she didn't particularly care what word we used. *Gay* was fine if we preferred.

We assured her of our love. We said, We loved you before, we love you now. *Maybe even more, certainly not less.*

But if I claim the icon's gravity and harmony for the occasion of our daughter's coming out, I certainly cannot claim its serenity. She was nervous. She spoke slowly and carefully, consulting her papers, and beneath my held-calm exterior, my guts were roiling as I grasped what she'd said.

That evening, my husband and I had to attend a barbecue with friends at Birds Hill Park but it was impossible for me to make cheerful party talk. I was heavy with thought and the need to be alone. I wandered away to Pope's Hill, as it's called, where John Paul II conducted a celebration of faith decades earlier, in 1984. I saw that someone had left a bouquet of white roses at the hilltop's commemorative altar. The flowers were fresh. They seemed intended for me. I broke one rose off its stem and held it. It felt plump and cool in my palms, it was spectacular in its perfection. *Oh my dear dear beautiful girl.*

And its creamy whiteness—hadn't she always seemed in her essence like alabaster?

I cradled the rose, then pressed it with a prayer into a crevice in the grey altar stone.

I'd released my fears via the rose, but then I took them back with me too, and that night I slept poorly, my stomach worrying over our daughter's news, hurting over what *gay* must have meant for her during its long secret existence in the Mennonite environment in which she'd been raised, not to mention our home's blithely heterosexual assumptions. I ached over what her truth—now finally spoken aloud—might mean for her, for us, for me.

.   .   .

I'd realized immediately that her coming out, as well as our affirmation of her, would put us at odds with our church community. The branch of Mennonites to which we belonged wasn't even fully persuaded of women in ministry leadership, never mind same-sex attraction. Even worse, I was filling in for the editor-on-leave of the denominational magazine that year; I was part of the church's institutional bureaucracy.

Since she'd decided to come out gradually, first to us, then siblings, then friends, her identity could remain my secret too for the rest of the year and I mostly kept quiet when the so-called homosexuality issue was raised at work. But I was now keenly alert to what was being said. Discussion on the matter generally involved a stern doubling down on the traditional church position in the face of culture's growing acceptance. There were reminders to be kinder to gays, yes, but the dreadful word *abomination* still echoed like oily backwash in their wake.

One leader declared that if the denomination ever affirmed same-sex relations, he would leave. Another told me, almost breathlessly it seemed, about a young pastor-theologian who'd written a paper reinterpreting the Book of Romans verses that belonged to the church's seven-text anti-gay arsenal, and it was going to be published in a theological journal, and what in the world could be done about this? I was struck by his agitation, his near-panic.

An irrevocable wedge opened between me and the formal apparatus of our church because of our daughter's news. While I experienced a crisis of church, however, there was no crisis of faith. Not this time. I'd had several such crises already, as I moved through an evangelical Mennonite upbringing into adulthood, through a pilgrimage that both embraced and let go. I'd (mostly) relaxed into more ambiguity. Mystery. I'd discovered practices not learned as a child. Practices like Lectio Divina in which one considered Scripture—*the Word!*—not as rigid theological superstructure, but alive and whispering and intimate, fresh for today, individually specific. Practices like listening in prayer, rather than just kneeling and jabbering on and on, then getting up with high expectations and another daily duty done.

It may seem surprising—even ironic—that I now drew my profoundest consolation from the very book usually wielded to condemn people like my daughter. But my maternal energy—fierce, protective, stubborn—had geared into overdrive. I studied the seven bludgeon texts, quickly accepted better interpretations, then left them alone. Arguments about them seemed as useless as the question of how many angels dance on the head of a pin. Theology might be a magnificent endeavour in the abstract but it was personal now, autobiographical, as author Frederick Buechner once remarked. I grabbed for the deeper, wider truths I'd learned from my earliest memories, heard them with other ears, seized them—for her, for us—with a certitude approaching vehemence.

The psalmist had written, *You knit me together in my mother's womb ... I am fearfully and wonderfully made ... How precious to me your thoughts,* and I heard no distinctions there, the words were surely inclusive.

And the womb being referenced was mine.

When our daughter said, I had to be willing to lose everyone and everything to be who I am, I thought, That sounds like the gospel's notion of conversion. When I read at Sacred Space, an online prayer site, *The narrow gate is the gate of love which leads to life,* I thought, Yes, of course, this is the meaning of the narrow gate! And, *When we enter into the world of love, we find that it is a wide world, with its own energy, strength, and beauty.*

Don't interrogate her, my husband cautioned, but I did. I had so many questions. I needed to hear our daughter's stories again, as if by absorbing them I could enter the past, be present with her there, but wiser than I probably would have been if she'd voiced her intuitions as a child. I longed for her to be, say, four again, so I could gather her onto my lap. Longed for her to be in junior high, in high school. I wanted to hold her through university and her architectural technology studies. I could hardly bear the pain of knowing she'd been alone in the unique complexity of her coming of age. If I'd failed her by ignorance then, I would *not* fail her now.

Like many gay kids raised in a religious community, she'd agonized before God. She'd pleaded, she told me, for a way to reconcile her feelings and the negative attitudes of her environment.

And, she said, God never answered. So she'd reached a place of self-acceptance, and now that was answer enough.

But I was her mother and I would continue to plead on her behalf. My parental assignment, after all, had flown at me from the pages of Isaiah, chapter 58, where it says that God's acceptable fast is justice—to break yokes, free the oppressed, clothe the naked and *never turn away from your own flesh and blood.*

And one day I'd looked up from my computer in my home office at the painting of the Madonna and Christ child hanging in front of me. I hadn't really noticed it for some time, as tends to happen with the pictures on one's walls. The Madonna stared at me, her expression formidable, earnest it seemed, and I stared back and her gaze continued steady and piercing, as if to say, *Yes, be mother.*

.   .   .

One evening after tea at her house, my daughter and I sat and talked on the floor because she didn't have a sofa. I ended up crying a little and she comforted me. I asked if I could hold her, and she said I could, so I put my arms around her and rocked her retrospectively for all her twenty-six years, for everything she'd borne on her own.

The floor was hard, the position uncomfortable; the rocking could not be sustained.

You need some furniture, I said.

Both of us burst out laughing.

.   .   .

In December I booked a weekend retreat at Saint Benedict's Monastery near Winnipeg to mark the end of my editorial stint at the denominational headquarters. Besides my responsibilities at the magazine, besides the knowledge of our daughter that brooded inside me, there'd been other challenges those months: the deaths of two sisters-in-law to cancer; another relative's suicide; my elderly mother's surgery and subsequent immobility and her needs and demands; the relentless toll of my father's Alzheimer's disease. (He would die less than a month later.) I'd travelled to Paraguay to cover the Mennonite World Conference. I'd done final edits on my upcoming novel. I needed to regroup.

On the morning of the retreat I made the mistake of checking the denominational online forum, where I encountered a rant about the "slippery slope" from women in ministry leadership to homosexuality in the church. The writer's language, bluster, confidence distressed me. Once again I felt defensive, and in turmoil with this community. I borrowed a line from the psalms, wrote *My bones burn like glowing embers* into my journal.

But evening arrived and our daughter dropped me off at the monastery and I slipped into the circle of retreatants, ready for whatever. A song played in the background. I couldn't catch the words except for a line about the loveliness of my soul and before I knew it my eyes had overswum with tears and I thought, Uh-oh, I think I'm going to be crying again this weekend.

I was assigned to Sister Catherine as spiritual director for the retreat. When she asked what I'd come about, I said the future, the switch from outside employment to writing at home.

I paused.

No, I admitted, it was actually about our daughter and what she'd told us. And the church, I continued, isn't really good with that.

We need to pray for the church, the sister said. Her voice was soft but very sure and the sentence startled me with its recognition and sympathy. The church wedge was a pain but she was on my side of it. With her I would be safe.

She gave me a text from the prophet Zephaniah and told me to ponder it, pray it, record any movements—of spirit and Spirit—that I experienced.

I left her and read the passage. It disappointed me. I tried again but I couldn't rouse any mood to respond to it. I was too wrung out, too tired. I went to bed.

The next morning I found myself a cozy room facing south, the best light possible on a bleak wintry day, and I read Zephaniah's words again.

Shout for joy, daughter of Zion,
Israel, shout aloud!
Rejoice, exult with all your heart,
Daughter of Jerusalem!
Yahweh has repealed your sentence . . .
Driven your enemies away.
Yahweh is in your midst . . .
Have no fear . . .
[Yahweh] will exult with joy over you . . .
dance with shouts of joy for you
as on a day of festival.

I could not shake my resistance, however, could not surrender to the joy. My head ached. I talked to God about being a mother, the *standing between* it involved. Then I was prompted to speak the Zephaniah words over my daughter as if she were in the room.

She was a gift, it was as simple as that.

DORA DUECK

I went for my second meeting with Sister Catherine and she blessed what I'd done in praying the motherly love of God upon my dear one. But she probed. What did *I* want?

Suddenly I knew. Mother was inescapable. Necessary. Praiseworthy. Mother was me and I could never—would never—abandon it. But I was at the end of my strength with mother. I was exhausted with mother. I wanted to be *child*.

What is it like, Sister Catherine asked me then, to be a child?

Not worried, I said. Happy.

So ask, she said. Ask to be child. Joyful, trusting, without concern.

The gentle sister sent me off with another text to ponder and pray: the Magnificat of Mary in the Gospel of Luke. She told me to notice how much the Lord desired me to have what I wanted.

I did what she said. I came to the text as a child and this is what I heard: *Mother God is mighty. Is merciful. Lifts up the humble. Sings over me. Quiets me. Delights in me.*

Relief, release, my dormant joy gave way. I felt like John, who'd been wild and unfettered even as a fetus, who'd leapt in her womb, his mother Elizabeth exclaimed, when Mary had greeted her.

· · ·

How distant they seem now, these events of eight years ago. Our daughter flourished, and her father and I have too, I think, in our roles as allies and advocates, and if I've written here of the churn of beginnings rather than the contentment of endings, it's because those early months were, for me, intense and spiritual. Too much carrying and wrestling, I notice, but spiritual nevertheless—*soulish*, I would call it—where strongest memory sits down and resides.

And looking back I see the triads, shadowy imitations of the Trinity in our storytime unity, and if we never achieved the delicate serenity of the Rublev icon, there was a bending toward the other, and a current of love. She and her father and I that first afternoon. Then she was tucked along with me, as it were, into my Saint Benedict's retreat, both of us a child and both of us wombed in our Mother, we three leaning, listening, leaping, laughing.

I Am Karenahti:ne

CAROLINA ECHEVERRIA

My friend Ateronhiatakon (Francis) Boots asked me, How did your people explain the universe?

My people didn't, I said. My people said children did not need explanations. You were just told. I was told to pray every night for my mother, my father, my brothers and my sister. I added such a long list of names after them, plus dolls, teddy bears and pets, I could not sleep, ridden with anxiety—what if I forgot one?

I was told that God lived in the sky and he could read my mind.

I was told I had un *angelito de la guarda* who made sure nothing bad would ever happen to me.

They lied.

. . .

I don't think my parents ever thought to be careful not to teach me to be racist. Being born into a colonial battleground was something they were simply not aware of. They believed they were the rightful owners of the land, descendants of la *Madre Patria España*, whose ships landed in Tili in 1540 and who named it Chile.

Spaniards arrived to the *fin del mundo* to expand their colonies and find wealth to bring back to their kingdom and because they wanted to improve the slave trade. Spaniards preferred Indian maids to black ones; Indian maids were *más obedientes*. The conquerors were on a mission. To impose Catholicism and to exterminate, export or assimilate the offspring of their invasion.

. . .

My parents did not bother to verify the fact that our actual ancestors were not only a mix of conquerors and conquered, they were not even Spaniards. I confirmed that when my DNA results showed that we were mostly Basque.

My parents saw themselves as landowners, as part of the privileged class. In reality, they owned nothing, and whatever their ancestors owned was never theirs to start with. That did not change the notion they were privileged. Such is the fate of the colonized when they don't know that they are.

.   .   .

I was born in 1964 in Clínica Santa María, and right then and there my privilege started. Chile separated those born in hospitals from those born in *clínicas*. A hospital is usually public and poor, which in Chile means dirty. To be born in a *clínica* meant you are born in a clean, affluent place where your mother gives birth with proper care and recuperates in a private room where family and friends can visit regardless of visiting hours.

I screamed for air for the first time in a proper place, a clean place.

My parents had problems—white people's problems, and so they had maids. The maids lived with us, knew everything about us, which is why they were kept separate. They even had their own bathrooms. We used the white-tile-and-black-marble-shiny kind, the proper, clean kind. Those other bathrooms were *asquerosos*. I was not allowed to sit on the toilets. We were privileged and stoic. I was taught to hold my bladder for a very long time.

At my grandparents' house we used potties, and the maid emptied these potties every morning. Once in the night I saw the nanny pee in my potty under the moonlight.

I never peed in the potty again.

.   .   .

Every summer at my grandparents' house I felt at home. Viana 681 was my ground—across from the *catedral* and the *estación del tren*, the house trembling each time a train rolled by. Stepping out a window onto an art deco balcony, you knew you were the centre of that universe.

That house had held my mother as a child. She also had a nanny—to hug Mamita Raquel was like hugging a mother. She smelled safe and sweet like her baking, sweet sweat drops rolling down her forehead while she stirred the *dulce de leche* boiling in the copper pot, Mamita perched on her little wooden ladder.

So much action in that house, it was infectious, so I organized my cousins like a *mini sindicato* and found them odd jobs, but they were lazy and they tired fast, so I acted on my own. I bought a pastry and cut it into four and sold the four little pieces and bought four more pastries, and cut them up and sold them. My uncle called me *La Judía Chica*.

My mother hit the nanny, called her stupid because she could not speak Spanish.

My mother hit me and called me stupid. *Estúpida, estúpida, estúpida, estúpida, estúpida, estúpida, estúpida, estúpida, estúpida, estúpida, estúpida, estúpida, estúpida, estúpida, estúpida, estúpida, estúpida!* I recorded her saying it seventeen times, then played it out my window, where her boyfriend heard it. My mother hit me after her boyfriend left.

I did not cry.

I learned to cry without a nanny to dry my tears.

.   .   .

Miguelina Paillaleo is Mapuche. I asked her to teach me her native language, *mapudungun*.

Mari mari papai, mari mari chacha, ke me le cai mi? Miguelina is a *chacha*, my mom would not let her little girl live with us. Miguelina and I cried a lot in that house.

Miguelina finally left our house and family.

Many more maids and nannies left too, one after the other.

Then one day I left too.

.   .   .

I met someone whose family left Morocco for Canada when he was only a child. He asked me to come and live with him in Montreal, and be born again. I left my mother, my father, my brothers and my sister. I left home, my dolls, my pets, my boyfriend, my culture that was never a culture, my church, my god.

I told *el angelito* to go screw himself.

This man loved me. His mother, Mamie, loved me. His friends loved me. We married *en français* at the Palais de Justice, in the heart of old Montreal. We drove all the way down Avenue du Parc, stopping for flowers on the corner of Pine.

Not a soul from Chile came to my wedding.

.   .   .

Eight months pregnant and covered in a large white sheet, I went under the mikveh waters. Three times I went under. Lea bat Avraham Avinu. Lea is the name I chose. The last names were given. Daughter of Kahina. Born again *La Judía Chica*.

My new people believe that man is made in the image of G_d, so I asked Rabbi Joseph that if G_d is all intelligence, we humans are all intelligence too, right? Right. So, all intelligent beings can disagree, right? Right. So I can disagree about the existence of G_d, right?

Right.

I believe men wrote the Torah so they could leave women out of the game. Which they did. That is what I told my son when he came running home from school, saying that sin was the fault of a woman and a first bite. Still teaching the apple story? Wow.

I told my son, Look, think for yourself. If you do something stupid, do you take the blame or do you blame your sister?

This is a lot to ask a little boy.

Or is it? Mamie makes the *boulettes* for Shabbat while the men pray and gossip about business. My son loves her *boulettes*, she has been sneaking them into his tiny mouth since he was at my breast. Sensual Moroccan flavours. Belly dancing instead of lullabies. Roots as old as Abraham.

.   .   .

I give birth to a daughter and have to abandon my first studio. Still, I paint and paint. People buy my paintings. Teacher disapproves. I am not formed as an artist yet, I should not be selling. Shaming my success—an immigrant making a living without crashing her soul? So I crochet dresses out of fine wire and call them Garments for Survival, to be worn between body and soul. It's installation art, so, no money involved, ever, right?

Wrong.

There are international shows, media, sales, talk.

Meanwhile, Quebec and Canada are bickering; they want to be a country, they all do. Parizeau calls us *les ethniques, les immigrants*. More labels, a life of constant self-identification. Tell them who you are so they know who *they* are. Am I a Jewish artist? A former Catholic artist? I am an artist, I tell Peter Gzowski on the CBC. Isn't that enough?

Rabbi Joseph takes me out to lunch, he laughs at my radio rantings, he tells me he knows I have a pure heart.

Rabbi Joseph is not allowed to convert women anymore.

Rabbi Joseph has a stroke.

I give birth to a second daughter. My son has his bar mitzvah. Rabbi Joseph calls it a double simcha. I knit kippahs and paint with a new baby on my back. When it's time for a bat mitzvah for my eldest daughter, she says she would rather have a laptop.

. . .

I gave this land three children. I came to Montreal, thinking it was Canada. Turns out I was in Quebec. *Vive le Québec libre*! The lost children of Peter Pan, immigrant children forgotten. You don't give up your suffering so easily after that.

I learned that Quebec is Mohawk land, the land of Ateronhiatakon.

Ateronhiatakon told me that the Mohawk language has over three hundred million words.

How many words are in the English language?

Around a million and a half.

You cannot comprehend what you cannot name.

I drove my children from Montreal to Halifax so they would know their land, this land. You cannot love the land you do not know. There was nothing between Edmundston and Halifax, just a long straight road. All we could see was road, road, road.

. . .

I visit Chile in 2015, and travel south, deep into Mapuche territory. Others from Canada come with me. A sheep is slain in honour of our arrival. I swallow and smile after having quietly washed in the blood that watered my homecoming.

Blood stains my hands, splashes on my shoes, before seeping into the ground.

A bloody welcome.

A bloody massacre.

For me, a turning point.

In the night, I hold Susan's hand out on the land as we swing in our new ponchos and greet the *wetripantu*, feeding the earth, drumming and dancing, our hands joining friends from Temuco to Ontario.

. . .

I take Ateronhiatakon to my place up in the mountains, to Les Laurentides. He says he did not know that name. But he knows the little towns and places and communities in the small hour between Montreal and Sainte-Lucie.

He shows me strawberry fields in my own mountain yard.

Strawberries are the first fruit to bloom in spring.

Mohawks don't have hell or heaven. They have strawberry fields, forever.

Ateronhiatakon told me never to feel alone, even after Mamie died and people back home forgot my name. He told me I had Grandmother Moon and the birds and the wind. He cleared my voice with the purest water so I could speak again. He cleared the dust out of my ears so I could hear birdsong again, he wiped my tears with the softest hide so I could see clearly once more. He combed my hair with the finest comb and wiped the stain of pain off my chest with the same soft hide he used to wipe my tears.

He taught me that sumac grows at the woods' edge and that the secret to children growing up to become healthy adults is to keep them happy as children.

He told me to never lose hope, that Mother Earth will always heal herself, and he gave me a little pouch of tobacco to carry with me, everywhere I go.

Ateronhiatakon says each Mohawk has a unique name, names are used only once and you must ask the elder when a name becomes available again.

I am an immigrant artist, painting is my voice. In my paintings, I use red a lot.

Karenahti:ne is the Mohawk word for the first-leaf-changing-colour-in-a-tree-in-the-fall. Yes, there is a word for that. The leaf that leads red out into the tree.

I am Karenahti:ne, the one who leads red into my tree.

Repent, Sinner

EUFEMIA FANTETTI

My religious past is a typical "Girl meets church, girl loses church, girl spends rest of her life trying to figure out what the hell happened" story. Introduced to Catholicism before I could form words, the relationship has been tense from the start. At my baptism, everyone had a marvellous time eating cannoli, drinking anisette and smoking cigarettes in the same room as baby me. In photos, I have the floppy-headed gaze of a newborn taking in her surroundings—staring up at the people seated next to me with interest. I imagine my infant indignation and skepticism: "Original sin? Who, me? Listen, I just got here and I'm not buying it."

For at least five hundred years, my family lived in a tiny hillside village called Bonefro in the region of Molise, a rural, mountainous area in the middle of Italy, about four hours southeast of Rome. I'm part of an exodus generation, those first born on foreign soil. A sampling of the lifestyle perks I took for granted included supermarkets, fully stocked cupboards, running water and immunization. Guilt? My body secretes the stuff faster than red blood cells deliver oxygen to tissues.

Everyone in Bonefro believed in the same god and followed the same faith. Belief was the fabric meant to hold children close to the clan, so I was trundled off to Mass every Christmas and Easter; I squirmed in uncomfortable tights and black patent leather Mary Janes, waiting for a miracle, a message or a visitation: no such luck.

My folks believe in the devil, destiny and damnation. If my family had a motto, it would be Repent, Sinner. A battle cry: He died for our sins. A mantra: Bless me, Father, for I have sinned. A slogan: Stop pestering us, Satan.

I'm the misfit—the lapsed-and-recovering member of the tribe. What I wanted from church was community, connection and compassion: a temple where my spirit could rejoice. I found only sharp disapproval and customary rejection. Some days I wonder if I'm on Catholic *Candid Camera*. Will I get to the end of life only to view a documentary playback of all the times I lacked kindness, imposed judgment, ignored restraint?

Here then is a tour through the Stations of my Sins, a Greatest Hits compilation of shortcomings, according to my mysterious childhood faith.

Lust

I wore my first wedding gown when I was eight years old. Technically, it was a First Communion dress with a pink rose pinned to the centre. The long, see-through sleeves shaped into angel wings when I raised my arms. My unruly hair was blow-dried and curled by a hairdresser to be bridal beautiful. I wore a veil crowned with a tiara of tiny white flowers. I wore lace gloves and carried a mini pearl-shaded purse with my missal inside.

At Sunday school, the priest who was brought in to prepare us for the sacrament of Communion asked us to recite the Hail Mary.

Silence.

He berated us for being unschooled, questioned if we attended church, blamed our parents and public schools for our ignorance. Finally, one kid who knew most of the prayer put up his hand. We spent the rest of the class reciting it in unison, tittering at the "fruit of the womb" line because it sounded like Fruit of the Loom—an underwear brand in a room full of eight-year-olds was bound to be a giggle-fest.

If I've suggested that more time and effort was given to my outfit than the value or meaning of Communion, that's because it's true. It's also a pattern I'd repeat as an adult—two more (real) wedding dresses, parties with well-dressed loved ones, fancy chicken dishes and chocolate desserts—planning the marriage rite more than contemplating life with the men I chose. I wanted a family I could rely on for love and support. I wanted to create the stable home I'd never had as a child. Instead, fuelled by fear, old-world ideas of whoredom and incapable of assessing my own worth (my dowry was stockpiled with sheets and linens from age five), I recreated the conditions of early chaos. Sex with someone meant staying with that someone—period.

Both choices resulted in busted relationships partnered with significant financial setbacks.

The last time I complained about being single to my dad, he said, "Can't you just find somebody to live with?"

We've come a long way, Jesus.

Gluttony

Weekend grocery trips when I was a kid followed a comical and repetitive script: I'd whine for Creamsicles and Fudgsicles and my father would relax his negative stance once I promised to eat the ice cream pops slowly and not ruin dinner. At home, the boxes would be stuffed in the upstairs fridge with a warning not to repeat my previous binges. I'd say thanks and have one, then another and another. My mother could hear the freezer door being yanked open and would yell that I was *doing it again*. My father would give me grief about breaking a promise; I would shrug and stuff my face. By Sunday night, the treats were gone, meaning I ate my way through twenty-four iced Popsicles in under twenty-four hours. Untouched were the virgin arugula, cucumbers and zucchini harvested from our suburban backyard.

This is the sin I feel most shameful about carrying over into adult life. During the ice cream years, I had no appetite. My mother ruined most of our meals. She would fry green peppers and save the oil to reuse for another dish; the acrid smell permeated the house and lingered in our hair. For years we ate what she put in front of us—an experience my father refers to as "burning our stomachs"—with nerves of Teflon and a stainless steel gut. I learned to suppress a gag instinct when a plate was slapped down in front of me.

Hungry ghosts whisper in my ear whenever I find food rotting in my fridge or indulge in the luxury of a restaurant. In an ordinary week, some days I starve my body and other days I binge, feeding the cravings with junk food: the mother of false nourishment. The esurience feels ancient, an ancestral famine embedded in muscle and coursing through my blood.

A mother's inability to show affection, a father's malnutrition as a young man, a soul starved for direction—my body contains them all.

Greed

I was working behind the counter at McDonald's when my dad came in to tell me he had to go to Italy, his father was dying. He wondered if he should book a ticket for me as well. Did I want to say goodbye?

I was sixteen and burst into tears. The previous trip, when I was eleven, had been disastrous. I'd been stranded for a month in Bonefro with my mother, two outcasts from the modern world shipwrecked in a medieval realm, when my father had to return to work in Canada.

I said no.

On the night my grandfather died, a hearse came to the drive-through window minutes before closing. That's how I knew.

My dad came back to Canada and gave me two gold necklaces purchased with the small inheritance he'd received from my grandfather's pension. I rejected the gifts. He hadn't noticed I detested gold and always wore silver. Gold represented everything I hated about being Italian—flashy, loud and overbearing, the embodiment of tacky.

My normally calm father lost his cool and shouted at me. I understood the value of nothing, he said, spent my earnings on food I didn't finish and bought plastic gems I rarely wore. He raged at my excess, this tendency to treat money like a crop that would replenish on its own, while I stared at him, my jaw slack from shock. His crumpled brow was lathered with sweat. Worry wrinkles lined his cheeks. I looked into his amber eyes and saw the boy he'd once been—a workhorse youth, his childhood consumed by scarcity, the use of funds dictated by the endless vices of my indolent grandfather. I saw my existence reflected in his face. My stockpiling stuff from the mall wasn't a sign of abundance or success—it was evidence of careless greed.

Sloth

My last confession was when I was fifteen, the week before my cousin Vico's wedding. As a member of the wedding party, I had to present myself to a priest and admit all my sins. My last conversation with a man of the cloth had been right before Communion. The priest in the confessional thought he'd misheard me.

"*Seven* years since your last confession? This is terrible. Do you go to church?"

I took the laziest approach I could with God—a cafeteria Catholic, I showed up for the big days, birthdays and Crucifixion anniversaries. Aside from the fault-finding priest of my Communion and a few classes before my confirmation, no one tested my knowledge of scripture or ensured that I understood the tenets of faith, the purpose of prayer. As a result, I rarely called on God and when I did it was petitioning for favours.

The last time I repeatedly called his name I was ten, when my mother, having lost her temper and all reasoning, doled out a biblical-style beating. I had to cover my arms and legs for weeks until the bruises paled from raisin purple to a sickening yellow. I sweated through summer vacation as friends squinted at my clothes and slowed down their walk for my stiff-legged limp. The memory of that day is lodged in my skin like shrapnel. My soul grew around the wound, cementing a belief in a system of reward and punishment.

I judged myself unworthy of saving because the hand of God didn't intervene on that agonizing day. I didn't doubt his existence; I lost faith that he cared about me.

I agreed to multiple Our Fathers, several Hail Marys and endless rosaries with some remorse. Not enough to complete the soul-saving assignment, but aware that penance might be required down the road.

Wrath

By the time I was twenty, I'd broken all the rules of first-generation children: left home unmarried, had a boyfriend from a non-Mediterranean background and rented an apartment with two male roommates roughly three thousand miles away from my parents.

My move to the West Coast reunited another branch of the family, my father and my uncle Rocco, close first cousins who hadn't seen each other in over thirty years. My parents flew in to celebrate the yuletide season. I helped with the dishes, set the table and said I'd prefer to skip Mass on Christmas Day.

My father took the resolution as an insult. My uncle demanded obedience. The more they pressured, the more adamant I became. Salvation was a slippery slope—accept Jesus Christ as Saviour and admit blame as a wicked wrongdoer: I was done.

"That's enough. What if I say to you I'm the father and you going to Mass?"

"I would say I'm your daughter and I am not."

My mother, the usual instigator, was consoling in her tone. "Why you no come with us?"

My aunt Eileen interceded. "Oh, leave her be," she said, in her Irish lilt.

Finally, I thought, the voice of reason. I smiled at Eileen, my uncle's second wife. She was a poster child for my idea of a former Irish nun—bowl-cut brown hair, Atlantic-blue eyes, with a quick tongue that lashed out at cobra speed.

"It's her soul," Eileen continued. "Let her go to hell if she wants to."

"Excuse me?" I thought she couldn't be serious—this, from a woman who'd *divorced* Jesus? I decided that if the day ever came to pass where we were being herded along through fire and brimstone by demons with pitchforks, I wouldn't lift a finger to help her. I would not stand next to her in the lunchroom line, nor sit with her on that awkward first day. Icicles would be chandeliers in hell before I would consider letting bygones be bygones in the damned afterlife.

Everyone headed out to the car without me. That year, I was the loose cannon who wrecked the festivities faster than anyone could say amen.

Envy

Kevin, my first serious boyfriend, assumed every woman was envious. I learned this after he awkwardly greeted another young woman with a hug and talked for ten minutes without acknowledging me. They discussed all the people they knew in common, what their old friends were up to and how many had left the rural community they were from. Minutes passed and every so often the young girl and I would smile at each other. As we parted company, almost as an afterthought, Kevin said, "Oh, this is Eufemia."

When we walked back to my apartment, I asked why he hadn't introduced me sooner.

"I knew you'd be jealous."

"What are you talking about?"

The young woman was an ex-girlfriend.

"So?"

Kevin rolled his eyes. He refused to consider that I hadn't felt threatened.

My mother struggled with jealousy and lost the fight over and over. I watched her cave to every envious impulse a person could have. She was an abyss of rage when she was jealous—nothing could appease her.

As our relationship progressed (I hesitate to use the word), I noticed Kevin seemed intent on provoking envious reactions. I wondered, did he think the toxic emotion was the only scale to measure love? My mother was an extreme example and an enormous lesson: jealousy was an energy vampire draining all sweetness from life.

This is not to say I never struggled with the feeling. In my worst moments, I did. I also recognized envy when it showed up, and I learned to wrestle it to the ground with every scrap of awareness I could muster. Kevin's insecurities made him look for a jealous reaction as proof of my love. This was Caveman Love. Club-someone-over-the-head-and-take-away-their-freedom love.

I understood from early on that everything I envied was misplaced desire, an unquenchable yearning to stop the never-ending ache from childhood. This sin was saved for one longing—a mother who would love me.

No surprise then that I avoid all social media around Mother's Day. Unchecked envy would unleash destruction that could surpass the eruption of Krakatoa.

Pride

Late in the fall of 2000, I walked into Holy Rosary Cathedral in Vancouver to decide if that was the year I would return to a regular service. I was feeling aimless again, trying to figure out how to move my life back in the direction of being motivated to get out of bed in the morning. It was a portentous time, the cover of every magazine heralding the two-thousand-year anniversary that marks the calendar of the English-speaking world.

There must be something to Catholicism, I thought. There must be something wrong with me—a tuning fork for shame, guilt and hypocrisy, where others found acceptance, forgiveness and mercy.

I sat near the back, at the edge of a pew. The church had a familiar aroma—Eau de Criticism, and I left feeling ridiculous. I slept through New Year's, and worked and slept and worked and slept some more.

Months later, I met a guy who broke up the monotony. He was an actor. More melodrama ensued. It kept me busy and distracted.

Four years later, I applied to attend a ten-day silent retreat, vipassana meditation, an event my actor-turned-husband referred to as Mission Impossible. My dad worried that Buddhists would "wash my brain."

My father was heading into another breakdown, my second marriage was draining both my finances and my spirit. I desperately wanted to change my life and break the vise grip of blame and recrimination. There was always a bad guy, it seemed, and frequently, it was me.

Nine hours a day I sat, accompanied by backache, stiff joints and misery-soaked thoughts. On day five, I sat on my cushion at the back of the meditation hall crying as quietly as possible while I circled the same problem mentally—my deeply unhappy and unfulfilling marriage to a man who put me in constant financial jeopardy. I had recently co-signed a loan for his enormous credit card debt and discovered he was lying about using credit, again. Then, on a slow exhale to regain composure, a simple thought occurred to me. That thought was the beginning of serenity and the end of the relationship—change.

You maybe know this from yoga classes—the instructor saying, *Change is the only constant in the universe, we are always in a state of transformation.* During meditation, I was catastrophizing about our economic future. I couldn't figure out how we would handle the bills, in particular, rent. My husband had an exacerbating teenage approach to paying for the roof over his head—contributing a paltry portion, then begging off his share of hydro or the phone because he was scrambling to pay off his debt. Cheap when the money was his, and extravagant when it was mine.

I got off my cushion at dinner break, shaky from the day of tears, and asked to speak with the meditation teacher. The next day, in a small room off to the side of Dhamma Surabhi's Dharma Hall, I met with the tiny powerhouse who guided the session for a couple hundred people. She asked about my meditation experience.

Instead of launching into a story about my mother, my father or my husband, I said, "I think I'm addicted to suffering."

The instructor grinned. "Interesting. Are you able to sit with your thoughts without judging their quality?"

Her generous grin was contagious. "I don't know about that. I was raised Catholic, we judge everything."

In her presence I felt focused. I returned to my cushion and watched other thoughts arrive. Insecurities came up one after another. Emotions I recognized and greeted as old friends: "Thanks for showing up, Anger, but you are not needed at this moment." "Good morning, Sadness, you shadowed every dream I had last night." I was cheerful with hubris. "Look, Pride, we both know this can't continue." I stayed focused on how frequently my thoughts tried to attach themselves to unhelpful states of being.

I left the retreat clear-headed, determined to stick to a new payment plan.

The marriage dissolved in less than eight months.

I had no clue what would happen with vipassana but had been cautioned by my yoga teacher that my world would shift in ways I might not be ready for. In the end, the lengthy meditation helped me let go of a harmful match because I'd spent the days in a bothered, problem-solving state.

Not exactly a Bodhisattva, but give me time.

.   .   .

This is what I imagine will happen when I die. Saint Peter meets me at the pearly gates and demands an account of my life. I can't come up with a decent reason for him to let me in, so I offer a joke instead.

"How do you know Jesus was Italian?"

Saint P., an elderly Birkenstock-shod hippie in need of a haircut and beard trimming, wears the perma-frown that results from working long hours. I carry on undeterred.

"He lived at home until he was thirty, he hung out with the same twelve guys his whole life and his mother thought he was God."

"Is that supposed to be funny?"

I'll look down at the cloudy floor covering my feet. "What, too soon?" The saint wants me to wait another deuce thousand years before I can repeat a wisecrack or be myself? Forget it.

Two millennia of holy wars, inquisitions, pogroms, multiple massacres, residential school victims, violated children, disempowered women and genocide—sundry crimes against humanity—will stand between me and entry into eternal paradise. Real sins that have not been absolved, offences of an epic and ongoing nature, barbarous atrocities committed in the name of God by men who professed to be devout. The Catholic Church will still be fighting restitution when I face a humourless Peter, thinking about hundreds of years of institutionalized abuse.

I'll ask him to pass on a message to my paternal grandmother, a pious, benevolent soul whose time with me was much too brief. In every memory, she emanated light. Her saliva cured a scraped elbow, her embrace alleviated sadness—she was a devoted presence missed long after she was gone.

"Please, tell her not to worry when she doesn't find me here. I'm fine, in fact, I'm happy. Tell her that my life outside the church has been blessed."

My Uterus Is a Tree

MEHAROONA GHANI

Be like a tree, let the dead leaves drop.

—Rumi

Dear Rumi,

I am a tree.

May 23, 2016, I turned forty-seven. My birthday wish was to walk the Pacific Spirit Park trails near the University of British Columbia. I had a vision to fulfill—a need to mark changes. I invited friends to what I called my spirit walk. Barbara was one of the first to respond.

"Do you have a shovel?" I asked, then added, frantically, "It's not for a body—I have a pine cone to bury."

.   .   .

January. At a workshop co-led by a shaman healer, I worked on one of the exercises—write about how you arrived today, and a promise:

> I caught the #99 UBC bus and rang the bell. I jumped off and ran toward Alma and Tenth to catch the blinking hand at the intersection lights. Must be at Sophia Financial Office for 9:15 a.m., I told myself repeatedly, so I could be in a spot where … [breathe in and out]. I. Felt. Present. I entered. I'm stuck. With a decision. About my uterus.

The light played off the shaman holding her drum painted with animals, flowers and a tree. I recalled the Greek word, Sophia, for wisdom, and the relationship the office had to Sophia as "the voice that expresses our intuitive,

55

creative nature, sees the interconnectedness of all things and honours the sacredness of all life." This evoked a knowing calm inside my heart, a confirmation of the sacredness of a woman's body, of me.

My uterus is sacred.

. . .

Shaman. Drum. Chant. Wisdom. Listen. Share. Tears. Carried inwards—guiding us into a self-hypnosis—a vision. The Divine Feminine appeared.

"Where will you be if the uterus is tampered with?" I asked. I had always believed the womb to be the place of the Divine Feminine—the essence and power of a woman. My stomach tightened, waiting for her answer.

I am there and everywhere else.

The shaman brought us back, gently, into the room, then circulated a brown paper bag filled with pine cones. We were each to pick one and hold it in our hands, then release our thoughts and prayers into the cone. "Where and how would you like to return the cone to the universe?" the shaman asked. Eyes closed, I saw my hands digging earth. I knew exactly where.

Later that evening—a dream. From my Fallopian tubes bloomed large violet stargazer lilies. My uterus, replaced by a garden.

Rumi, I am a tree.

. . .

February. I awoke after a non-invasive procedure—an endometrial ablation—to news of complications. My gynecologist laid her hand on my leg. The corners of her hazel eyes crinkled. Wisps of light brown curls peeked out from under a sky-blue surgical cap. "Your choice," she said. "A new drug or hysterectomy." The white sterile blanket on the cot felt soft. "No need to answer now."

I checked in with my heart. "It's a hysterectomy then."

. . .

February onwards. "Why are you doing all this research?" Mom asked while she drank her tea. She was looking out my apartment window toward False Creek, contemplating her return to Victoria.

"I need to know what questions to ask my gynecologist." I flipped through various pictures describing reproductive anatomy, hysterectomies and sex.

"You need to rest," insisted Mom. Two weeks since the surgery and I was on a quest.

"How's it going to impact me?" I started to ask. She watched me impatiently. I put away my laptop and walked toward the kitchen. I just couldn't bring myself to say it.

I tried to talk to other women about the impacts of a hysterectomy on their sex lives. It amazed me the number of women who wouldn't talk—what I was asking was so personal. Too personal perhaps?

. . .

"I have questions about sex," I finally blurted out one day on the phone now that Mom was back in Victoria.

"Why are you so focused on sex?"

"I'm not, but if you don't answer my questions, who will? Only you understand the way we grew up."

"I'm listening."

Then came the torrent. I yelled. At the divine. At life. At the universe. At every man I had ever met. "I've read that in Islam, sex before marriage is a sin. And when I did my MA thesis on forced arranged marriages of Muslim women, I read a few testimonials of Muslim women who dated and were judged to be unmarriageable or promiscuous, and in some situations violence erupted. But a man? Oh, if he dated it was okay and if he is Muslim and has sex—even though it's a sin for him too—you know who's judged? The woman! I wonder, how much is religion and how much is about power?" I took a breath.

"Yeah, it's unfair." Mom's patience floated through the phone.

I shifted the receiver to the other ear. "I don't have a problem with people dating or having sex, but aren't violence and inequality sins, and isn't Allah the one to judge?"

"Don't worry about these things. Only look after yourself."

"I'm just trying to come to peace with the path I chose. All I ever wanted was a nice guy who was serious about a committed relationship leading to marriage, and not sex first."

I listened as Mom clicked her tongue in a "tch." She, too, was annoyed. Lips quivering, I held back my tears, relieved she couldn't see me. I cursed the many who assumed my choice was only about religion. Yes, it had influenced my early years, but as I began to explore intimacy, my beliefs centred on respect for my body and my choice. Some people—even some doctors—made me feel like I was strange for choosing not to have sex.

The act of sex shapes our world so dramatically, there is shame imposed on those *not* engaged in sex as much as those who are.

Now, with my body being cut open and my uterus removed, I questioned my beliefs.

Something had been lost. I mourned my sacredness. My desire to have babies in a committed relationship. I mourned the babies from whom I'd turned away. I reached for a tissue. I wiped my tears and blew my nose.

"Was it all too much to ask for?"

"No, no, *munay*."

I smiled at the nickname only my mom was allowed to say. *Munay*—a connection to *muna*, reserved for my dad—was a term of endearment for *little boy*. I was not called that because they'd wished for a son but because of their pride in my being the first child, equal to a son. I loved the nickname like I loved my name, a Persian derivative meaning *light of the moon* or *sunlight* or *love*, depending on how Meharoona is pronounced.

"It was not too much," Mom continued. "Don't ever down yourself. Your happiness and health are more important than these men or marriage."

"Yeah, you're right. I'll be okay. But I'm still pissed."

Mom stood fast, a tree in my storm. Mother and daughter caught in a gale. "If I was you," she said, "I'd be angry too."

Rumi, I am a tree.

. . .

"I've been reading *The Essential Guide to Hysterectomy*," I shared with the men in my life: my naturopath, my acupuncturist, my dearest gay friend, whom I lovingly called my "husband," and a second dear friend whom I called my "open man" because of his practice of open relationships.

My alternative doctors helped me decide what to remove and what to keep: ovaries, Fallopian tubes, cervix, etc. "You have MS. Your body can't handle any more irregular bleeding and low iron. You must let go of the idea that you wanted to find a man, get married, then have babies. There are other ways to have a family—there's adoption. Your health is first."

Inhale, exhale. I understood.

Husband listened patiently to my spiritual angst.

My open man helped me understand male and female intimacy, including orgasms. It was so easy to speak with him. At one time, we had considered a relationship. Then he revealed his interest in having multiple committed partners; I said I believed in a monogamous relationship leading to marriage. We understood and accepted each other's boundaries. We remained in an intimate, soul-sustaining friendship—not a friendship with benefits, and no intercourse.

Eventually, I found the courage to ask more of my older women friends and my gynecologist. They confirmed what I had read. "In one way you're lucky because many women have less pain during intercourse without the cervix and the uterus. Everything will be fine," said my gynecologist. I felt relieved.

· · ·

"Do you mind if I ask what kind of intimacy you've had?"

"I've been waiting for someone to ask."

Séverine's intense blue-green diamond eyes enhanced her dimpled smile. I felt safe, sharing freely with my friend.

No intercourse.

No oral sex.

I shared how bodies were held and cherished, that I had cried and said to the man I loved, "I don't know what's happening. All we are doing is holding one another and suddenly I have a wave of tears. I feel so overwhelmed, so with you …"

"You're having an epiphany of love," he'd said.

I shared with Séverine that it was in that moment that he and I bonded, that even fully clothed there was internal union, and I'd realized love came from a sacred spiritual intimacy and partnership that encompassed the entire body, mind, soul. Sexuality was more profound than sex alone. Sex, I said to Séverine, should be redefined.

"Wow! You've experienced intimacy in a way that every woman wants."

"Really?"

"Oh yes! And most importantly, you respected your body by saying no to what you didn't want."

A light went on. I felt ecstatic. Anger dissipated.

It took many people—including men—in the most gentle, loving, non-judgmental way to convince me to let go.

Rumi, I am a tree.

. . .

Barbara sent smiley emojis in response to my saying we were not burying a body. "Do you need to dig the earth?"

I was surprised. *Oh, is she concerned about hurting Mother Earth?* It would be months later, post-surgery, before I learned she was actually concerned about park rules!

I told her about the journey with the shaman. I shared the prayer that we were given. I shared that what I felt I needed to do was thank the universe not only for giving a gift but also for taking it away. I shared that my desire was also about respecting the land, that the vision of digging with my hands and burying the pine cone in the park was sacred—and should take place on First Nations territory. For some reason, I knew it had to be there.

"Well then," Barbara said, "we can't mess with that vision. We will dig. I'll bring sweetgrass and sage to thank the Earth."

May 23. Morning prayers. I surprised myself by saying, "I am no longer asking You to stop the MS. I realize now that You have a plan, so let it be. I love You and I love me. I only ask for continued support, love, courage and strength. But. Secretly. MS. Disappear."

Barbara and my friends Aliya, Kamal and Cara walked with me into the forest of Pacific Spirit Park. My hands snuggled to keep warm in my fleece pockets. Although the early spring sun was out, only a sliver of light crept between the branches of the many trees. A fragile morning breeze kept us alert. At a crossroads, we saw one sign that read Salal, while the other said Cleveland. I liked Salal. It sounded Arabic, like halal—meaning permissible, similar to kosher—and I chose the kosher route with an internal smile.

Eventually, I came upon a huge tree. I slowed down, stared at the tree. *Go deeper into the forest.*

"Did you notice the circle?" Barbara asked. I stopped and looked back. "The circle around the tree. Circles are very powerful."

"I noticed the tree. I don't see. Oh wait, I see."

I walked toward the tree, alone in the centre of a circle of ferns. Other trees also formed part of the circle. I touched the bark as I circled the tree. I listened, opened, hugged it. Pressed my face to its trunk. Closed my eyes, asked, Is this it?

I was swept back to another time, another vision quest. The year 2011. Sitting in a lotus position, surrounded by a violet aura. A yellow beam appeared. I was asked to take it to my future self. She—I—stood on the ocean, surrounded by green, as the lower part of my body became a trunk. She—I—was a tree. "I have MS," I said. I asked my future self the question, "Will I still be able to walk in the future?"

Yes. You are strong as a tree.

Tearfully, I opened my eyes, turned to my friends. Pointed to the earth in front of the tree. "This is it," I said. I looked around. The unexposed root of the large tree, covered with dirt and moss, lay like a large mound across from a smaller, shrub-like tree, its roots exposed, entwined, intertwined, connected. Halfway between the two trees a stick pointed to the heavens. An antenna. "I'm going to dig here," I announced. I sat down, cross-legged and prepared to remove the cone and the prayer from the pouch.

Barbara crouched down to sprinkle sage and sweetgrass, then turned the space over to me. I said again what I was doing. Looked each friend in the eyes. Then looked at the ground. "*Bismillah*" (in the name of Allah), I said, "please, Mother Earth, forgive me and accept my dig." I dug the earth, positioned the cone at the mouth of the hole, unfolded my paper and read. "Thank you for taking this from me and transmitting it to love and light." I envisioned the pine cone holding my uterus and everything I had held on to.

Then I let go.

I swept the surrounding dirt over the cone and over the hole, loving the feel of dirt against my palms. I buried the cone and everything it held. I repeated the prayer. I felt profound release.

"This felt right. I'm done," I said. I stood and each friend hugged me as we began to walk away. Then I stopped, and turned back to the tree once more. Circled my arms around its trunk. Pressed my face and breasts, my heart, my breath against the bark. I closed my eyes again. Smiled and cried, "I'm done."

I'll take care of it, said the tree.

"Thank you." I walked away, this time without looking back. I watched my friends walk and talk. I felt an incredible spiritual surge from them that brought us all together.

"What does 'salal' mean?" We were back at the crossroad when I asked Barbara the question. She looked at me, calm smile in her eyes. Her silver braid, which fell to just above her shoulders, was tied with a beautiful buckskin tie from her mother's traditional Cree territory.

"It's the shorter trees. See those with the shiny leaves?"

"Yeah."

"That's salal."

"Too funny. I had no idea! You know why I chose Salal?" I said I had connected it with halal/kosher. We laughed.

Later, when I told the story to my sister, Sabha, she said, "Where you were is Musqueam area."

"Yes, that's why I wanted to be there."

"It's been said there is a First Nations cemetery somewhere," she continued. "Maybe it was the ancestors speaking to you."

"I'd like to think so."

What I did not say was that this park also felt deeply important for other reasons. Women in the past have been sexually assaulted in the park. In my ritual to reclaim our feminine power, I was transmitting love and light to all women. I still wonder why the park chose me.

· · ·

MEHAROONA GHANI

Underneath my feet, I felt green grass, dried twigs, small soft stones.

Toes wiggled into arid dirt. Heart lowered, head forward. Entry prepared—an opening. "Thank you for my body. I thank you for being with me since a fetus, since birth, through womanhood. Thank you for being of service. I did the best I could out of love and respect."

Epicentre in front. I walked in, out, to labyrinth's core. Shed what was. What could no longer serve, no longer be. Layers dropped away. With gratitude I left what once was and accepted what is. "Thank you." I smiled into warm glow.

Released into centre. She appeared. Divine Sacred Feminine welcomed me, her hair long, black, straight to the waist of her gossamer blue gown. Her look gentle, her face formless. She reached forward with a ball of light—crystal, bright, blue, white, Milky Way light—and asked, *Are you ready to receive the light?* I felt my arms and hands pulled forward. Head and gaze lowered, I nodded yes. She placed the ball in my open palms. My fingers over the circle; her long fingers placed over mine. I arched forward, pressed the ball of light into my chest. Light transferred into my heart. Warmth flowed in veins, cells, bloodstreams, limbs, feet, hands, spine, brain—everywhere. I felt loved.

Us. Her arms, faceless face, upper body, breasts draped over my body, we formed an arch—we stood, me in Her. I wept. She released me.

She presented new gifts, on the grass before me: a pine cone—perfect geometric Fibonacci sequence—and a pearl-pink scallop shell. With gratitude I picked these up and thanked Her, then turned, and returned slowly with heavy feet. I looked back once more. She smiled. I wove out, sidestepped sheddings, and left.

Rumi, I am a tree.

Love always,
Meharoona, your light of the moon

Poetent

SUE GOYETTE

a gopher maybe, a catastrophe, a muskrat, a family, or maybe a river otter

I respond, without thinking, to most situations with fear. This happens when you grow up with trauma. My house was erratic. It could motor along for days in its quiet but off-kilter way and then, out of nowhere, the volume would increase, its intensity and its intolerable, compacted fucked-up-ness would hit the fan. In this way, I was wired as a first responder and I often found myself in the trenches. I know how to move fast despite feeling paralyzed. I've known this feeling for decades because it's so deep in my wiring it feels normal. It's a familiar and reliable reaction. Necessary, protective and, at some point, a fair and worthwhile response to the many situations I experienced. It's got a drone voice and narrates most things with downward dread: *holy shit this is going to be bad, ack.* Don't get me wrong, I have great respect for fear. I appreciate how it shifts my gears to hyperalert, switches my headlights to high beam. But I've been noticing how persistent it's been, how it assumes authority and how much authority I give to it without question.

The Buddhists say we have two dogs in us: love and fear. We're asked by pretty well every situation we find ourselves in: Which dog do you want to feed? The answer is simple enough but carrying out that answer is a little more challenging. Responding to situations and to people with love takes practice. And a generosity I'm working on. Curiosity seems a realistic place to start. It is a reliable negotiator, it can mediate between my racing heart and panic, my dread, and invite me to consider other possibilities, other directions, while not quite demanding the outpouring of love that I know to be the golden goal. Curiosity initiates a bonus round or another chance. It's a gamechanger that widens the horizon line. When I follow its roots, I arrive at awe and the jaw-dropping, unbelievable genius that is our planet's morphology and work-ings. Awe and then love. The way I see things is refreshed then, invigorated with the resources that bubble up when possibilities are manifesting and anything can happen. And those things may be better than I can imagine. But some days, I can't even imagine that.

If awe is salve for our eyes the way Rumi says it is, then maybe it's balm for our curiosity. There is so much we don't know: how things will turn out, for example. And curiosity, I've been thinking, may be the best greeting for encountering the unknown, the unexpected. Fear has been my reliable first response but curiosity may be a more sustainable fuel. I lean out of myself when I'm curious, I perk up; fear diminishes my primary radiance. It erodes my spirit, it's a pesticide for options and perspective and it robs everyone else of their spirit as well. What first eradicated my fear were encounters with sea-horses and a Portuguese man-of-war, bats and hummingbirds. A singular pine hit by lightning but surviving with a crooked and vital reach. These encounters claimed me somehow, but I'm getting ahead of myself.

A couple of years ago, my friend was camping by a lake. She was sitting by the water in the early evening when she saw something swimming toward her. A gopher, she thought, no, maybe a beaver. Not a beaver, a muskrat? As it swam closer she thought maybe a fisher, a river otter. It gave a shake as it reached the shore, then it stood.

I do this all the time. Name things before they're out of the water. I think growing up in the house I did nourished the kind of vigilance that worked hard at making sense of a situation. If I named something, then I knew what I was dealing with. It was a way of keeping myself safe. I honed my observation skills, my intuition. *This* usually happens, for example, after *that*. I'd create equations for the unknown, and potentially dangerous, to stay ahead of that danger. And I get why I did it. I still appreciate the skill, the dedication it took. It was spirited. An early form of courage. I bow to that younger version of myself. *Well done*, I say, *and now you can rest.*

Sometimes naming is also a form of control, isn't it? If I name it *this*, it can't be *that*. And the quicker I name it, the faster I know what it is and what I have to do. Another way to stay safe. What would happen if I learned to wait a little longer? What would happen if something was given the space to claim its own name?

The creature shook and then nudged itself forward and up, sort of unfolding itself. A young moose, all legs, dripping the lake back to itself. A moose, my friend said, never would she have guessed a moose.

.   .   .

the moment in which I was lit

I was pedalling a bike with training wheels through two puddles, working on the wet trail of all the tire marks I was leaving. The making of the marks was engrossing, though I was circling something I knew intuitively to avoid. It soon became the hub in my circle, the point from which I navigated. If I had been stopped at this moment and asked what exactly that thing was, I would have maybe said: *wet Kleenex*. I would have said: *small clump*. I was four and can still smell the parking lot, see the weeds you can imagine would be growing near an apartment building in the suburbs: long grass, some wild chicory still fisted, new sprouts of goldenrod. The small clump was a bird, fallen from its nest. I remember squatting for a closer look at its workings visible through its translucent skin. Its eyes were planetary, dark and inward. I knew, beneath words, that I was in the company of something important and unexpected. Too important for my parents. I went to the woman who knew birds, the silent old woman on the ground floor who fed them in a way that expanded my idea of family. I don't remember what happened to the bird. What I do remember was the care she showed it, her reverence. It was the nutritional kind of care a child leans into and learns something from. If someone had held a match to her care, it would have lit.

.   .   .

an apparatus, a vortex

I had been conducting the wind to vortex around
our apartment and unearth the root of the basement

from the ground, sending the building swirling to another place
with darker trees and a wider green. The process involved
an open heart otherwise an audience with the wind
wouldn't be given so I put myself in its current
and with wide arms tried to get it to chase me.

This was a couple of years later. I was six or seven, running madly around our building convinced I could create an adventure by vortexing our building out of the earth. I had talked a few of my friends into joining me but gradually they got bored or distracted, so I was running alone.

The apartment building was solid with renters
who didn't have much furniture but had a heaviness
to them that involved shift work and souring.
It was like riding on the back of a mammoth
with nothing to hold on to. It bucked me close
to the bush with thorns but I held on and called it magic.

There wasn't much else in my life at that point. A television. A dark and heavy family. I was convinced I'd been born into the wrong one. Seriously. They just didn't feel right.

My sister yelled stop every time I blew past her.
It finally bucked me off and I rolled hard
towards the building, the thorn bush softening
and then stabbing my fall. When I sat up, I was in the same world,
the rocks hadn't grown, the sky still in a hurry. In the bush
above my head was the only clue that something was different.
The unexpected green of it caught my breath, freshened it with
    colour
and then gave it back to me so I could whisper: what are you?

The moment was a chandelier. I was alone in a new and vital silence. The look we exchanged was potent. Or poetent, I just typed by mistake. But that's what it was: the look was *poetent*.

The creature posed all angular and miracle. If it had been
a miniature horse, it would have whinnied and shook its head
at being seen. If it had been a miniature airplane, its propellers
would've started spinning, its engine pulling it down the runway
of the branch and then, unbelievably, airborne
into takeoff.

What moments like these share is an expansion and a sense of other, a blueprint for the mysterious and for the totally unexpected manifesting. I was part perk and part bow. Humbled and verging. Fear's blind spot has kept me from knowing that I'm part of this genius. That I'm unfurling with a delectable spirit honed to that awe, that genius of design all living creatures share. When I forget that, I find myself homesick for the wildness that is inherently part of me.

The creature I found had given me courage,
convincing me that it wasn't an insect but a portal
into the miraculous. If you think I'm special, wait
until you see what else is out here, it telepathed,
and I believed it.

I had to. There wasn't much else and my relief was palpable. Ennobling. The luxury of a praying mantis: its colour and unexpected angles, its extensions only hinting at what is possible and how very little I actually knew. I remember the gratitude I felt. My horizon line widened past family. Here was another clue that I belonged to something bigger and my curiosity quickened. Who invented these creatures? And who thought up the apparatus of these perfect and timely encounters? Now I wonder: How do we keep that vitality watered when we find ourselves in a palliative care unit or a mental health ward? How do we keep it fed when all we're given are forms and prescriptions to fill? Or when we feel the heart pain inherent to living on this planet at this time with the deep grief we're experiencing but can't even begin to articulate? What is salve for our care and for our kindness? Our generosity and restoration? I wonder if we're more important to each other than we think.

. . .

an attack only better

It was the Summer of Heart Attacks. One after another,
men from Quebec in Speedos, their cigarettes wilting

towards their commendable bellies, this electromagnetic force
in the middle of its enduring oui or non argument. The bodies, thick

logs of sullen nons and the hot tongue of sand licking its yeses.
I counted five attacks before the shark and then stopped counting.

I was eleven. The first man to have a heart attack on the beach was an event that afforded me some time to think about mortality. A voltage into an already present: *Ack, it's going to happen to all of us??* By the fifth attack, a pattern seemed in place. I'd have guessed that it would happen again. I would have bet on it. The next day, however, a shark appeared instead, beached, and still very much alive. A shark, I remember thinking, who saw that coming? I'd never encountered anything so streamlined and so condensed. It had washed up crammed with ocean and was the most primordial yet modern thing I'd ever met. It spiced my summer with something that removed me from the mundane and wrought company I'd been in. I forged with it, I melted. There are no reliable patterns, I was learning, and this was neither good nor bad and sometimes could be spectacular.

After years of therapy, I unzipped the wetsuit of shark
and found a heart attacking. My mouth to fish, breathing,

was replaced with ocean bailed from my eyes and sloshed
on gills. The fish fluttering like a bird, like a new love eager

for a glimpse of me, another beloved.

·   ·   ·

synchronizing our watch

I'm still learning to appreciate moments that defy the mundane with their singularity and brilliance. These moments are like dahlias, each detail a petal, contributing to flower. My vocation now is to watch for them, to take notes, to weed around them so they thrive.

An old friend and I were catching up, talking about our lives. Each of us needing answers more than we should have needed anything. Maybe we wanted safety or reassurance. Maybe we wanted affirmation or just company. We both were on our own, facing our singular and private loneliness. The pub we were sitting in was called the Nail and the Kneecap, which is what we were feeling we were up against, emotionally, spiritually even, we had joked. Life, eh? We had so many questions and weren't willing to admit how scared we were, how old we were to be so scared. Here we were, knowing so little. What was it she asked me? If I'd do anything differently? If I had any regrets? The pub's windows were generous: wide and open to the street. Summer was just emerging, the flowerpots vivid and active. My pause after her question was part bafflement, part consideration and a large part dread. And that's what he drove through on his bicycle. The young person, driving without hands, right in front of us, straight-backed and composed, wearing the biggest, white-feathered wings I'd ever seen: another species of response. His timing, as timing is, was perfect.

SUE GOYETTE

My Flannery

LIZ HARMER

I knew her name long before I read her. Like J.R.R. Tolkien or C.S. Lewis, Flannery O'Connor, with her public and unabashed Christian faith, was one of our darlings. Each of these artists was incarnate proof that it was possible to be a believer and an artist, to be a believer with an intellect. In our faith community, which, for my entire childhood and adolescence, was my only community, we needed these proofs. Belief in Jesus was perpetually under attack. Christianity was for people who needed a crutch or a fairy tale, who couldn't face reality; it ignored the good science of Darwin and Hawking. It was absurd to believe in such cartoonish things as hoofed beings with pitchforks and grey-bearded men in clouds; it was offensive to tell people they were sinners.

Meanwhile, we all knew that faith was not certainty. It seemed that atheists not only did not understand us but refused even to try. Just as none of us understood atheism as anything but cruelty and hard-heartedness, a lack of openness. We thought they were shackled; they thought we were shackled. One upon a time God had hardened the pharaoh's heart and it sobered us to imagine that God might leave us alone with our disbelief.

In 2013, Marilynne Robinson wrote that O'Connor "knows all the arguments against religion. They seem to have changed little in 70 years." We all knew these arguments, or at least flimsy versions of them, since no one I knew believed they had any force. But when I was seventeen, seventeen years deep into my religious education, the idea that someone could find Christianity distasteful was shocking. Religion was deep and moving; I loved Jesus genuinely and eagerly awaited his return. Christians had been cruel to me, yes, and we were all hypocrites, but the fact of our shortcomings did not diminish the power of God. I believed in a universe both well ordered and mysterious. My favourite metaphor in those days was what we called the Drama of Scripture: God was the author and we were all characters in a book destined for a gloriously happy ending.

Our catechism was posed in a series of questions and answers. The first was poetic. Q: What is your only comfort in life and in death? A: That I am not my own, but belong, body and soul, to my faithful saviour Jesus Christ.

That I am not my own, but belong. This sentiment is hardly cheap. There is plenty of value in this articulation of faith. Still, I think that many people committed to liberal ideals of the freedom and integrity of the individual would find the level of our dogmatism and submission shocking. When I look back I sometimes feel that rather than having been raised in covenant with Christ, I had been indoctrinated.

There are many different ways of looking at Jesus. Any theological question could produce a split, each split giving birth to a new denomination. Should one keep the Sabbath by refraining from working or by having a celebratory meal at Swiss Chalet? Should one be baptized at birth or in adulthood? Should women be allowed to preach? How should a person confess? What would Jesus do? Scripture is not airtight. For most verses there is a counter-verse. In the Bible, as it is according to the Beatles, all you need is love, but even such an apparently obvious and easily decided matter was difficult to live out.

We believed that God's word was inerrant and stood with authority. Even as we produced and reproduced interpretations, ever unsettled, we called this scripture "infallible." Now it strikes me as bizarre to call a book so full of genres and writers, with parables and narratives, myths and poems and prophecies, proverbs and commandments, infallible. How could a story tell us what to do the way a commandment did?

How was one supposed to know what any of it meant?

.   .   .

As it is with Jesus Christ, it seems there is a different Flannery O'Connor for every reader. Robinson called her "unloving" and "hard-hearted." A good many tweets rose up to dispute this. Some of O'Connor's early readers believed she was satirizing the very faith she sought to strengthen. About her first novel, *Wise Blood*, she said:

> That belief in Christ is to some a matter of life and death has been
> a stumbling block for some readers who would prefer to think it

a matter of no great consequence. For them, Hazel Motes' integrity lies in his trying with such vigor to get rid of the raggedy figure who moves from tree to tree in the back of his mind. For the author Hazel's integrity lies in his not being able to.

To her increasingly violent protagonist Hazel Motes, Jesus is that raggedy figure who will not come unstuck in his mind. Some readers find his efforts to dislodge Christ heroic; others find it tragic.

In her essay "Writing Short Stories," O'Connor writes that she prefers "to talk about the meaning in a story rather than the theme of a story."

People talk about the theme of a story as if the theme were like the string that a sack of chicken feed is tied with. They think that if you can pick out the theme, the way you pick the right thread in the chicken-feed sack, you can rip the story open and feed the chickens. But this is not the way meaning works in fiction.

Nor is it the way meaning works in scripture. But what are we to do if we can't feed the chickens? How will the chickens be fed?

"When anybody asks you what a story is about, the only proper thing is to tell him to read the story," O'Connor writes.

The human mind works in such ways that we are pattern makers, ordering all we see even while we believe things were ordered such before we came along. What we see in an ink blot tells us more about our state of mind than it does about the ink blot.

In 2000, I took a single introductory course at our local Christian university. My professor was sympathetic to my views of God's authorship, ourselves as part of a book, and he adored Flannery O'Connor.

In her stories, I found kinship. She was a peacock farmer, deeply southern and ill for most of her life, but she and I shared an intense longing for the blaze of mystery lighting everything up if you would only stop to look. I believed that she, like me, was a person indifferent to this life and this world and this body in favour of the heavenly ones to come. My interpretation of her work, if it is indeed a kind of ink blot test, makes my beliefs then look pretty frightening. Faced with almost any atrocity, I would have said, perhaps somberly, "God's will."

O'Connor's world is a brutal one. Her stories are filled with ugliness and evils both petty and large. Granted, her setting is the poor, Protestant South; her genre is Gothic. Few of the characters—not even the children led off to the woods by men who will kill them in "A Good Man Is Hard to Find"—are sympathetic. Many readers feel moved by her less to pity than to shock. It didn't bother me at all back then, this world view in which small moments of insight are overwhelmed by disastrous violence. In "Revelation," Mrs. Turpin must be attacked and insulted by an unhinged person in order to see her own meanness, and in "Everything That Rises Must Converge," the character most like the villains in the other two stories (an older chatterbox who doubles as a racist hypocrite) is so despised by her own son that *she* becomes sympathetic. Everyone is small and puffed up with hubris; everyone needs knocking down.

Back then, in the early days of 2000, I was happy with these stories. They did not disturb me in the least. Sometimes violence is required. Original sin is our inheritance. God needed to shock us from our complacency, or, as O'Connor writes in a letter in 1961, "I don't know if anyone can be converted without seeing themselves in a kind of blasting annihilating light, a blast that will last a lifetime."[1]

Let's go ahead and call Flannery O'Connor a strong believer. We know that she wrote in order to reveal God in the concrete, to reveal mystery in manners. In the universe according to Flannery O'Connor there is true and false, good and evil, heaven and hell. The world is infused with grace. The life of Jesus is not only an idea we might draw from but a series of events that actually happened and have real consequences in our lives. We might be tempted to apply the words *fundamentalist* or *dogmatic* to her beliefs, and perhaps we would not be wrong, though those words carry with them a faint stink. When we think a believer is fundamentalist, we are usually pretty sure that we are not: her beliefs—not mine—are crazy.

When someone who left the church of my upbringing once called it fundamentalist, I felt I'd been slapped in the face, or, like a character in "Revelation," had had a book hurled directly at my eye. I felt she was calling me unthinking, which was far from the truth. My own qualms and doubts centred on problems

....

1   Sally Fitzgerald, ed., *The Habit of Being: Letters of Flannery O'Connor* (New York: Farrar, Straus and Giroux, 1979), 427.

of logic. (The first serious non-believers I met were incredulous: "You believe in the immaculate conception?" I was incredulous at their incredulity. The Virgin Birth—*that's* your stumbling block? If we're talking about the author of the universe, a miraculous insemination is no big deal.) Where the so-called inerrant text contradicted itself—there was the problem. Most damning (if you'll pardon the pun) was the thing that stuck in every Calvinist's craw: How could we have free will when our lives were utterly known and predestined by the One who made us? Why would a good God bring in to the world people whom he knew would fail, and then punish them for failing?

Fundamentalism was a movement reacting against an increasingly liberal American Christianity after the First World War and continues to be deeply influential in conservative territory. The interpretive focus of fundamentalism is a nearly psychotic literalism. Find an injunction of Paul's and make it so that no woman is allowed to speak in church. There actually was an Adam, an Eve and a serpent in the trees. Most of us in liberal society find this sort of thinking immoderate and distasteful, as it requires not simply submission to authority but the submission of some more than others. Fundamentalism came along purposely to oppose secularizing tolerance.

It would be inaccurate to call Flannery O'Connor a fundamentalist. A fundamentalist reads a parable only for its moral lesson; such a reader of an O'Connor story takes with her only the flimsy theme—*don't be a blowhard! Don't lean so much on your own crutches!*—leaving behind all of the good and complex richness that might have fed the chickens. The literary equivalent of eschewing well-cooked meals in favour of a daily vitamin.

So what kind of believer was she? A strong believer is often a dogmatist, a person who refuses to change her mind. I once had a professor who used the phrase *come what may*: What do you believe *come what may*? At the time I was a rather dogmatic believer and would have scoffed at weak faith—any faith that wasn't *come what may* was no faith at all. I thought agnosticism was a cop-out: just perform Pascal's wager and choose a side!

Weak belief is what I have now, in my thirties, humbled by a long relationship with a skeptic and the daily battering of my domestic challenges. I miss my certainty. I miss my strength, the belief that allowed me, always, to close my eyes and to jump. Everything was in all-knowing, all-powerful, all-forgiving hands. A friend points out to me that perhaps seeing oneself in a kind of burning, annihilating light can only lead to radical uncertainty, that radical uncertainty is more likely the position of any character at the end of an O'Connor story, as though even one's beliefs have been burned away.

"You may ask," O'Connor says in *Mystery and Manners*, "why not simply call this literature Christian? Unfortunately, the word Christian is no longer reliable. It has come to mean anyone with a golden heart." This slam is why it is possible for Robinson to see O'Connor as unloving. But God is always present in her stories, even if instead of tidy conversions we have self-mutilation, violence, ugliness, delusion and all sorts of insanity. One of her most tweeted quotes is "The truth does not change according to our ability to stomach it." Take that, ye who are repulsed by us! She also said that "for the hard of hearing you shout and for the blind you draw large and startling figures." She had a pedagogical purpose, but she wasn't going to preach. Her teaching strategy was demonstrative. She was going to show you and, by God, you had better see.

. . .

Before her comeuppance, Mrs. Turpin of "Revelation" ensures that it will come: "'If there's one thing I am,' Mrs. Turpin said with feeling, 'it's grateful. When I think of all I could have been besides myself and what all I got, a little of everything, and a good disposition besides.'" We see Turpin's type everywhere in the Gospels. A Pharisee went to the synagogue to pray: "I thank you Lord that you made me nothing like *him*." No Pharisee in a Flannery O'Connor story comes out unscathed.

But here's the thing: in 2000, I didn't see that I was a self-satisfied Christian. I had true faith, and didn't know I was a Pharisee, lacking charity toward others. I could not see the irony in reading "Revelation" and thinking, Thank God I'm not like Mrs. Turpin. In 2000, strong believer, dogmatist, I wrote in my essay for that English class in the Christian University that not only in a Flannery O'Connor story but in life, grace must sometimes give you a thrashing.

The story under consideration was "Parker's Back," in which a man goes from secularized to awestruck. It is full of smacks upside the head: Parker falls off a tractor at some point, and loses his shoes. Parker marries a Christian woman he's convinced he doesn't love. To anger his wife, he has an enormous "byzantine Christ" tattooed across his back. The story, written shortly before Flannery died, is less typically O'Connor in that Parker is pitiable, not certain of anything and rather helpless. In 2000, seeing God's thrashings everywhere, I saw Parker as a character stupidly trying to flee God, like Jonah of the famous whale-swallowing, who finds he's bumping up against God's power at every turn. You think you can just sit up there on your tractor?—think again! You think you are invisible to God? There he is watching you as though tattooed to your flesh. At the end of the story, Parker's wife beats him up and he is left "crying like a baby."

People need knocking down, I wrote. I would have included myself—I need knocking down, too, I'd say. Looking back, I see that it was an attempt at inoculation. I thought by knowing how broken I was, I could prevent the actual breaking.

·　·　·

Twenty-some years into believing *come what may*, I finally discovered the beauty of the opposing position. In 2005, my young husband and I took a trip to New York City and went to a planetarium show, my first planetarium show. At the time, I believed my knowledge of science to be fairly strong. I had learned about the discoveries of DNA. Few of us had a problem with the idea that God created the world through a "big bang." "Evolution from monkeys" was a larger stumbling block. The planetarium show we saw concerned the question of life on other planets. We were surrounded by ten-year-olds on field trips. I was completely unprepared, in the moments that followed, for a sudden loss of faith. The show moved quickly through the basic physics of the universe's origin, and then *boom*. Harrison Ford gave this epigrammatic zinger as, all around us, cooled rock and ashes began to sprout from trees: "As soon as it was possible for there to be life, it was there."

The revelation was immediate. We Christians did not have an exclusive claim on beauty or mystery. Humans without God were still capable of the range of human emotion, including awe, and love, and kindness. Shaken, I sat at the cafeteria afterwards, looking at my fork. "I'm no more important to God than this fork," I told Adam, woefully. "Even if there is a God, the universe is so vast."

I began to call myself an atheist, though Adam, who had spent most of his life with no particular relationship to religious experience, laughed gently and said that I was far from an atheist. I would find myself thinking that God had predestined this phase of disbelief toward some end, I was so unable to shake the sense that I was important to Him. I tried and failed to picture the sky as if it were not filled with watchfulness and care.

Around that time I was sitting in a movie theatre when I had a sudden oceanic feeling of fellowship with all the other people in that theatre, all of them strangers. I realized that I had always felt set apart—pit against—and that really these were just other people.

Now I say, perplexed, that the less devout I've become, the more loving I am. "I would question your use of the word 'devout,' then," my father says. But I really was devout back then, in a daily and continuous conversation with God, immersed in the scriptures, thinking always of Christ. Certain, doctrinaire, judgmental, unkind. The farther I get from God, the more vulnerable I feel, and this vulnerability, like the loss of a wooden leg in an O'Connor story, is what makes love for others possible. But humiliation—the wellspring of humility—can lead to all kinds of other things too, like rage, like reactive bigotry. All sorts of things might have happened to the characters at the end of an O'Connor story, if it were real.

.   .   .

All avid readers know how a book you thought you knew changes upon subsequent readings. Books like *Beloved* and *The Road*, both of them dealing with how hard the world can be for our children, will affect you differently before and after parenthood. But we, of course, are always changing, in ways subtle and not, converting, deconverting, reconverting.

Fourteen years after that "thrashed by grace" essay, I was in a graduate seminar discussing *Wise Blood* and realizing that her theology was much more difficult to understand than I had once believed. Not only a darling of the Christians, she is a darling everywhere, a strong believer who writes in stark and uncompromising terms, admired by those who don't share her beliefs, loved for the elegance and wit of her prose, for the shock of her reversals. It is her craftsman's devotion to the sensory, the particular, to *show, don't tell*, that make her such an excellent Rorschach test. There will always be interpretive wiggle room; these are stories, not sermons. Now, in stories where I once saw a cleansing and annihilating light, I see instead God speaking in a small, still voice.

In a review of O'Connor's *Prayer Journal*, Carlene Bauer quotes a letter she wrote to Andrew Lytle in 1960:

> I have got to the point now where I keep thinking more and more about the presentation of love and charity, or better call it grace, as love suggests tenderness, whereas grace can be violent or would have to be to compete with the kind of evil I can make concrete. ... At the same time, I keep seeing Elias in that cave, waiting to hear the voice of the Lord in the thunder and lightning and wind, and only hearing it finally in the gentle breeze, and I feel I'll have to be able to do that sooner or later, or anyway keep trying.

Most believers do not possess a static faith that sits unchanging throughout their lives. Flannery herself wants a faith that is plaintive and searching, not merely raging or dogmatic. Perhaps it says more about me than about her work that I see grace operating more quietly and with less shocking efficacy than I used to. I am, like Flannery, "vulnerable to all sorts of intellectual quackery." Now I am more confused than ever, unable to shake Christ, lover of the world. "Parker's Back" was written by a dying woman scribbling under her hospital sheets, told she was too weak to write, and now when I read it, I don't find myself hovering over the character, hoping that Parker will fall so that he can rise. I find myself with Parker under the tree, bewildered, horrified.

Embracing Impermanence

SHENIZ JANMOHAMED

One petal folding over the other, twirling into a centre so perfect it seems unreal.

One petal falling after another, draping the ground with reminders of what is real.

The simplicity of a crepe-thin bougainvillea flower in the heat of the sun, part shadow, part light, like the folds of the tissue paper my maternal grandmother wraps and unwraps around her heirloom jewellery. She does this as a ritual each year, waiting for me to come to her room, then lifting the jangling keys from her gown pocket to find the right one, opens her drawers of silk purses and pouches, plastic heart-shaped and felt ring boxes. She brings each drawer, one by one, out onto the bed and proceeds to unpack each carefully wrapped package. Her glasses slip to the edge of her perky nose (the nose my sister inherited, unlike my crooked one) and she hands over a piece of jewellery without looking up. "If you want it, take it." As if there are no memories attached to these pieces of her life, as if she hadn't worn them in happier days. An amethyst as deep and luscious as a grape sits in a large ring setting. I tell her to keep this one. She tries to put it on her gnarled finger, lamenting, "My fingers are too crooked now."

Crookedness.

Her mother, practically a saint, was bent over for most of her life—the result of a painful labour. By the time she passed away, she was nearly in the fetal position—returning, to begin again.

. . .

There are stories of saintlike women in our family, stories that swirl like wisps of smoke from a dying flame. I can only grasp what remains, I have no way of reviving that fire. I gather the ashes in ways that make sense to me, or don't make sense at all. Maybe that's what it means to come home to oneself.

.   .   .

Ash and dust appear and reappear in family stories. It was rumoured that my dad's grandmother, Sukaribhai—a title that means sweet lady—would spend hours sweeping the local *jamatkhana*, a place of worship for Ismaili Muslims, in Old Town Mombasa, then gathering up the dust she would fold a pinch in wax paper and take it home to sprinkle on her grandchildren's clothes, claiming that the dust would keep them humble. One of her friends would collect the dust and swallow it. Some might say that prayers swirled in that dust, that a tiny taste would allow a faith glutton to ingest the blessings of these heartfelt devotions. The realist in me leans toward a less rose-coloured explanation. Perhaps the dust was a reminder that all things, ourselves included, one day turn to dust.

> *"Die before you die," said the Prophet Muhammad.*
> *Have wings that feared ever*
> *touched the Sun?*
>
> *I was born when all I once*
> *feared—I could*
> *love.*
>
> —Hazrat Bibi Rabia Basri

.   .   .

When Sukaribhai died, close to a thousand people lined the streets to take turns carrying her body to the cemetery. Sukaribhai would do her charity work quietly and without praise, visiting one community after another to assist with living costs, food, health care—anything that was needed—yet even her own husband was unaware of the extent of her good deeds until she passed away. To quietly do the work, despite challenges and trials, despite limitations—this is the work of my women ancestors, many of whom never had the chance to pass on their wisdom to those of us who would follow them.

The lilt of my grandmother's voice when she sings familiar hymns, the cloud-grey obscurity of my great-grandmother's eyes in photographs, the silence between the flick-flick of tasbih beads, the reminder of death each day. These are my inheritances.

> *Let sorrowful longing dwell in your heart,*
> *never give up, never losing hope.*
> *The Beloved says, "The broken ones are My darlings."*
> *Crush your heart, be broken.*
>
> —Shaikh Abu Saeed Abil Kheir,
> "Nobody, Son of Nobody"

. . .

What does it mean to encounter the world with a broken heart? What does it mean to be born with a hole in the most vital part of yourself? A place you will speak from, create from, love from. A place of knowing. A place that will break itself and mend itself, the pulsating red joy that beats in spite of you. What does it mean for the heart to feel empty before having the chance to be whole?

My mom recalls a time when I would draw my heart in the darkest crayon colour I could find and demand an answer to the one question that plagued my little self: Why is my heart bad? She admitted to not having the answers, and so she gave me books about every religious and spiritual tradition she could think of. Stacked on my shelf were stories of Krishna and Siddhartha, meditations on nature and tales of Sufis—reminders that the questions that riddled me were questions people have been asking for generations, millennia, eons.

I have always known that my heart needed to be healed, even if I had no idea why it was broken in the first place.

I was nine months old when it came to light that I had a hole in my heart. The hole was repaired, but then the doctors noticed that my natural pacemaker wasn't working properly. My heart had doubled in size, could barely be contained inside my tiny chest, so I was hooked up to an external pacemaker until my heart could contract enough for an internal pacemaker to be inserted. My pacemakers have changed over the years—clunks of metal that inspire nick-names like Bionic Woman—to pieces the size of my fist. I often forget I have a pacemaker, and when I remember, I'm humbled and disturbed to know that I owe my steady beat of vitality to the reliable pulse of a machine.

Thanks to my heart, for the first ten years of life, the hospital was my second home. A home where childhood joy met untimely illness, and some-times death. A home where eating my favourite comfort foods and watching my favourite shows almost made me forget the panic of anaesthesia or the prick of a needle. Visiting the hospital now as an adult can be humiliating—being poked and prodded while trying to keep your dignity intact—but as a child, I had no concept of dignity and control. I had yet to develop that self-cherishing part of myself. As a child, I had no choice but to surrender.

When I was fifteen or so, I faced another routine replacement surgery. Being a teen made me even less trusting, more unsure of my confidence and courage. The night before the surgery, I could not sleep. My imagination conjured up grotesque images of what could happen during surgery—of all the things that could go wrong. Exhausted and unable to shake those fears, I retreated to the living room and turned on the TV.

There on my screen was a turbaned man dancing barefoot at a shrine somewhere in the heart of Pakistan. Wearing a jewel-toned robe reminiscent of Joseph's technicolour dream-coat, he played an *ektara*, a one-stringed instru-ment, and danced to the beat of bells draped about his ankles. He was singing the words of famed humanist poet and Sufi saint, Bulleh Shah:

The path of love is long and difficult
full of pains and punishments

Love has its roots in all realms of heavens and earth
love is in every heart …

I didn't understand the words. And, it didn't matter. A seed of peace had been planted in my heart. I felt comforted by the rasp of his voice, able at last to fall asleep, then rise the next morning to face another day of surgery.

A few years later, while pursuing an undergraduate degree in religion, I saw a documentary on Sufism in one of my classes. There it was—the same film I had watched the night before my surgery. I learned that the singer's name was Saieen Zahoor, a modern-day Sufi bard, travelling across Pakistan to revive the words and message of Bulleh Shah. After that class, after searching for Saieen Zahoor on YouTube and bookmarking his performances, I found myself hunched over translations of Bulleh Shah's poetry for hours and hours in the library, in the heart of the downtown campus.

I was delving deep into Sufi poetry and music when a rare opportunity presented itself. Saieen Zahoor was coming to Toronto for one weekend only, to play an open-air concert celebrating the music and lyrics of Bulleh Shah. Through my work as a freelance journalist, I had miraculously landed the task of writing his biography for the concert program. That meant I would have backstage access, for an interview.

On a balmy day in July, I sat in a glass-panelled room when Saieen Zahoor arrived in a white salwar kameez—loose-fitting pants paired with a long tunic—and wearing a black turban. He walked toward me and placed his hand over his heart. Introductions began, and the interview followed. I was nervous, aware that my window of opportunity was shrinking. I wanted to express gratitude for his inspiring me at such a challenging time in my life. I caught the kindness in his kohl-streaked eyes and collapsed into my notes, in tears. Wet-faced, I blubbered my gratitude to him—with the aid of a translator.

What happened next felt impossible to translate into words. Bulleh Shah's message had survived religious intolerance to be lovingly revived with the gravel-rich voice and hennaed fingertips of Saieen Zahoor. Now, these same hands were placed upon my head to impart a blessing—a blessing for healing, a transmission of poetic memory. A handful of water to sprinkle on the seed in my heart.

.   .   .

When I was a child I stuffed my pockets with maple wing nuts, peeling them to reveal the rubbery seeds within. I collected gravel pebbles that glinted in the light of the sun before they dulled when night descended. I gathered hand-fuls of glistening river rocks with vibrant colours that faded by the time I got them home.

SHENIZ JANMOHAMED

And yet, I still lined my windowsill with them—these disappointments from the earth, imperfect mementos reminding me that nothing but memory remains intact, and sometimes, even memory fades.

In my late twenties, sick with writer's block, I would stare at my blank pages, willing myself to perfection. My words fell short of the magic I envisioned in my mind. The joy of writing soured. The inner critic screamed louder and louder in my head. I was obsessed with becoming more profound, to the point that I could not write.

You read to become all knowledgeable
But you never read yourself.

You run to enter your mosques and temples
But you never entered your own heart.

Everyday you fight Satan
But you never fight your own Ego.

Bulleh Shah you try grabbing that which is in the sky
But you never get hold of what sits inside yourself.

Stop it all my friend!

Stop seeking all this knowledge, my friend.

—Bulleh Shah

So, I returned to nature.

Leaving perfection behind, embracing impermanence, I gave myself permission to be made and unmade in each moment.

I held vigil for the brokenness of my perfect, imperfect heart.

Silence replaced speech. My heart led my hands.

I created art from the land, for the land, to be left on the land.

Standing, sitting, settling in to the discomfort of freezing temperatures.

Kneeling, heaving, sweating until it became too dark to continue.

Offerings of gratitude encased in a sand-dusted mollusc, maps of mind traced in the sand, full circles dotted with oblong pebbles, seeds scattered to sprout for others.

Pockmarked pebbles, faded leaves, soft twigs, shards of ice, curled peels of birch bark, capless acorns, loose moss, straggly lichen, bruised petals, sand, snow, silence—

A fallen bougainvillea flower lies by the side of the road, faded to the colour of parchment paper. A gift wrapped in the dust of remembrance—a hand-cupped reminder of death every day.

A handful, a full heart.

SHENIZ JANMOHAMED

Second Chakra

PAM JOHNSON

A rhythm pulled at me as soon as I entered the park. I'd been doing data entry at my temp job, and I needed something to calm my agitation. Vic stared at me and raised an eyebrow when I told him. I was like an addict hunting for a hit.

Lately, I'd felt the pulse of an internal snare drum insisting on change. It was a constant, trying to keep up with the drum. Keep moving, keep watching, keep marching. This was the pace of the city and this was me, the loyal soldier, trying to find my way. Constant motion, constant beat, constant rhythm. What I couldn't find was the beat of my own heart. It felt brassy, tight, the drum's head pulled taut. Keep moving, my head told me. This is how a person progresses. If I put in more effort, if I keep moving, it will all work out.

Thud, thump, trot, march.

Keep the beat.

Snap, pop, click.

That day in the park, I fell constantly, failed repeatedly in chi kung practice. "Fall seven times and stand up eight," the Japanese proverb says. There I was in tree pose, arms extended, legs in a half-squat as if sitting in a chair, thighs gripped, quads burning. My eyes struggled to focus. Time slowed down. My legs wobbled and shook and in an instant they collapsed, knees crackling on the way down. There was a force below the rhythm, an undertow—I was in deep water, feeling the sand give way beneath my feet, not wanting to smash to the ocean floor.

"Go to the ground, Pam, focus on your breath," Vic instructed.

So I squatted, hands on the cold earth, and found myself staring at the trees. Something about their rooted detachment forced me to pay attention to the ground beneath me. There was no getting lost in dramatic views or metaphors, my focus was steady: tree bark, roots, green space. The trees themselves were our instructors. Last week we crawled on logs, eyes closed, and I learned that I needed to get down on my hands and knees to move forward, to learn to trust. Our focus had been tested by a woman walking her dog. She didn't like what she was seeing.

"You crazy sons of bitches," she shouted. "Take your voodoo movement the hell away from my park. You hear me?"

What did we look like to outsiders? To the city? The trees didn't seem to mind. Or did they?

. . .

My practising chi kung with Vic and the group in Dufferin Grove Park was new, really, only three months old. In the early stages of practice, we did propriocep-tion exercises, sensing the relative position of the body parts during movement. Side to side, back and forth, up and down. Slowing everything down to feel the interconnectedness of breath and movement. The practice was filled with discipline and shifting perspectives, physically and mentally. I was learning how to be present in my body. During these times I started with a head full of ideas, threads of conversations, worries, plans. My breath circulated only in my upper body. Full, deep breaths were elusive. It was difficult to feel my legs or feet. I could feel only the dull, prickly sensation in my chest, as if I were winded. My mind flitted, jolted, from one sensation to the next—cold fingertips, stiff upper back, exhaling from my mouth, a constricted feeling in the chest.

Vic's instructions were simple, and he gave us small amounts of informa-tion about each exercise. Occasionally he would talk about the meridians, the interconnected, internal energetic system, but he kept descriptions brief and encouraged us to focus on the breath in our belly, or the palm of our hands. Overintellectualizing the process would distract us from the experience of being in our bodies.

"Allow your breath to move into your belly. Find your centre," he'd repeat, lesson after lesson. "Where your mind goes, your ch'i flows. Everything returns to the centre."

Vic was part spiritual warrior, part five-foot-seven panda in a T-shirt and loose cotton pants. His own experience was the foundation for his teach-ing. After a car accident years earlier, he'd discovered chi kung as part of a therapeutic journey. Vic was direct and honest, with a deep laugh and a soft belly. His observations and insights were astute. He took his time as he led us through exercises, talking about moving from our centre, our Tan Tien, and listening to the internal guidance it provided.

"See the practice as a way of taking you back to who you really are. Teaching you what you already know."

Something shifted in me as I stayed in the squat position, feeling earth beneath my hands. My breath found new spaces in my torso. The sensation in my heart had dialled down ever so slightly. My mind flitted a little less. I was a smidgeon more aware.

Eventually, I rejoined the others and we began to walk in circles, circling our arms, opening our hearts. I found myself yawning uncontrollably to suck in air. Words circled through my mind—*trust*, and *surrender*, and *let go*. Over and over and over, they circled through, like Vic's voice. "It's not about 'getting' somewhere, Pam. It's about process and moving in circles. Let go of your habitual linear thinking and follow the circles. Feel the surrender."

I would hear these ideas again and again in the six years I worked with Vic but in the beginning they were enigmatic concepts. It would take years of practice to embody—and discover—the meaning of those words.

.   .   .

The walk to Vic's from the Dufferin subway station was short enough, but as I turned down his street, I felt my inner adolescent rearing up again, the girl who's resistant to the unknown. It was the first time I'd met Vic outside the park for a lesson. I stood awkwardly in his front hall pulling up my socks, as Vic indicated the empty room to our left—the dojo, he called it, a spare room with no furniture and caramel-coloured floors. The facing wall had blue wallpaper with small pink and white flowers that brought to mind the honeysuckle bush from my Calgary childhood. An upright piano stood in one corner, and across from it, a side table with a small altar with a feather, a rosary, a crystal. A small vase with three sturdy shoots of bamboo, tufts of green leaves coming out the top.

Vic sat cross-legged beneath the window. Outside, the light was dim. Upstairs, tenants were walking on the creaking floorboards. A muffled woman's voice seeped into the space. I felt the hardness of the wooden floor beneath me. I sat across from Vic, knees cracking some, my breath stilted. What was I doing here?

Vic began in his slow, deliberate speech. "You've shown real dedication in the past three months. At first I didn't think you'd last." His voice was steady, clear. I sensed there was something significant about this lesson. I needed to pay attention. My stomach tightened.

Next step: lie on my back, for deep breathing exercises.

"Focus your attention," Vic said, "on the sensations in your body."

I began with my feet, gradually moving up my calves and thighs until I reached my hips. "Focus your breath into your hips."

Almost immediately I felt an intense desire to wail.

Vic's voice was steady, reassuring. "Breathe into your lower abdomen and hips, Pam."

I felt a concentration of energy in my left hip. Tears welled beneath my eyelids. My head felt like it was moving away from my body, and there was this heavy feeling, as if my abdomen and hips were filled with silt, as if my sacrum were draped in heavy sand while my head bobbed out at sea. A huge space separated all these parts. On top of that, something essential was missing. My lower abdomen and womb were void, empty. A moment later, my mind flashed to a child, to losing a child. I felt a catch in the throat and sternum. A wave of emotion ripped toward my heart. Tears flowed. I wanted to get up and run, to stop the breathing, to leave whatever *this* was behind. My right leg began to shake. My ears pooled with tears.

Holes, spirals, tunnels.

Vic's voice cut through the sensation. I was safe, he said, reminding me to focus on my belly, to feel the rise and fall of breath. "I know this is difficult, Pam, keep coming back to your breath."

Eventually, as the waves of emotion subsided, my breath and focus began to move more easily, back into my belly.

I took several minutes to settle.

Vic spoke quietly. "Be gentle as you come to sit, you've had quite a ride."

He then went on to talk about the energetic movements I had just experienced. "Your sacrum and pelvis, your second chakra, is dull, it has been numbed over the years but it's gradually coming back to life. You'll notice dull pain as the sensation comes back into your body." In a soft tone, he talked about the second chakra's connection to my heart, how I was inclined to take responsibility for others, how I liked to please. He was right, I was a "good" girl. The result, though, was repressed sexual and creative expression. Then: "May I ask you a very personal question, Pam?"

"Uh, yes."

"Have you ever experienced trauma in association with a sexual experience? Or have you ever had an abortion?"

My mind flailed as I tried to take in what he was saying. I could hardly make sense of the intensity I had just experienced in my body. "No … no," I blurted.

Talking about the energy of my second chakra, I began to think about patterns around creativity and sexuality. We talked about the fact I hadn't fully explored either of these areas in my life. Some of the concepts were, of course, familiar. An energy healer I'd seen a few months earlier had talked about an energetic deficit in my second chakra, that I needed more fluidity in my life, less control.

Vic and I talked about the second chakra's link to relationships. We talked about my dad's struggle with his sexuality, the shame he'd felt, being gay in a time when that could not be openly acknowledged. Unknowingly, unwittingly, I'd inherited that shame. "You have a pure heart," Vic continued. "You're energetically sensitive, Pam. You would have picked up on your father's feelings at a young age."

I sat still, very still, on the cool wooden floor.

"There is power in your creative centre which you are not using. It's time to stop holding on to something energetically that is not yours."

As I left Vic's house and stepped into the crisp fall air, I felt both more in my body and more apart from it. Had I ever felt this way before?

·   ·   ·

Lucy's laundry dominated the apartment's clothesline. Lucy, with her chartreuse bras and Walmart towels, her lingerie, her latest conquests. All out there, all on display. I knew the details of her love life from our shared clothesline— that and the pulsating music. Chartreuse bra and "It's Gonna Be a Good Night" signalled a new man on her radar.

I had never hung lingerie on that line.

Thinking about my second chakra—the numbness, and the coming alive—I realized I'd made some correlations to my relationship with Dad and the men in my life, but I'd never considered all this from an energetic perspective.

How had I let myself be numbed?

My youthful romantic history had been a running theme of unrequited love. Sad songs and one trajectory—the heartache of never being picked. Gin and tonics at house parties, Roberta Flack's "Killing Me Softly" after getting home. Drinking orange juice and vodka and passing out in a garden, waking up with dirt in my ear. Dancing to "Red Red Wine" and "Suspicious Minds." Phil Collins's "Against All Odds." My twenty-year-old defended heart studied women's literature, read stories of heroines drowning themselves, searching for that feeling of release.

The men in my life wore Converse sneakers. They were fun-loving free spirits with boyish grins and life-of-the-party energy. They were hoops-shooting guitar strummers who wore their baseball caps backwards. My naive heart mistook friendship for love, drunk calls from a pizza joint at midnight as something to pin my hopes on. Longing and yearning and almost-but-not-quite and lemon gin with the COULD CAUSE BLINDNESS warning on the label.

I was obsessed with being a virgin, terrified of the intimacy, the energy it would take not to be one.

And the patterns had continued until sex had become a distant idea of a life force, a frozen pulsation, and I in perpetual winter. I couldn't sense the flow beneath the ice. I longed for melt and thaw, for signs of growth. Green spears on the tips of trees. Spring. Warmth and moisture in alignment.

What I realized now was that a season has to run its course.

It would take time to come back into the parts of my body I had shut down.

I had separated myself from sex for years. It became something I had learned to live without, so much so that my mind had stopped registering the need for sensuality. I had treated desire like an antigen my body should fight off. Sensuality was that foreign to my system.

Here, now, change could begin.

Vic's words played in my head. "It's okay to be creative, it's okay to be a woman." Intellectually I understood this, but more breath, air and warmth were needed before I could embody that knowledge to the fullest.

I ran my finger over the Formica tabletop where my journal sat. The sounds of guitar wafted down from the apartment above. I cradled my mug of tea, the whiff of cardamom, cinnamon, allspice drifting up in waves. A calm air permeated the kitchen. I could just make out the colours of the dimly lit maple tree outside—its coppers, pomegranates and golds suspended in the fading light. There was a smudge on the windowpane, where the leaves tapped against it, and for an instant I mistook the leaves for someone peering in.

I wrote in my journal. *I am going gently today.*

Thinking about Vic's words, about "everything being perfect" and that I am not wrong—that the failure, the small steps and feeling wobbly are okay—I commit to moving forward.

To being with what is, just taking the steps.

To being creative, to being woman.

Are You There, God? It's Me, Talking to Mary Karr

TAMARA JONG

Dear Mary,

I just read *Lit* and want it tattooed on my body. Wait. That didn't come out right. I want "Stay Lit" scribbled on me. You wrote that for me when we met at HippoCamp in Lancaster, Pennsylvania. I didn't have the guts to mention the letter I sent you about your changing the way I view faith. Though I'd like to think if I did it would be as good as when a fan said reading your book was like coming home and you came off the stage to comfort her.

My letter was typed although I considered writing it (cursive writing and all) but didn't want to subject you to my serial-killer chicken scratch, seeing most times I can't read it myself. I did not inherit Ma's beautiful handwriting. All big loops and ball gowns, I swear. She was a poet like you. What kind of poet, it's hard to say. We only have some lines she wrote that my brother found twenty-nine years after her other poems ended up in the landfill. That was back in 1987. I'm undecided about whether I can forgive the person who tossed 'em. That's the year Ma drowned and I was the one who dragged her poetry in boxes to the curb.

Aunt Margie tells me that all the kids in their family were writers; Ma included, that'd be seventeen Catholics from New Waterford, Nova Scotia. There's a doctor and Taoist monk (so religion was bound up in me) on Daddy's side but no scribblers. Ma ran away from the farm at twelve. Her dad used to beat them all pretty regular and loved the racehorses more than kin. The dooziest tale was the one where my uncles Alec and Peter came back to see their dad when their anger was all grown up and beat him so bad he couldn't walk.

So, yeah.

Reading *Lit*, so many childhood memories came back of Ma. I was riveted to the pages. The words seemed to want to stay with me, reminding me to revisit stuff, no one can hurt me now.

Religion and spirituality have been a struggle lately. See, for starters, I was baptized twice. First, as a Catholic and later, as a Jehovah's Witness. It's curious what a mother's love will do to keep a child from certain types of hell. My first, the sprinkling, took place fifty-one years ago at the 187-year-old Saint Patrick's Basilica in downtown Montreal, by a Father John Bobinos. The second time was full-on immersion in an Assembly Hall of Jehovah's Witnesses in the city's west end. I don't remember Ma there but she must've come. I was seventeen.

Before Ma converted to the Jehovah's Witnesses, we used to celebrate Christmas and birthdays, all that heathen stuff. Then she got religion in the not-joking-around-anymore-hard-core-serious-type way. She'd heard about the Jehovah's Witnesses on the radio around the time my little bro came on the scene. When the sisters showed up at our apartment door with the *Watchtower* and *Awake*, Ma took it as a sign from the Almighty. Ma's great-aunt Sister John of the Cross must've taken it like a slap to the face.

I took solace in having Jehovah around, gotta say. I was a real Mama-and-God girl. A crybaby too. Kindergarten was all gerbils, hot dog days, Barbies, cookies and juice. Grade one meant whole days away from Ma in a strict get-down-to-business kind of outfit. I would get math all jumbled in my brain. I couldn't tie my shoes and got scolded for chatting. I would fret about my punishment once Ma heard I got put into the corner. Once, I was so upset I told Mrs. Cohen it would help me if I could pray to Jehovah. She let me go and get in a good old chat just outside our classroom door.

So, I started off real little, being a big old believer, thanks to Ma.

Take the pictures in our children's book, *From Paradise Lost to Paradise Regained*, of unbelievers—the naysayers and do-nothings—destroyed for not choosing Jehovah's side at Armageddon. Those images were etched into many of my nightmares as a kid. Buildings collapsing. People running and screaming, falling into pits where earthquakes had split open the ground. My sister tells me these prophecies cross her mind from time to time.

Ma's family being what it was, I guess it's no surprise that she handpicked a new mother. Her name was Virginia and Ma brought her into the Jehovah's Witness fold. Us kids viewed her like a grandmother, but then Virginia went and died of a heart attack and all that had been stable in our lives died that day too. Ma started hitting the bottle like her old days. I was nine, my sister eleven and my little bro seven. Ma left me on a train trip to Toronto and would go on drinking binges and sometimes hitchhike with me. She'd send us to the store to get her beer and cigarettes. Ma sitting at the edge of our kitchen table after school let out, sipping her Brador stubbies and listening to the same records over and over again is something I just can't forget. I feel myself triggered right back to kiddie-hood when I hear Supertramp, Jessi Colter, Kenny Rogers, K-Tel's *Emotions* or Tom Jones.

My dad didn't convert. He studied the Bible with the elders in the congregation and he'd entertain the brothers and sisters by cooking for them. Years later, he told me that he was "too bad to change" but that being a Witness was good for us kids. He tried to pay the bills, but wasn't home much. He liked to hang out with his friends in Chinatown or play basketball. He had lots of affairs, according to the paper trail of phone bills my mother found. When they were home together, there'd be full-on fights. When he had enough of it, he'd switch to Cantonese so we knew he was real mad. Eventually he didn't want to be a husband or a father so he checked out for good.

Ma went on welfare when they split. Some lady came to our digs to check-mark the box that said, *Yeah sure, they're poor.*

I know all this JW stuff sounds like a bunch of hooey, but I wouldn't be here now without Jehovah or the brothers and sisters in the congregation. Everyone viewed us kids as orphans. It didn't help that Ma did a stint in the mental ward of the hospital and wrote scary things in the Bible and on the floor of her room. Even though my home life was less than ideal, when you're living it, you're not wondering what's going to happen next, you're just trying to get through it, aren't you?

It's only now that I have the courage to ask my brother and sister about their versions of truth. Even then all it takes is for my sister to say, "Remember when Mummy was up all night making popovers and she never got up in the morning?" and I'm fourteen again.

Your honesty helped me understand Ma's alcoholic ways. I hated her because of the drink. Sure, she got sober through AA, and even though I sat through a baker's dozen of her speaker talks, I never really listened. (I was in therapy before I listened, replayed her talk on cassette.) The Alateen meetings where I went, we were supposed to take turns talking about our problems. But those took place in churches and since I had been taught that the devil is the ruler of Christendom, I was creeped out just being in there. In Kingdom Halls, there are no icons, no robes, and there definitely was no Jesus hanging around on that cross, looking like he'd also like to be anywhere but staring down on us sorry sacks week in, week out.

Jehovah made me feel safe and cared for in his congregation and with his commission to preach about his name and his kingdom. Being a part of the brothers and sisters worldwide who were committed gave me a job that would keep me busy for a lifetime. I felt that at the Kingdom Hall things made sense. I could count on the regularity of Jehovah and his rules. If I stuck to Jehovah and his written word, I would be written into His Book of Remembrance. I was a real keener when it came to pleasing others, especially Jehovah. I'd do whatever it took to please him, believe you me.

Things really started to click for me in my teens. I'd get into religious debates with my friends and try to offer them Bible studies because I didn't want them dead at Armageddon. I got rid of my records that seemed unchristian and I wouldn't watch sex, drugs or the violence in movies. I didn't lie or stand for the national anthem and celebrate holidays. I didn't date boys and would wait until I was marriageable age. Didn't want much to do with Ma either, since she'd veered off the path. There were many rules to follow and I was happy to comply because the faith reminded me of a time when our family had been happy (mostly), united and stable.

I was seventeen when I decided to dedicate my life to Jehovah. First—I had to study the *Organized to Accomplish Our Ministry* book with the elders to see if I was ready for baptism. I had to be a good Christian example in the congregation and an active preacher of the good news. (I was better at being a Jehovah's Witness than I was in school, too, other than in English.) Once the elders approved, I'd be getting baptized at the next Circuit or summer District Assembly where I would take my vows before Jehovah and my fellow Witnesses, sitting in one of the first few rows saying yes (loudly) to the two questions asked. After this affirmation of faith, we would be baptized one by one, fully submerged by a brother. The actual day it happened, I was baptized by an elder named John in the pool at the Côte Saint-Luc Assembly Hall. John-the-Baptizers times two, considering a Catholic priest came first. My non-religious father came to see the momentous event but missed my actual dunking.

Ma was finally disfellowshipped for smoking and shortly after that, my sister and I left home. I was eighteen. Ma's and my relationship kind of deteriorated then. We weren't talking on a regular basis on account of her spiritual state, then suddenly, she drowned on vacation in Cancún. She had bought me a T-shirt and I wondered why when I more or less refused to speak to her. I was always taught that Jehovah came first, family second, and I was determined to serve loyally as a faithful servant.

I guess Ma raised me too well in the faith.

It would only be later, in my late thirties, when I blamed Jehovah for the bad situation with Ma. I started leaving Jehovah much like my dad left us, slowly at first, then deliberately. I thought I'd return to the Witnesses after a pause but I couldn't. I don't remember when I stopped talking to Jehovah either. I used to pray several times a day and sometimes fall asleep in prayer. Maybe I stopped when Muriel told me she couldn't promise that I would still be a Jehovah's Witness at the end of our therapy work together. Inside, I scoffed at the idea. She didn't know me or my faith; I was a *rock*. But the reality was, I was working a lot, hardly going to meetings and in the ministry even less and I guess I felt guilty being half in, half out. I have never been a fence-sitter, me. If I hadn't isolated myself from Jehovah's congregation, the truth of his word, and become wise in my own eyes, then things might have been different. But you really can't go back once you get far away from a thing no matter how familiar.

I just wanted to let you know that *Lit* hit me straight in whatever heart I had left to even hear about spirituality.

After being on stress leave, I ended up in the hospital because of a suicide attempt. I was taking Paxil and Ativan and I felt like a failure. I was still a Jehovah's Witness, although I can't remember the content of my prayers then. Honestly thought the world would be a better place without me. Jehovah standing right in front of me could not have convinced me otherwise, I was that despondent. I started changing slowly then, and the change altered my relationship with the God and father that I knew.

Not that I realized it at the time. I thought it would be easier just to be religion-free.

These days, though, I really feel a need to be *in* something, to believe in something.

Oh, and I didn't run off to become a stripper or a wild drug addict or get covered in body tattoos like some ex-religious girls do. And honestly, even if they did all those things, I think being all judge-y is the most un-Christlike thing of all.

I thought I would turn out to be some kind of atheist, but I can see now that's not me, not even a smidgeon. Your examination of the whole "higher power" thing, and not wanting to give in to it, also made me think. I was at one time a faithful dress-wearing proselytizing Jehovah's Witness and when I threw in the towel I thought, *That's it, I'm done*. I don't know if I can be a part of anything with such a huge commitment again. I just don't.

Recently, I felt called to go to Montreal, my old hometown. I wanted to see the church my parents had taken me to when I was an infant to get God's stamp.

And wouldn't you know, I get lost trying to find Saint Patrick's (my phone showed me the way) and when I finally see the 226-foot-tall building, my heart is beating fast and then the bells are chiming and I realize it's taken two therapists and eleven years to find my feelings.

Earlier that morning, I woke up several times, afraid that I'd miss Mass. Then when I got there and paid four dollars to light a candle for Ma (she's never far from my thoughts), none of the lights would even turn on. *A fine start*, I'm thinking. The sermon was about Doubting Thomas, the skeptic. Go figure, I never questioned while I was in the faith. Muriel used to say maybe it's not about the answers, maybe it's about the questions.

Now all I have are questions. I want to go back to the beginning, to where Ma started my spiritual journey. She was only twenty-three, probably hopeful, maybe even happy about my future. I wonder what commitment she made that day, trying to start me off right, trying to save my soul.

And ya know what? Even though everything fell apart, it's kind of a beautiful mess after all.

Daughter, sister, searcher, believer,
Tamara

Star Women

JÓNÍNA KIRTON

I come from strong women, all of whom chose very different spiritual paths. My Icelandic grandmother, Jonina, had seventeen children, all home births on the farm, and even though she was surrounded by family who loved her, she felt something was missing. When the Jehovah's Witnesses came to the door, she asked them in.

Some say she became a Jehovah's Witness because she enjoyed the intellectual stimulation of weekly Bible study. She did love a good conversation.

There are no stories about what brought my mother, her eldest daughter, to Christianity. I suspect it was my Métis grandmother, her mother-in-law, who introduced her to church. All my life I knew my mother to be a devoted Anglican, an active member of the congregation. She was a Sunday school teacher and later, when I grew older, president of the women's association, the organizer of many teas and craft fairs. As a young woman, I jokingly referred to her as "the church lady." Even the minister had a nickname for her. He called her his "Passionflower."

The spiritual path I have chosen—or that's chosen me—is different. Eclectic. One that included ritual and ceremony, mainly with women.

Each of us built community based on our spiritual lives.

. . .

As a child I attended church each Sunday. I was the oldest so would sometimes get to stay for the service when Sunday school started. I felt so grown up sitting next to my mom on those hard wooden pews. I would watch for cues and was fascinated by the synchronistic raising and lowering of the prayer kneel. I learned the Apostles' Creed and rested comfortably in the things that we would sing and say. *The Lord be with you* felt like a blessing, which I was so happy to return with my full-throated *And with thy spirit*. I was pulled in by the reverence displayed by those in attendance, none more so than my own mother. My child mind would be awash with the possibility that someone like Jesus was real and that he loved me. I would sing with all my heart.

Jesus loves me! This I know,
For the Bible tells me so.
Little ones to Him belong;
They are weak, but He is strong.

The words "Little ones to Him belong" reminded me of my step-grandfather, Fred, and the way he folded me into him saying *little one*.

"They are weak, but He is strong" made sense to me. I felt weak. In fact, I was already drowning. But my mother was a vision in her shift, good shoes, nice purse and hat and, on occasion, gloves. How I loved standing close to her.

For a time, I found comfort in all that happened in church.

Perhaps it was the sweetness of her ways and the momentary peace she found there that made me feel safe. Church was her sacred space, away from a life filled with four children—one girl, three boys—and an alcoholic husband.

As a young girl I wanted to go to church, to sing the hymns and feel close to Jesus. My connection to him was so strong, there was an air of mystery to it. It was as if he and I had a secret. I never told anyone about this. Years later, several past-life practitioners told me I had known Christ in a previous life. My name was Mary—not that I was one of the famous Marys, just a simple Essene woman who taught prayer and meditation. I never knew what to think of these assertions. I do wonder what our bodies hold and believe in blood memory. Perhaps it was my ancestor these seers were seeing, and the memory of Mary and her time with Jesus was ignited whenever I read the Bible. All I know is that the stories of his kindness had always made me feel so safe.

For many years I looked forward to Sundays—my time with my mother. But later, when my brothers became altar boys, I began to question why the women had to organize and host teas or teach Sunday school—all background stuff—but were not up at the altar, doing ceremony.

Although I felt at home in church, I also felt the pull of the forest and what I now feel were the calls of my Indigenous ancestors. Whenever I could I would spend time alone in the woods behind my house in Goose Bay, Labrador. Barefoot, I would become a warrior. I'd close my eyes and feel my way around the forest, touching tree bark, feeling the crunch of dry leaves underfoot, careful not to trip on any fallen logs. I would practise pulling my energy in, so I could sneak up on someone silently without sending out energy ripples to warn them of my presence.

The people around me did not think much of "Indians," but my instincts told me otherwise. Somehow, I knew it was good to be one.

My time with the trees ended with our move to Winnipeg, and in my teens, church soon faded from my life as well. I refused to go and filled that hole, at first, with Beatles records and crazy, mad crushes on boys with pimples and Paul McCartney haircuts.

Eventually I discovered alcohol and disco and completely forgot about spirituality of any kind—unless I was visiting my grandmother. It made her happy to speak about the Jehovah's Witness teachings, and I had great respect for her devotion to her chosen path. I would ask questions and listen carefully, but while eventually a few of my aunties and uncles joined her faith, I knew it was not for me.

To my knowledge, neither my father nor my grandfather attended church or congregation. They were manly men who loved their sports. The highlight of my grandfather's day was wrestling matches on TV. My dad, he had hockey, the rink was his church and the theme song for *Hockey Night in Canada*, his hymn. A goalie in the days before masks were worn, he continued to play on local teams until he was well into his forties and, once my brothers began to play, my dad became a spirited spectator. While their women called out for God or Jehovah, the men called out to the gods of blood sport. Without their team sport, the men remained loners.

It fell to the women to be strong for the children.

In my twenties I rejected the need to be a "good woman," and took to the disco. For many years the dance floor became my church, the music and the dancing, my hallelujah. Nightly I would lose myself in the sex-infused air and what I now recognize was trance dance. Between dances I filled myself with the alcohol from men looking for company. I felt powerful, connected to these clubs. Until the age of thirty-two, when I realized I was getting too old for club life, and alcohol was becoming a problem.

I needed to make changes. I married a man I met at Bogarts and did what some call a "geographical cure." I moved west, to Edmonton, to start a new life, one that did not include nightclubs and alcoholic drinking. Suburbia and marriage were going to help me slow down.

Nothing went as planned.

My mother's cancer had returned, and now I was miles away from her. As she planned for death, she called me home—being the only daughter as well as the oldest, I was often her sole source of support.

She spoke of her wishes, that she wanted to stay home as long as possible and once in hospital, she was not to be left alone. Even if unconscious, she wanted me there. She showed me the AA pamphlets she was leaving in her drawers, in hopes that my father would see them. She said it was important, so very important, that I understand that she truly did love him. I was deeply humbled by this fact. I realized I had judged her for hanging in there with my father. And there was more. She had written her obituary. She wanted to know if I was okay. Was I happy in my marriage, she asked, and did I think I drank too much.

I could not answer truthfully and, in her way, she accepted my denial. I left, promising to come when called.

Six months later I got that call. She was in hospital and not conscious. "Come now," the doctor said. "She doesn't have long." I packed my bags and caught a plane, not knowing I would be ten long days at her side.

Every night during that time, I would watch her chest rise and fall. No words came from her lips even though what I most wanted was one more "I love you." I wanted her to put her cheek on my cheek the way she would when she'd lean over me seated in a chair. The silence and absence of her being made me question everything about my life. I had already lost two brothers in their teens. I had wondered if, as a family, we were cursed.

I began to pray. I prayed day and night, as I had learned in church. I prayed without ceasing.

Each day my dad would come for a few hours so I could shower and eat. He would ready himself at the door with a cheery "Good morning, Lorraine. You look beautiful today." Her appearance had always been so important to her. We would comb her hair and put on her lipstick before he arrived. She did not look beautiful, she was dying, I could smell the cancer, but to him she was truly still beautiful. It's true, I thought, his love for her was undeniable.

Once my dad took over, I was free to head outside, and surprised to see the world still moving.

In the stillness of the night and the closeness of death, I'd forget how vibrant Winnipeg is in summer. There would be the sun shining, offering me its healing warmth. Everything was talking to me. The hum of the traffic on Portage Avenue became a vibrational hymn. As I showered, I experienced the gentle cleansing that only water can offer. I felt some of the heartache and the cancer smell that infused my nostrils wash away. I would think about how good the water felt on my skin and how my mother would never feel that sensation again. Even food tasted different, as if it were infused with healing light.

My senses had been heightened by all that prayer. At the same time that my senses were awakened, I began to think how ungrateful I was, that there was so much good in life if you could just let it in.

The night she died, I experienced unexpected bliss. I felt her spirit leave her body and fill the whole room with peace.

. . .

Her passing left me with many questions. It left me with an urgency that I no longer feel. I was in pain and needed answers about our spirits, which clearly outlive our bodies. I thought that I needed to know what happens after we die. What I did not know and would later find was that I didn't know how to live. I was in need of guidance.

I began my quest with my mother's minister. She trusted him, so I thought I could trust him. She had turned to him, he must be wise. Entering the church that day I felt weak and, really, in need of saving, I was so very lost. Memories of Sundays with Mom, my first wedding, and all the funerals rushed in as I entered that familiar space. I could feel my mother and my two brothers, Murray and Gordon. I felt home. And yet the meeting did not go as I'd hoped it would. The minister sat barricaded behind his big desk, fidgeting with papers. His eyes would not meet mine. Perhaps it was his own grief. He had loved her too. Undaunted, I pushed for answers. I needed to understand, I said, what I had experienced. He was a man of God—shouldn't he know about these things? Couldn't he see I needed spiritual guidance? Some reassurance that what I had experienced was real, that my mom and my brothers were not completely *gone*?

He had nothing to offer me.

That was my first falling-out with Christianity.

There were many more to come.

.   .   .

After her death, I tried to settle back into my life. At the same time, I continued to seek answers. The first one came in the form of a presentation by the renowned death-and-dying expert Elisabeth Kübler-Ross. Just thirty-two, I had already known death as a significant part of my life. Elisabeth offered some answers, but I was still desperately alone. I was already attending Adult Children of Alcoholics Anonymous (ACOA) and was familiar with the twelve-step programs when I met a man who was thirty days clean with the help of Narcotics Anonymous (NA). I told him of my father's alcoholism and that I was doing the steps in ACOA. He smiled knowingly, asked for my number, and the next day my roommate said, "He really liked you and wants to take you out."

"Pretty sure he wants to take me to a meeting," I said.

We were both right. The next day he took me to NA.

Although drugs were never my thing, I was happy to hang with this crowd. NA was new, so there were few members, and we were a tight-knit group. And we were young, not like the old farts in AA. I did not feel like I was giving up too much until grief hit me hard. Thankfully, I had a great sponsor who helped me get through "the steps" quickly. I was encouraged to pray daily and to ask for God's help in all matters. I was back at church—inside.

Still, I needed more.

I joined an evangelical church, where I happily studied the Bible and had what felt like vivid remembrances of being with Christ. I became close to the pastor, who baptized me. I was born again, made fresh, made new, something I desperately wanted as I felt so dirty. I asked the pastor if the "normal" men in the congregation would accept my "made clean as snow" status. Would any of them want to marry me? To this day I am thankful for his honest answer. "No," he said, "you will probably find a man with a history like yours."

I never went back to church.

If I could not be seen as "new," what good was it being "made clean as snow"?

My feelings about church and AA were mixed for other reasons, too. For one thing, men always seemed to dominate. Some were predators as well. I knew I had to go to meetings and I knew I needed a spiritual community, so I was very grateful when my dear friend Hemangini took me to listen to Joseph Chilton Pearce talk about Siddha Yoga and meditation. Although sober, I was still deeply troubled. All I had to hear was that the practices offered via their meditation intensives would help our thoughts, feelings and actions line up—and I was in. I had been all over the map with PTSD. This path sounded wonderful.

I left the lecture and signed up for the next retreat, by satellite intensive. My first introduction to Gurumayi was via TV in a hotel conference room, where I experienced her omnipotence. The drumming, the chanting and the shared silence when we meditated saved my life, and I don't mean metaphorically. They saved my life, offered me a safe container where I could grieve the loss of not only my mother but my brothers as well.

I no longer attend satsang, but I have my favourite photo of Gurumayi on my bed table. I light a candle in gratitude for her and the teachings she provided daily.

Eventually, I entered the world of women and sacred circles. Here, I found my gifts as a facilitator useful and I welcomed the opportunity to create and perform my own rituals. Over time, I began to explore my Indigenous ancestry and I reclaimed my Métis status. For many years I prayed daily and offered tobacco for my ancestors. I attended ceremony and sought their stories. I waited ten long years for a name from an elder.

I knew to be patient.

Some things take time.

At sixty-one, at my first sweat, I was given a name, *Star Woman Who Looks Down on Us from the Sky*. The two-spirited elder who gifted me with this name had known me for only an hour and yet they had sensed my interest in the ancestors.

We consider the stars our ancestors.

I look back now on three generations of women—each choosing a different spiritual path and yet all of us choosing to live out our lives in a spiritual way. I am thankful that we had choice. We are truly blessed to have lived in a time and in a land where we could follow the beliefs that resonated with us. I am grateful that I have been able to reclaim some of the teachings of my Indigenous ancestors. I may one day feel comfortable using the name that I was gifted, *Star Woman Who Looks Down on Us from the Sky*, but for now I will continue to lean into the name that my grandmother and I share, Jónína. I have reclaimed the accents for us both.

Being mixed blood, I feel the pull of all my ancestors; for the longest time it was the women that I heard most clearly. They asked me to heal for us all. But they did not ask me to do this alone.

I have always felt them walking beside me and today they whispered . . .
one day we will all be Star Women in the Sky.

The Places in Between

AMANDA LEDUC

The first woman I loved was another writer, a woman I met in my second year of university. Let's call her Emily. She had blond hair and blue eyes and when I first knew her she wore her hair long, parted straight down the middle. She looked like she was fifteen. She had a boyfriend and she wore shorts even when it was cold. She was sarcastic and angry and hopeful and sad. She was an excellent writer.

Is an excellent writer. She isn't dead.

.   .   .

When I was ten years old the Vatican issued an edict allowing girls to act as altar servers. I was the first girl in my church to don the robe. We had white robes with hoods and belts of red rope. You doubled the rope around your waist and pulled the ends through the loop so that they hung at equal lengths. We wore rough wooden crosses round our necks, carried the Bible, rang the Eucharist bells. When my sister became an altar server too we fought over who got to carry the chalice. One year she tripped and fell as she was carrying communion wafers to the altar. The wafers spilled out of her dish like confetti.

The priest kept a large square of white cloth at the altar. When he drank from the chalice after blessing the wine, he'd use the cloth to wipe his spit away. This didn't make sense to me even at ten; surely priests had germs too. Surely, I thought, priests had insides that bled and purged and rotted just like the insides of everyone else.

. . .

Once, in high school philosophy, I tried to argue that gay people shouldn't be allowed to get married.

"Why not?" asked my teacher.

"Because," I said, "children need the influence of both a mom and dad."

"Well," he replied. We were debating à la Socrates. "What about single moms, then? Or single dads? What happens when a parent dies? Do you think they shouldn't have children either, simply because they have to raise their kids alone?"

I had no answers. I tried to talk and the words just fell between the chairs.

I stopped talking in class after that day. Don't open your mouth, and you can't say stupid things.

. . .

My parents were not really religious. When we talk about it now, sometimes they admit they went to church mostly because we kept asking questions. Mummy, where do we come from? Daddy, how does God hang the stars?

When my mother was pregnant with my youngest sister she converted to Catholicism. She went to catechism classes with my father on Wednesday nights. I remember this because my cousin came to babysit—I was the oldest, so I got to stay up late. Later. We drank fruit juice and watched *Unsolved Mysteries*. The music from the show gave me nightmares, but I never told anyone that.

. . .

When did I fall in love with Emily, exactly? I don't remember. I was twenty-three, or twenty-two. Sometime after we had the long debate about the pope. It wasn't fair that a woman couldn't be pope, couldn't be a priest, couldn't have a *say* in things, how could I call myself Catholic, how could I believe in God at *all*, she said.

I only shrugged. "I don't want to be a priest," I said. "So that doesn't matter to me."

One summer morning I woke up wanting to kiss her very badly. It felt like I woke up in love but of course the feeling had been growing, bubbling, simmering for much longer.

I did kiss her, eventually, one night when she came over for dinner. She had kissed many women before me but when I took her face into my hands she squeaked, she was so surprised.

. . .

When I was twelve or so, I asked my mother about lesbians on the way to the doctor's office. "Men like watching lesbians in movies," I said. "But then they make fun of them in real life. How come?"

My mother didn't answer right away. "Why?" she said. "Are you having ... feelings?"

"No. *No.* I'm just curious. That's all."

"Men are very visual," she said. "For them, it's all about what they can see."

Years later, when I told her about Emily, she didn't seem surprised at all.

"I knew," she said. "Just something in the way you talked about her."

. . .

I did entertain thoughts of becoming a priest for a while. Or I entertained thoughts of becoming the female equivalent of a priest, which is to say, a minister that no diocese would ever use.

The female chaplain at my university was an ordained Catholic minister. When she went on maternity leave the diocese terminated her employment, told her to reapply for her job when her leave was over.

. . .

I believe in God, the Father, the Almighty.

What does that even mean?

. . .

AMANDA LEDUC

For my twenty-second birthday, Emily took me out for Chinese food. We ate potstickers drenched in soy sauce. She was graceful with her chopsticks. I was a failure. She'd cut her hair and streaked it pink. Now and then our knees would touch beneath the table.

"Celibacy," she said. "I just don't get it. I mean, how can you survive so long by only masturbating?"

"Well." I coughed. "Actually, I've never done that either."

She laughed so long and hard that other patrons around us smiled.

"That's what's wrong with you!" she said, finally. "Jesus Christ. That's fucking *insane*."

She was newly in love then, with a man named Paul. It shone so brightly on her that every time I was around her I felt intoxicated and small. Her easy talk of sex and death and love made me feel stupid and sheltered but also excited, like I'd been wrong about the world my whole life and was finally getting to learn.

· · ·

When I was twenty-nine I went to Iona, the tiny Scottish island off the Isle of Mull. From Edinburgh, you take a train and then a ferry and then a bus and then another ferry. The journey takes about seven hours. Saint Columba landed there in 563 BCE, and built a monastery that was burned in later centuries. In the early 1900s the church was rebuilt and the island reclaimed its status as a place of pilgrimage. George MacLeod, who founded the new spiritual community on the island, called it a *thin place*—an area where the veil between this world and the next was thin as tissue paper.

I did not really believe in God anymore when I went to the island. But what I remember most from that visit is sitting in the abbey during a rainstorm, listening to the wind lash against the roof so hard I felt sure it would break. A tiny spot of calm in the middle of a hurricane. I couldn't stop crying.

When I left the island a day later the feeling went away. I actually felt it retreat while I was on the ferry, watching the island recede. Like waking from a dream about flying only to discover that you're rooted firmly to the ground.

· · ·

Before I fell in love with Emily I was in love with a man we'll call Jim. He'd been my English teacher in high school and the crush lasted from age fifteen until about twenty-seven, give or take. It still flares up now and then, this doomed crush, so wonderful and terrible in its implausibility, that sometimes I wonder if it used up all of my romantic energy, if parts of myself burned out too soon. Though of course that sounds silly now, on this other side of thirty. Aren't we endless? Isn't our capacity for hope and love the most infinite thing we have?

I don't ever remember loving God in this kind of headlong way, even though I wanted to so badly. When we met for Christian fellowship at school I would sit and bow my head, pretend to pray, when really I was just repeating things that everyone else said and hoping, deep down, that one day they would take.

Fake it till you make it. At the hospital where I work, the psychiatrists sometimes say this to their patients. Pretend to be happy and eventually you'll feel it.

Pretend that you love God, I told myself over and over. Pretend that you believe it all of the time, not just in your dark moments, and one day it will all come true.

. . .

For two days after the first night that Emily stayed over, I walked around feeling like the most beautiful girl in the world. It was so much better than any God I'd ever known.

. . .

Ipse se nihil scire id unum sciat. *I know that I know nothing.* We call it the Socratic paradox and attribute it to Plato. It is maybe a paraphrase, maybe a lie. The full line comes from Plato's *Apology* and runs something like this: *This man, on one hand, believes that he knows something, while not knowing. On the other hand, I—equally ignorant—do not believe.*

We cannot know, except to understand that knowing itself is dangerous. Except to understand that the world is at its shadiest with you in exactly those moments when you think that everything makes sense.

· · ·

As a child I was known for taking two helpings of dessert. *I want a little bit of both*, I always said. *Why do I have to make a choice at all?*

Alfred Kinsey says it this way: *The world is not to be divided into sheep and goats.*

· · ·

Here is a secret I've never told anyone: when I was thirteen I rented an X-rated movie from the variety store near my house. I still don't know how I managed it. Maybe the clerk wasn't paying attention. Maybe he just didn't care. In the movie, a woman is kidnapped and brought to work as a maid in a house filled with other women. One day, the matron ties her to a bed and takes her clothes off. I think she fucks her with a yardstick, although I'm no longer sure. The memory blurs.

I brought the movie home and kept it hidden in my closet. I set my alarm late that night and watched it in the basement after everyone else had gone to bed. I watched and rewound that part on the bed so many times it was getting light outside by the time I turned off the TV. My throat so dry it hurt, my fingers cramped from clutching the remote. I hadn't touched myself. I washed my hands anyway, then took out the video and boxed it up and tiptoed back upstairs into my room, the space between my legs so heavy I felt like my heart would drop right through if I wasn't careful.

· · ·

In grade twelve, during the height of my Christian phase, my philosophy teacher threw a Henry Rollins tape into the VCR.

"How awesome would it be," Rollins said in that particular skit, "to be bisexual? To just walk into a room and go, MMMMM, ALL RIGHT!"

Everybody laughed. I did too, even though my insides were hot with disapproval and shame.

That was years ago and I still think about it. Sometimes I think it's the truest thing I've ever heard.

· · ·

I broke my heart over Emily, eventually. I did not know how to tell her what I wanted because I did not, at the time, really know what I was asking.

"I don't want you to be *with* me," I said. We were sitting together on the couch in my tiny little bachelor apartment. It was hot outside and hot inside and I was very young. "I just want … you. That's all."

She did not want me back, which was something I think I had known all along. At the time I thought I'd never hurt so much, but this is always what you believe during that first flush of grief. Emily and I would stumble through the breakup-that-wasn't and go back, eventually, to being careful friends. There would be other women, and other men. People who made my heart burn just as hard. But right then it felt like I had wanted something I was not supposed to have, and even God had turned away from me.

· · ·

Once, at a bookstore where I worked, a lesbian co-worker told me that bisexuality wasn't real.

"If you're with a man," she said, "then you're heterosexual. And if you're with a girl after that, you were never really heterosexual in the first place. You were always gay."

That didn't really make sense to me then. Or now. But maybe I was wrong—maybe the belief that you can love a lot of people is just another name for not committing.

You believe in God, or you don't. There is no in-between.

· · ·

What I want to believe in, I think, even more than God, is *goodness*. The ability of people to stand up and do the right thing over and over again. To reach inside themselves and find the universe.

· · ·

AMANDA LEDUC

That's a lie, mostly. I want to believe in God, too. But the space between the two seems very big now. The path back almost invisible, like realizing one night that you lost an earring at some point earlier in the day. It could be anywhere. Stuffed under some papers at work. Crunched on the floor, forgotten by the garbage can. Dropped into the kitchen sink and gone forever, waiting for water to flush it back out in the open, for someone else to find it.

Somehow my faith slipped from me unannounced. Now it lies waiting somewhere in Scotland or Canada or somewhere I have yet to be. Waiting for me, wishing me back. Or maybe it's tucked away in my parents' basement, nestled among macaroni necklaces and handmade cards and other forgotten, childhood paraphernalia.

. . .

Still—in 2013, at a book festival, I spoke on a panel about faith and belief, and how that plays into fiction.

"I grew up Catholic," I said, "though I'm not Catholic anymore."

"Yes you are," said the facilitator.

Everybody laughed, including me.

. . .

Does it ever really go away? *Give me the child for seven years*, say the Jesuits, *and I will give you the man.*

When I was thirteen my aunt and uncle convinced me that I needed to welcome Jesus into my heart. Baptism and confirmation hadn't been enough.

"The Catholic Church," my uncle said, "is the largest accepted cult in the world."

I sat in their basement and repeated what they said and waited for Jesus. *My only Lord and Saviour*. It felt true. It also felt wrong, somehow, because I didn't believe it. Not wholly. Not entirely.

You don't know, said a tiny little voice. As my aunt and uncle cried and hugged me and welcomed me to God. You want to know, but that's not enough.

You're a liar.

And still, here I am all these years later, somewhere in the space between lying and the truth.

.   .   .

Sometimes I remember Emily and my arguments in that long ago philosophy class and I think: If there is a God, then that God has a wicked sense of humour. Funny, isn't it, the things that make sense and then don't anymore. Or the things that don't make sense and then do, the thin veils between them all.

Maybe *infinite* sense of humour is the term I'm looking for.

.   .   .

There once was this time when I thought a co-worker of mine wanted to kiss me. He was married. We'd left a night shift early because there was nothing to do and he'd walked me home because the street I live on is nice but maybe not so nice at 11:00 p.m., maybe the kind of street where anything can happen when it's dark and everyone else has gone to bed. He came up to see my apartment and we talked for a while and then he got up to leave. We hugged on the porch a little too long, and for an instant of time I thought he might *actually* kiss me and I pulled back and said, "*Shit.*"

He said, "What?" like he wasn't quite sure what had happened.

"Nothing. Never mind." And then he left.

When I look back on it now it feels like maybe there were no kisses waiting in the first place. Like maybe I have always been so desperate, so eager to believe in signs that are not really signs at all. Like I have been waiting for the universe, or God, to kiss me back in situations where that is so clearly not going to happen.

I am not sure what this says about me anymore.

.   .   .

A year or so ago I left a burner on my stove unattended for a time. After a while I smelled the gas and fixed the knob—I had turned it off but it hadn't clicked shut properly. It was too late in the night to sleep at a neighbour's house so

I opened all the windows and turned on all my fans and went to bed, and I prayed the whole time I was awake. Please don't let this be the end. Please.

Mostly, though, I prayed—to God? to myself?—so as to fight the overwhelming urge to go to the stove and light a match, to stand in the centre of my little kitchen and watch the world ignite, pull aside that tissue and reach out for God's own face, or nothing. To *know*, once and for all.

I stayed in bed, not burning. Eventually I fell asleep, and while I was dreaming the air cleared and all the gas blew away.

Yoga Rage

KIRSTEEN MacLEOD

I've been a student of yoga for thirty-one years, and a teacher for fourteen. In case you think I'm about to make a case for my own enlightenment, I'll soon tell you how I came to swear at an eight-year-old. After three decades on a yoga mat, I'm oftentimes a raging yogi.

It's not always the most peaceful people, after all, who are drawn to this ancient practice. Witness the eighty-two-year-old man doing poses in the aisle on a flight to Tokyo who was asked to return to his seat. He pushed his own wife, threatened murder and head-butted and bit a marine who tried to assist flight attendants in making him sit down. He'd recently taken up yoga. Maybe if he'd started in his seventies?

We so identify with the relaxed, peaceful side of yoga that we forget what it's for. Yoga—one translation is "union"—is a transformative path for integrating body, mind and spirit. Yes, relaxation is part of the equation, but over time, you'll also be brought into close contact with "negative" states—if the yoga is working.

Everything is bound to its shadow.

For me, yoga has often been paired with anger, the most afflictive of my darker emotions. Yoga helped me deal with the after-effects of a childhood with an angry father as well as with my own anger: our family inheritance, likely passed down for generations along with our dark hair and blue eyes. Hard-won knowledge about my demons was the fruit of countless hours doing yoga, which generates insight through the physical body, opening up space for change.

As a yoga teacher, I've had the opportunity to observe my process and recognize many other angry yogis. I'm not talking about Rage Yoga— which promises to be "Zen as fuck," involves swearing, listing to Metallica, drinking and doing downward dog in a bar, and was invented by a Calgary contortionist and juggler during a painful breakup. I'm talking about classical yoga, which often induces meltdowns because it's a path that changes our unconscious patterns.

There's a Zen story that explains how this works. A man gallops by on a horse. "Where are you going?" yells a curious bystander. "I don't know," he replies, "ask the horse." Similarly, yoga philosophy holds that we're born with a karmic inheritance of mental and emotional patterns known as *samskaras* that we repeat without realizing it during our lives. On our yoga mats, we can calm down enough to learn to guide the horse, to see where our conditioning is taking us and then to make new choices.

Over the years, I've noticed that angry people pass through three main levels of yoga rage. Beginners' yoga rage is when you are driven and unconscious and hate to slow down. With Intermediate, you've experienced some peace, and then feel deceived once you realize that yoga is not all bliss—which is when the infuriating, hard work of change begins. Advanced yoga rage is when you think you've achieved some mastery of your emotions and issues—and then a tiny affront makes you explode. For me, this journey has felt epic.

Yoga Rage for Beginners

My first yoga class was in 1986 at the downtown YMCA in Toronto. I was twenty-five, an avid aerobics queen and runner. When the doctor examined my badly sprained ankle and said, "You just have to rest it," I was mortified. I craved speed in all aspects of life. I had to be moving, doing *something*. That's why, despite my sneering disdain, I went and tried yoga.

Hobbling into the Y's studio one sunny afternoon, I was welcomed by an impossibly supple old woman, probably in her fifties. The teacher told us to lie down on our mats and breathe, and for a full hour led us in quiet, slow movements—reclining, sitting and standing. I seethed with impatience. Afterwards, limping past my aerobics classmates lined up in the hall for our usual workout, I saw smirks. I hopped on one foot down the athlete's staircase to the change rooms, the indignity more painful than my swollen ankle.

Two days later, pent up from physical inactivity, I returned for a second yoga class. This time, the teacher was a weedy man in white clothes and turban with an incongruous Scottish accent. Simran was the first vegetarian I'd ever met and fit my stereotypical idea: thin, frail, pale. A practising Sikh who lived in an ashram on Palmerston Avenue, Simran, or Jimmy in his Glaswegian incarnation, taught kundalini yoga and told unintentionally hilarious stories. "Yoga saved my life, man," he'd say, segueing into tales about his druggie days, which were easy to imagine since he still spoke like a hippie stoner.

Leading us in washing-machine-wringing movements, he'd say yoga wasn't for the faint of heart, and tell about his friend the weightlifter who swore by yoga, and found it really challenging. Yeah, right! I'd think dismissively. After the hippie song that marked the end of class, "May the Long-Time Sun Shine Upon You," I wanted to bolt, but had to settle for skulking slowly thanks to my ankle.

Undeniably, after a few weeks, I noticed greater flexibility in my body. And an unfamiliar sensation: fleeting calm. But yoga was so quiet, so uncool. For years, I'd raced around the gym, and worked as a journalist in frenzied, deadline-driven environments. My personal life was a state of emergency, just the way I liked it. Fast-forward hyperalert was normal. I wanted to cram more into every waking minute, to race against the clock, to be so busy I'd never catch up.

Yoga, by contrast, was lame, something to do while lame. My inner carping about wasting time peaked as I drummed my fingers during the interminable relaxations at the end. Doing nothing made me impatient, angry. Why? It was non-productive. Also, like most people, I preferred to practise mindlessness: instead of becoming calm and watching my emotions, I ignored them until something actually went wrong.

After a month my ankle felt better and I returned to running and aerobics. To my surprise, I kept doing yoga. I even went to the one place in town you could buy a yoga mat in the eighties, the Sivananda Centre on Harbord Street, where they cut me a six-foot length from a huge green roll. None of my friends did yoga. It was a pursuit for flower children or old folks, not edgy media types.

Resting in *savasana*, the corpse pose, at the end of class, I'd observed new things. My head was noisy, filled with incessant, anxious chatter. My body was rigid with tension and my heart raced. I felt I'd been holding my breath forever—and now, I was finally learning to exhale.

In retrospect, I can't overstate what a revolution this was. Consciously, what I wanted was to be sweating in step class, Billy Idol's "White Wedding" blasting. But by increments, I was being seduced by stillness.

Intermediate Yoga Rage

Frankly, if I'd known that yoga brings you face to face with your issues as an individual and a human being, I'd have tried aquafit instead. I never suspected that I might unravel. I thought I kept doing yoga because my body felt good. I had no idea that calming the body and breath is level one, or that yoga poses and pranayama are only two of the "eight limbs" that make up the wider path of yoga, meant to provide equanimity for the challenges of a spiritual life.

In those early years, my yoga mat slowly evolved from being a place where I stewed about wasting time into a peaceful refuge. No matter how crazy things got, I could enter the calm, sunlit studio, lie down, come back to myself, unwind. I discovered one of life's most underrated pleasures: breathing at ease in your body. Yoga was dependably divine, as peaceful as floating in the ocean.

Time passed, and unwelcome disturbances began to stir the waters. First, small bubbles of unease, and soon, bad memories, up from the deep. One evening, resting on the gleaming hardwood floor in *savasana*, I was swept back to childhood: my father's savage tongue, black moods, red rages. I was a kicked-dog spirit, biting if he came too near, but mostly trying to hide, scared stiff. Tears ran into my ears and onto my yoga mat. Where is my bliss? I felt like my peace had been snatched back, another of life's cynical tricks. That's it, I thought. I'd roll up my mat and never return.

Who appeared then but the teacher. She'd noticed my breathing was erratic during final relaxation. "Are you okay?" she asked.

"No," I said, wiping my eyes. I told her about the tsunami of bad memories. Obviously, I concluded, the yoga had stopped working.

She was quiet a moment. Had I considered, she asked then, that I might stay with what was arising, gain insight and respond, versus reacting by running away? The idea of yoga, she added, is to build a base of calm so you can look at your own anger, or pain, whatever arises. When you work deeply with the body, unresolved emotional issues come up—it's normal. By staying with them, you gain insight, and grow.

So this is a kind of success? I asked, incredulous. She gave the sweetest smile and nodded yes.

The idea that the body could teach me something was like seeing the first photos of Earth from space, a revelation. We are the embodiment of our experiences.

Over many difficult years, I began to see that physically, I was like a caterpillar poked with a stick, curled into a protective posture. And that unconsciously, I'd replicated high-tension family life, manufacturing chaos with a workaholic, druggy lifestyle. The more insights I gained on my mat, the harder things got. I began having panic attacks. Life felt more and more out of control.

I was volcanically angry. At my father for attacking rather than protecting me. At myself, because I'd taken over the job with self-hate. And at yoga, which had led me to this hellish place. Once I realized that neither yoga nor the right teacher was going to solve my problems, I got even more poisonous. I felt I'd been duped, that no one had alerted me to the Warning, Rough Road Ahead sign.

Through my thirties and forties, on my yoga mat, I breathed my way through. I also tried, with various degrees of commitment and success, psychotherapy, quantum healing, liberating my ancestors through Buddhist meditation, consulting tea leaf readers, astrology, and exorcism through poetry. But it was yoga—gentle, incremental, over years—that provided the safe space I needed to see reality and sit with it, to heal, and integrate. It still amazes me, the simple power of intentionally breathing and intentionally moving. You go inward, the waves settle, and below the tossing surface, you see more clearly.

Yoga's system of the eight-limbed path provided a foundation to remake myself, in awareness. It gave me a way of dealing with the toxic effects of rage in body and mind, a way to learn calm and self-acceptance. Slowing down has the power to transform. It was often painful, but yoga let me go deeper, let mask after mask drop away. I reconnected with myself, ditched my lucrative but unsatisfying job and crazy lifestyle, and moved toward what sustains me: a life in yoga where I can be at home in my body and the world; and a more creative life, the antidote to childhood fear, tension and silence.

Advanced Yoga Rage

Three-plus decades in, I can say with certainty that a life in yoga remains far from all peace and calm. Though much of the grace and beauty I experience in my life continues to be on my yoga mat.

Now, I've become that woman in her fifties teaching yoga, though not so supple as that first teacher at the Y. Instead of embracing the "frenetic steeplechase toward nothing," as William Faulkner described it, a chase that's gaining speed in the twenty-first century, I do my best to step out of it.

Yoga practice has given structure to a chaotic life, as well as discipline and steadiness that support my haphazard working life as a writer. I've learned something about my propensities and issues, particularly the destructive power of rage and its killing effects, and how yoga can help. Yoga let me contain my emotions so I could look, and let go, stop reacting or hiding.

It's odd to think I was led by a twisted ankle. Forced to slow down. Yoga isn't magic—I still have to deal with my aggression and suffering—but it's a path that makes sense to me, one with heart. And I'll never be finished. Recently, a student suffering panic attacks responded angrily to my advice about daily breathing practices: "It's easy for you, you're so relaxed!" The truth is, with one small spark, my temper can still flare, spontaneous as hiccups, or wildfire.

About swearing at an eight-year-old. It happened this way:

After teaching yoga
I steer my bike
through the brilliant blue day,

at one with vermilion leaves
that scuttle like crabs before
the windwave of my tire, rubber
merging with new tar on the black street.

The skateboarder doesn't see me.
I swerve magnanimously;
he falls off, his board gliding
between my back and front wheels.

Braking hard, I speak kindly:
You must watch where you're going.
The red haired, gap-toothed kid
says: Fuck you! *exploding*

my om into orange and toxic yellow:

No, fuck you … sonny!
Silence. Delight, this retort:
Take a hike, ass-wipe!

Be careful, *I say*—not to
get any more brain damage,
and I push his skateboard,
pedal away to the coffee shop.

My yoga friend, noticing agitation,
asks whether I want a decaf.
I just swore at an eight-year-old,
I say. But he started it.

Yes, blindsided by a kid on a skateboard. Now at least I know enough to realize I'm reacting to my past, my ingrained habit energy. Like the rider letting the horse choose her destination.

To intercept conditioned responses, you have to have speed and clarity of perception. In yoga, you breathe, pause, reflect—you respond instead of react—and begin to embrace freedom, erode your conditioning. Or so I tell my students.

The temper of our times, so angry and brutal, makes it feel vital that we try to train and educate ourselves to respond instead of lash out. Yoga's beauty is that it helps us encounter our shadow, but also our virtues—courage, wisdom, compassion, reverence. It's about finding peace and inner change, which transforms your relationship to others, and the planet.

We're all works in progress, physically, emotionally and spiritually. As for me, I'm still angry, reactive—though less so. I still fight with my father, who died six years ago. Nowadays I'm practising this: watching my emotions arise and pass away, and using the energy to motivate positive action. Trying to turn heat into light.

I'm still far from enlightened, whatever that is—perhaps being liberated from neurosis? Meanwhile, when a skateboarder cuts me off, or someone says "no efforting" in yoga class, or people grab their cellphones like addicts the moment we finish our peace chants, there's an excellent chance new epithets may fly.

KIRSTEEN MacLEOD

The Seraphim

EMILY McKIBBON

Beacon pinched the sheet between the thumb and index finger of her hand. "This paper," she said, her words punctuated by the rattling of the page as she twitched her wrist, back and forth, back and forth through the air. "This paper—see how I've written love on it?—it represents all of the love that you have in your heart. All the love that you were born with, and all the love you have to give."

She paused, flipped the sheet of 8½ × 11 paper toward her body and gripped it in both hands, held close together along the top right edge. One decisive movement and Beacon's right hand ripped one long section free. "And this is the love that you gave your first boyfriend. You met him in high school and he was so cute—*so nice*—and you thought it was going to last forever." Holding this orphaned scrap up and out, Beacon released her fingers and the fragment dropped. We watched it fall, our minds testing this scenario against our endless catalogues of preteen crushes. "But he broke your heart," she said. "And that part of your heart is gone."

Beacon said, continuing, "You didn't date much in high school after that; it was too painful, seeing him every day in the hallway with his new girlfriend. So you study and get good grades, go to church, hang out with your camp friends. You go to university, join some student groups. And you meet a new boy—maybe at a prayer group. And you think: *This is the one. He won't hurt me.* So you go on a few dates, date for a year, maybe even two years. But he loses his path, loses his faith—and you lose him." Her soft voice, its slow cadence, was interrupted by a sharp, ragged sound: Beacon had torn another strip from the shrinking sheet. She dropped it. "Gone."

From the camp kitchen I heard trays of melamine tableware being stacked, hot and quick-drying from the commercial-grade dishwasher. I smelled wet pine needles, the Muskoka breeze and "dip," buckets of ice-cold, diluted bleach they made us rinse our hands with before we entered the dining hall. All of us girls were silent, most rapt and—in hindsight—tender young.

I longed to be in my cabin instead, in the tight flannel fold of my sleeping bag, listening to the rain. I'd discovered the Song of Solomon in my father's Bible, discovered *let him kiss me with the kisses of his mouth,* smuggled whole passages of it while we were supposed to be reading the Beatitudes, wanted to return to the Song's lethargic sweetness. But, instead: "You struggle with the breakup." Beacon continued: "Maybe you go out drinking. Meet someone. Make a mistake." Another rip, and another piece of paper fluttered to join the two already on the floor.

Beacon continued, listing bad decisions and rash choices. After a few more heartbreaks Beacon paused and held her meagre sheet in front of her chest and breathed deep, looking at the sheet and us in turn. "This, girls, this little sheet of paper? This is all the love you have left in the world. All the love you have left after all of this for God."

Beacon paused again: "God, and your husband."

.   .   .

When I performed this camp anecdote for drunken friends in my late teens and twenties, I rarely appended it with my repressed hope that giving love was more like spending your magic penny than a slow attrition. And I told this story often, in the types of shady bars that can be reached only by rickety staircases, dives loved only by kids who loved most where one must love defiantly and against all good judgment. In telling this story, I affirmed my allegiance to a cynicism that I thought might suit me, might allow me to navigate romantic love and sex more confidently. I would laugh: *How naive to conflate love and sex!* I would roll my eyes and say: *What uptight prudes. What puckered Christian spinsters.*

But I tell this story less often now, and when I do it's often inflected with a sense of sadness and loss. Admittedly, a part of me still wants to be sneering and dismissive: surely the summer camp Christian is just as casual and superficial in her engagement as a classic Super Bowl Catholic. But the truth is that faith once pulled me in and along a tightly circling orbit, and camp was once a place to reaffirm this love of God. In the years since losing my faith, I feel as though I am spiralling out with no centre to hold. It was summer camp that crystallized all that I found narrow-minded and judgmental about my family's religion and allowed me to dismiss faith entirely. But I loved that place, too; loved and hated it, and I might love it still had I fit in better.

I am reminded of one of my first Bible studies at the camp. Our leader brought us icy-cold glasses of milk, the glasses first fogged, then sweating in the heat of the summer day. "Take a sip," she said, "and close your eyes. Really feel it." I tracked that cold swallow down my throat, a cool line travelling down my esophagus, noted the way I lost the singularity of that swallow as it passed, diffuse and chill, through my chest and downwards. "That's like the Holy Spirit," she said, "moving inside you."

And this: an unsettling song, sung in the round, to the tune of "Frère Jacques." A chorus of young girls chanting, starting soft and gathering steam, harmonic-cacophonic at its peak, fading to silence as the voices fell away: "Revelations (*Revelations*), twenty-one eight (*twenty-one eight*), liars go to he-ell (*liars go to he-ell*), burn burn burn (*burn burn burn*)."

It was the most beautiful place on earth. But it was dangerous, too.

.   .   .

Even as I grew rebellious, I was never fully immune to the emotional and narrative power of forgiveness, to what this summer camp did best: summertime redemptions.

These rituals of public confession and collective forgiveness were no less gripping for being completely formulaic. Each morning we'd finish breakfast and break into small groups for Bible study, an earnest forty-five minutes of conversation about God's role in our lives. Afterwards, all the girls would return to the dining hall for worship—a heated session of soft rock and pop Christian songs with lyrics lit up by an old-school overhead transparency projector. A band would play at the front of the hall, the tables pulled back and stacked, benches lined in rows.

It's hard to explain to a layperson precisely what happened next. Girls who might have started worship seated, testing out the first few songs, would soon get to their feet. Eyes closed, girls crossed their wrists over their chests, palms against their rib cages, pointer and middle fingers hooked and held in the hard ridges of their clavicles. We'd start moving from the waist, tracing a figure eight with our shoulders, necks and heads. By the end of worship, the most devoted girls would raise their hands, palms up to the sky, singing. And it's here—this moment, this precise moment—that someone would start weeping. Others would notice and put an arm around her. Those around her might start crying, too. Ritualized confession would follow, sometimes taking days to tumble out. There was a glamour to having sinned, the girls who did it best lit with faith, tremulous and glowing.

The same hierarchies that existed in school were remade, automatically and intuitively, at camp. The coolest girls had the best redemptions, the things that made them popular and powerful were the things they tended to confess most openly: kissing a boy or two and terrorizing other girls. We might have forgiven their real and imagined sins, but there was also a pragmatic function to these disclosures: we hopeless losers would invariably be jealous of their prowess with the opposite sex, and we knew they could terrorize us if we pissed them off.

These beautiful once-sinners occupied the upper echelons of camp society. Below them were the sporty girls, crafters, pastor's kids and most other campers. I, on the other hand, was the worst kind of camp pariah: distinctly not athletic, prone to crying jags when slighted, and liable to make and beat to death a promising in-joke in a day or less. I was also guilty of subtler sins: a propensity for kittenish female friendships, a tendency to forget myself changing out of and into my bathing suit, and a healthy cover of coltish fuzz on my mosquito-bitten legs.

I was camp friends with a girl named Andrea—Andrya, as she styled herself—who attended the same session I did every summer. She was a year younger, petite and quick to excite. She liked the Smiths, and she taught me to tease my hair out like Robert Smith using a fork we stole from the dining room. "If you use a comb it works better," she said. "My brother does it like this all the time." We were riding out what remained of the late 1990s alt-rock movement in what religious, preteen ways we could. Sometimes it worked. Morrissey's abstinence made our hellfire-scorched attitude toward sex seem healthy by comparison. In the movement's emphasis on female friendships, we soared. Andrea and I wrote each other endless letters illustrated with angry cartoons and spoke on the phone whenever our parents would eat the long-distance charges.

Our friendship was misunderstood at camp, particularly in our final years there. We walked the grounds wrapped around each other, her arm around my waist and mine around her shoulders. "Don't even joke about that," my counsellor warned me after my ecstatic, shrieking goodbye one evening, *Farewell, Andrea! I love you!* "It's not funny, Emily. It's a sin."

Another rebuke. A girl in my cabin, Melanie, frequently volunteered to join in on evening prayer. She was an athletic pastor's kid and what she lacked in glamour she made up in fervour. "I pray that you let her in," she said one night. "That you lay your healing hands on her, before it's too late." *Healing hands?* I thought. *Healing hands?* From the mouths of babes, such tiresome adult phrasing. *She thinks she's better than me*, I thought, fuming in my sleeping bag.

I never sought forgiveness or performed public redemption for Andrea's and my friendship. My relationship with Andrea was not integral to my person—it was only a friendship I was flirting with, nothing more—and so I walked away from their censure only cynical, and largely unscathed.

·   ·   ·

Nights at camp were inky black, a faint smell of incense rising from glowing mosquito coils. Where the trees grew close there was only a moving canopy of fir above us, but over the lake the stars spread thick and deep. The cabins had no electricity, and the bug-repelling brown bulbs over the communal bathroom spilt a paltry light. At the beginning of the two-week sessions the nights were terrifying, but by the final few nights I would welcome them, finding in their cool breezes relief from the oppressive midday heat.

One such night, late in the session, my counsellor, Aqua, didn't return to cabin for tuck-in. This was my first or second year at the camp, and I slept in an upper bunk, a long built-in shelf separated into two beds down the centre. I slept head to head with a skinny girl named Stephanie, and we used to sing songs from our respective parents' *Les Misérables* double albums to each other when either of us was homesick. Aqua's absence scared us, and Stephanie refused to sleep without her there. I was tall for my age and tall was close enough to stalwart to ape bravery, so I suggested to Stephanie that we look for her. "We'll find her," I said. "I'm sure it's nothing."

Voices carried far, as did the sounds of flip-flops scrabbling over rock. Stephanie and I looked for Aqua in the beach shed, startled by stacks of CPR Annies in the half-light, the black lake licking the shore nearby. We looked for her in the craft room near the older girls' section of the camp. We even looked for her in the head counsellor's messy cabin, recently abandoned, papers scattered. We called her name in hoarse half-whispers, ignoring the interdictions from other girls to return to bed.

Aqua came back to the cabin long after we gave up, after we ourselves had fallen asleep. The next morning, Aqua said she was helping an older camper who had accidentally drunk a glass of bleach. I recall the crystal clear specificity of it—just one glass—and my confusion. *How does someone drink bleach by accident?* "She was thirsty," Aqua said, "and wasn't paying attention. We gave her some milk and took her to the hospital, and she's fine now."

Remembering this incident, I recently looked up "bleach," and "suicide method."

What turned up was a message board on a website called Suicidemethods .net. Some of what the website contained was familiar—that bleach is viscous, slick and hard to drink. When consumed, it erodes the soft tissue of the throat and stomach. After the stomach wall is breached, the bleach will break down other organs. Side effects include intense stomach pain, vomiting and sometimes death.

Aqua had the appearance of a reed tossed in swift wind, shaken but straight, a thing that survives by virtue of being slight. I remember her being rattled, but not to a degree that scared a twelve-year-old. And the night: a deep quiet, no sirens, no telltale sweep of headlights.

. . .

I wish I could say this was the only search string that turned up results darker than those I expected. A Google search of the camp's name yielded a list of popular choices other users had taken. Most were what I expected: alumni, Facebook, activities. Others less so: tragedy, scandal. I clicked on the latter.

In 2009, a camp counsellor and popular high school teacher was summarily dismissed from his position at camp. There were accusations: two teenaged boys, an "invitation to touch." There was an op-ed in the *Star*, a brief passage of time, and on a Saturday morning in October, a suicide at Toronto's High Park subway station.

God will communicate through fire, we learned at camp. Soft, young and campfire scented, this notion made sense to us. Flames can lick your foreheads, cut through the babel and grant you speech—and comprehension. Moses learns from blazing bushes. And the seraphim, the highest in the hierarchy of angels, are a choir in conflagration: they lift their heartsick songs to the Lord, and burn.

The dead have no voice to sing, praise or repent, and I shouldn't replace this man's with mine. Let his actions speak: he jumped nimbly from the platform, agile enough that the conductor thought the man might be testing his fate, not sealing it. His body electric with shame, snapping and arcing under the stress of a venal "sin" turned mortal burden. He faced the train—pupils dilated, the headlights bright—and gave himself over to public death.

. . .

Seraphim are known as "the ones of love." They burn most because they love best and they never lack for fuel: each is an infinite inferno and all are love everlasting. Would that they—always they—had taught us more of seraphs, and less of hellfire.

. . .

In the granite-pink light at early morning swim, steam would rise off the lake. The pines dipped close to the water's edge, their hold tenuous on the shallow soil overlaying this part of the Canadian Shield. The water, barely rippled, was darker and deeper than the adolescent dreams from which I'd surfaced. It smelled of cold and clean, a trace of the autumn that arrived earlier here than it did back home. It was easy to be hurt into a prayer by a place like this, but when my grasping toes broke the thick meniscus of the lake, I learned only that the water was warm, and waiting. I dove in because I was braver in those days, but I was younger, too.

The Petrified Dancers

LORI McNULTY

On a warm June day, in a field scattered with poppies, the king of Kannauj trembled. His young bride, Rani Balampa, was with child.

The couple had met in Garhwal and married in haste. Too lovestruck to pay due homage to goddess Nanda, they had angered the deity. Disease and drought ravaged the countryside; the enemies of state gained strength.

Fearful that Nanda would kill the couple's unborn child, the priest recommended a religious procession to Roopkund Lake to honour Nanda. To the glacial lap of sacred peaks, the troupe advanced. The king and his wife, their servants, buglers and drummers, even the celebrated Hurkiya dancing girls joined the march, singing lewd songs.

But the showy display enraged Nanda even more.

As they whirled along a rocky alpine meadow, the Hurkiyas were hit.

Their bodies petrified. Turned to stone.

The bugles moaned, the bells shivered silent.

And the doomed procession marched on.

.   .   .

Low, low. My breath hard, heart thundering, legs stiff and sore. Low. Low. Our guide, Amit, pushes his palm to earth. Keep my boot flat on the trail to save energy, he gestures.

We're already a day behind on our climb to Roopkund, a glacial lake filled with human bones situated 16,500 feet above sea level.

Yesterday, hail the size of cricket balls blasted our trekking party, forcing us to set up camp below the snow line. Shivering in my sleeping bag, I wore every piece of clothing in my pack. Bone cold. Bitter winds. Snow and hail force many to turn back on the trek to Roopkund, located in the icy lap of sacred Nanda Devi peak. Get the timing wrong and you'll face blizzards. Overstay your welcome, and you won't make it back.

My friends Nisha, Karthik and I are on a long-awaited trek to the Garhwal Himalayas, in northern India. Our guides are two Indian mountaineers, Amit and Guyan, and a local Garhwali guide, Kuari Ram. Amit hums as he walks, then slowly opens out into a lush, smooth baritone: the twenty-eight-year-old singing mountaineer. Guyan's slender bones and soft, sloping eyes give his face the perfect A-frame. When he laughs, I expect his thin moustache to slide right off his lips. Kuari Ram has the sturdy build of a Bulgarian gymnast. Tufts of jet-black hair curl beneath his blue woollen cap. I watch him walk, gripping the steel head and woollen handle of a pickaxe he keeps balanced across his shoulders. As we pass stone-stacked temples, he kneels before the gods in one of the most sacred and protected areas in all of India.

For millions of Hindus, the Garhwal Himalayas are the birthplace of gods, a holy ground stretching from flowering valley to shimmering peaks. Many come to visit holy shrines and restored temples, to walk through blossoming valley trails and feel the shiver of Lord Shiva stirring along their spines. Once every twelve years, Hindu devotees travel to Garhwal for the Nanda Devi Raj.

Thousands of Hindu pilgrims form a human chain across the countryside, most on foot, others riding mules, all carrying gifts and offerings for goddess Nanda. A four-horned sheep decorated as bride leads the procession to the Nanda Devi sanctuary, located just beyond Roopkund. Pilgrims cover 280 kilometres over three weeks, many walking the entire journey barefoot. Some play drums, or blow pipes, and carry ceremonial parasols. Some pilgrims are so old and weak, they die along the way. At final rest in the abode of gods.

We have no sheep. No gifts for Nanda Devi, the most sacred mountain in the entire Himalayan chain. Bliss-giving Nanda has been worshipped here since the fourth century. My friends from Mumbai came for adventure before settling down and starting a family back in Canada. I came to escape grief's grip on a distant slope and forget my way back.

By fifty-two, my mother had already survived two types of cancers. The disease wasn't done with her yet. On her fifty-sixth birthday, scans revealed another tumour, this time in her bladder. Chemo and radiation left her nauseous, vomiting bile. By then my mother walked as if the ground was forever falling from her.

In and out of emergency and hospitals my two sisters and I whirled. Near the end, our mother lay silent, barely a ripple beneath the blue sheets that billowed from her hollow ribs—a riptide, a shipwreck. We wouldn't let the tide take her in.

Wearing flat-soled leather shoes, Kuari Ram leads us along a curving limestone path. I watch his foot glide over the snow-patched shale, hover a moment, then find the sure path, like a diviner. As the trail rises, the temperature drops. The west wind breaks hard across our backs. I pull my toque down over my ears, tighten the strings around my hood. Up and up we march. Our minds turn loose, wander with high-altitude hangovers. A darkness that separates body from soul descends upon us as we trudge across a snowy ridge. Nisha, Karthik and I keep shuffling along, three children tottering along an icy sidewalk.

Entombed in my green hood, I dream of endings.

We drifted through the room. Saline drip, morphine, stat
My sisters and I. A trio. An ensemble cast.
Turn her over. Let her rest.
Watch the disappearing woman gorge on opiates and air.

The path disappears beneath layers of ice. All I want to do is to sleep. A cold knife between my shoulder blades. Blanketed in my green hood, I feel a sharp ache between my temples. Head full of hate. "We are not mountaineers" keeps pounding between my ears.

Deep, slow breaths. The snow-matted peaks surrounding us soon disappear in fog and cloud. Nisha hunches, struggling to breathe. She tries to inch her right foot forward, as if her entire body is being pulled through water. Her deep brown eyes, two stones surfacing, meet mine. I can't bear to look at her. Her lifeless arms, feet dragging the way my mother's right foot lagged behind after radiation, scraping the ground like a cement slipper. Guyan removes her small pack and straps it across his chest to lighten her load for the rest of the trek. He presses his hand to Nisha's back to help guide her forward.

Light-headed. Losing track. A storm in my stomach. Jagged peaks fill a ragged line on the horizon when the trail bends and folds, and then the mountain faces disappear. Nisha's face is ashen. Guyan and Amit exchange uneasy looks. Amit whispers to Karthik that they may have to carry Nisha on their backs the rest of the route. We're falling too far behind. Storms, the dark, are coming.

In our mother's hospital room, the days passed. Mouthfuls stranded on a tray. Her body shook, head pitched back, her eyelids fluttered. We held watch, held her shrinking form, and held our breath.

> *Our fingers caressed the bridge of her hand,*
> *tried to unfold the outcome, make a new map.*
> *We daubed moist sponges to her parted lips.*
> *Her eyes sank back into shadow.*

Nisha tries to smile as we push ahead. Finally, she stops speaking altogether.

The only weekend I took a break from my mother's care, she tumbled down a flight of stairs, breaking her left arm. She lay on the landing, a fine bead of blood spreading across her hairline. Later, under a running tap in the bathroom sink, I washed my mother's hair, feeling the last of her fine, wispy strands between my fingers, as tiny flecks of caked blood drained into the sink. Her left arm, a black wing pinned to her chest, was the only part of her body that would ever heal.

Amit checks his watch. The last push to Roopkund is a long climb over a snowy flank. I follow Amit's gaze to the steady slope ahead. Kuari Ram digs his pickaxe in, letting his shoe stutter-step, stutter-step, glide over the snow-matted slate. The final series of switchbacks is an hour's sharp vertical trek. By the time we reach the snow-covered steps, we find them loose and crumbling, many no wider than our hips. Single file. Eyes on boots. We watch for hidden patches of ice, taking uncertain steps. In silence, we turn up, brace for the final ascent. Twelve switchbacks in all. No one says a word.

Up and up the slippery slate we march. Every few steps we have to stop and catch our breath.

My twin sister flew in from Toronto, stared death down from her silent
*   mound—*
gave it the old evil eye.
Would stay to the end. In over her head.
Stutter-step, stutter-step—slide.

To avoid tumbling from the treacherous slope, when the path becomes too narrow to navigate upright, we are forced to drop down on all fours and crawl over snow and ice. Eyes down. A burning in my chest as we push toward the clouds. When I look up again, Amit has vanished.

Come back; come now, the nurses said
We slept in sleeping bags on the hospital boardroom floor, awaiting her
*   last breath.*
The doctors pushed steroids through her thin veins. And she sat up,
*   suddenly awake.*
*   Against all odds, held on.*

As the legend of Roopkund goes, when the king of Kannauj and his pregnant bride continued their pilgrim's procession across hard-packed snow following the Hurkiya girls' last dance, the trail became windswept and treacherous. Nanda soon unleashed her full fury. The buglers and drummers were hit. All were turned to ghosts. Struggling to find their footing along the tight-coiling switchbacks, the remaining party trekked on. When they reached the final ridge, a blizzard came storming across the path, pelting them with hailstones hard as iron. Snow-blind, the pilgrims were hurled down the slope to their graves at the bottom of Roopkund.

Without warning, we've reached the top. We embrace and shout. A surge of energy and we find our footing. Amit motions for us to join him at the ridge. On top of the world, Nisha, Karthik and I peer down at the mythic lake. The waters are turquoise grey, hidden by a froth of cloud. The oval pool looks like a huge vat of cloudy soup. Amit steps over the ridge and scrambles down to the lake edge, his red beret disappearing into fog. He crouches, scours the water's edge, gathers something in his arms. Scrambling up again, he turns toward us and we see he is holding bones. He shows us a man's tibia, and maybe a femur. Absent their histories, the moment is surreal. Exhilarating.

We take turns snapping photos against a pyramid pile of human skulls and bones by the lake. Pilgrims, the procession, the past pieced together. We scoop up snow, remake lives, turn history over.

> *Two men in white coats flutter down the hall.*
> *The surgeon's blue cap damp above the brow.*
> *My sisters and I stand in the doorway.*
> *"Your mother has eleven brain tumours."*
> *Now we are turning, turning, criss-crossing the room.*
> *One by one the lights went out and we wept.*
> *Dumbstruck. Numb.*
> *We were dancing in the dark all along.*

More than three hundred bodies were found at the bottom of Roopkund Lake in 1947. In the shallow depths, a mass grave, where cracked human skeletons, horse bones, jewellery, wood, coal and ash are still scattered. Unsolved for decades was the mystery of exactly who these people were and how they all perished at the same time. DNA tests later dated the remains of the men, women and children who died at around 850 CE. All had received fatal blows to the back of their heads from blunt objects the size of cricket balls. A deathly hailstorm, perhaps. No one knows for certain. The tall skeletons may have been of Iranian descent, the shorter, related to the Chitpavan Brahmins who acted as porters and guides. Yet the mystery of Roopkund remains, the pilgrimage to Nanda Devi endures.

Bodies shivering, soon after we arrive at Roopkund, we must begin the long descent toward base camp.

From the rear Amit croons a traditional Bollywood tune. Karthik and Nisha join in. I try to hum along, the song drifting above the summits before silence falls. Finally, we reach the grassy promontory at Pathar Nachauni, still an hour from base camp. Kuari Ram stops abruptly and points his pickaxe to a bald patch of rocky earth. He steps off the path and spikes the ground, scraping a large circle in the earth. I shake my head, not understanding. Stepping inside, he places one hand atop his blue wool toque, the other at his waist, and does a little twirl. Here is the site where the Hurkiya girls last danced. Pathar (stone) Nachauni (dancers)—the Petrified Dancers. He nods to me and turns back to the path.

· · ·

At base camp, Guyan and the muleteers stand and applaud our arrival. I close my eyes, feel the sacred mountains in my midst. The myth of Roopkund carries me forward across this holy ground.

Inside the kitchen tent, we sit cross-legged on the dirt floor while Guyan stirs a pot of chai, thick with Carnation evaporated milk. The scent of cardamom and cloves wafts through the tent, and steam fills the back of my throat, the way memories swirl in sorrow's mouth.

I stir the silky froth with my cinnamon stick and listen to the men laugh and exchange stories in Hindi. Their language an unknown path, I watch the grooves form around Amit's mouth, admire the silver pickaxe pinned to his red beret.

When night falls, and loneliness gathers around, I close my eyes and remember that fragrant air.

It tastes of eternity.

Spotted Dick

LINDY MECHEFSKE

Age 5½: My family has moved to Canada and I am at school in this strange new place. I am the only child in my class with an accent. I don't understand the teacher and I don't know many of the things the other children know. Though I can count well beyond ten, I stop there each time because I often mix up the order of eleven and twelve and am too afraid lest I get them the wrong way round. I don't know the names of the Disney characters or the games the children play. Baseball is particularly terrifying. The way the ball hits the bat and whips across the field. The way everyone runs and yells, changing sides suddenly. Nobody explains anything to me. I run when the other children run but I feel panicky the whole time. I understand nothing of what we are doing.

Eventually I learn that if I walk to the far edge of the schoolyard I can be alone in the trees and shrubs along the fence where it is much safer. In the classroom it is harder to hide. Mrs. Cunningham, our teacher, is short and wide and cross. She reminds me of a prickly hedgehog. She has no patience with me, is exasperated by all the things I don't know.

I don't tell anyone what I *do* know. How to get on and off an airplane, how to hold my knife and fork properly and place my napkin on my lap. How to set the table. I know my manners. I know how to appreciate food. I can roll pastry and make jam tarts and knead bread dough. I know how to peel an orange, as my grandfather does, in one long continuous strip, though I am not always successful. I can shell peas and tell cheddar cheese from Stilton. I know the call of the tawny owl and what a pheasant looks like, and a peacock, and a pretty little English robin. I know the English woodland animals: badgers, moles, hedgehogs, foxes and rabbits. I know many of the children's books on my grandfather's shelf by heart. I am partial to *The Wind in the Willows*, to Toad of Toad Hall.

At morning recess in Canadian kindergarten, we are served grape juice. Expecting Ribena, the tart blackcurrant cordial I am used to, I take a long drink and nearly throw up the cloyingly sweet juice. I hate it. I will never drink it and have not had it since.

In the classroom, I sit alone and cry—lost, lonely, missing everything I know, and most of all, my beloved grandfather.

At home, we live as if we were still in Yorkshire, the ancestral home of my family for as far back as records extend. We eat porridge and kippers and drink tea at breakfast time; and have Marmite or Lyle's golden syrup, *not* peanut butter, on toast when we come home from school.

My mother makes a long list of food we will never eat. "We are not eating fish from a can," she says. "Or peanut butter, or hot dogs, or Pop-Tarts, or corn on the cob," ruling out all the things I am busting to try—food that would let me fit in with my classmates. She enunciates clearly, never running the words together, putting the emphasis on HOT in hot dogs and POP in Pop-Tarts. In her spare time, she corrects the pronunciation on the CBC. "It's a con-TRAHV-ah-see," she says, tut-tutting, "Not a CON-tro-versy." After a while, both are so familiar to me that I no longer know which is right and which is wrong, which is English versus Canadian. The handsome *Globe and Mail* paperboy asks me what language my parents speak.

On Sundays, there is roast beef with Yorkshire puddings and gravy. My father, at the head of the table, says, *"Benedictus, benedicat,"* the Latin grace meaning "May the blessed one give a blessing." We three children—I am the youngest and the only female—have no clue what the words mean. It is merely the ritual, solemn moment of reverence before we eat.

. . .

My grandfather, patron saint of my childhood, was my introduction to love. He was a big handsome Englishman with smiling eyes and rosy cheeks, the sort of person you wanted to know because he was thoughtful, happy and phenomenally generous. He lived with passion and enthusiasm, insatiably interested in people. When anything awful happened, my grandfather was there, helping, bringing presents, flowers, food. He was whip smart, with a rare gift for friendship. And pockets full of candy. He was a little deaf too, so he was a touch on the loud side and known to slurp his food with more gusto than was strictly polite, but he lived life with heart and arms so wide open, he was impossible to resist. Kindness was his religion.

Age 3, first memory: My grandfather is standing in the kitchen of his old stone home on the banks of a river. A heavy white cotton apron over white shirt and tie and dark woollen trousers. His sleeves are held up with with elasticized silver arm bands. His hands are plunged in a large blue-and-white striped porcelain bowl. He is covered in flour and he is singing an old Yorkshire folk song as he works. I am standing on a wooden stool at the table beside my grandfather, a little English girl wearing buckled leather shoes, a hand-knit woollen cardigan and a dark tartan skirt. My hair, in braids, has ribbons tied at the ends. I am looking up admiringly at my tall, handsome grandfather—a great strapping man with astonishing deep blue eyes and a smile that lights up his face. He turns the raisin-studded dough onto a floured board and pinches off a small piece for me. Side by side we knead the dough. I am making my own very small loaf of bread—very serious business for a three-year-old.

What I remember is this: food, love, joy.

Age 4: My only cousin, Jackie, a shade younger than me, is visiting for my fourth birthday tea. My grandfather has produced a fruitcake covered in royal frosting and topped with beautiful, tiny marzipan fruit—perfect little oranges, apples, bananas, limes and cherries. The cake sits on the kitchen counter waiting for later in the day. My cousin and I are alone in the kitchen, we cannot resist sampling the marzipan fruit from the top of the cake. We know this is wrong but once we start, we eat them all. In for a penny, in for a pound. When my grandfather sees this, he laughs and calls us "a right pair of monkeys," then dips a knife in boiling water and smoothes out the icing before carrying the candlelit cake to the dining room table.

Age 5: My grandfather has entrusted me with the task of bringing ingredients from the pantry for a pie we are making. The old wooden door off the kitchen leads down four or five stone steps into the larder, where a bare light bulb on a long pull chain illuminates the space—he has tied a long white satin ribbon to the pull chain so I can access the light. The walls are stone. It is cool, quiet, slightly damp and surprisingly beautiful, a sacred place, practically magical, the best-kept secret in the house.

I stand on the bottom step admiring the provisions—a living still life. The open whitewashed shelves hold baskets of brown eggs from the farm, a loaf of bread, marmalade, jam and honey, cheese, a bowl of pears or plums, often a large leg of ham or a joint of beef. Sometimes a Victoria sponge cake dredged with sugar and filled with whipped cream and raspberry jam. Tea and sugar and flour in tin canisters. Dried herbs hanging upside down in string-tied bouquets on the walls, and spices in jars with labels I cannot yet read properly. There is chocolate. And Fox's Glacier Mints. Sometimes there are jam tarts or Yorkshire parkin or thick fingers of shortbread. Ginger nuts. Jacob's cream crackers. A domed glass dish of butter. Milk in glass pint jars. On the floor of the pantry are wooden bins of potatoes, carrots and onions. On the upper shelves rest beautiful china serving bowls and platters. And the big blue-and-white striped bowl we mix the bread in, beside its matching pitcher.

My grandfather believed in the sanctity of food. He ate as if every meal were his last, as if sustenance was a deeply spiritual, highly social matter. Food was the glue that held together relationships, families, societies. Food was a favourite conversational topic, a rightful passion. Before one meal was over, he was thinking about the next.

A continent away, decades long past, the memories surface and resurface. Every time I sit down to write, I think of my grandfather. Every time I start to cook, he is there with me. I bring him forward, and very likely his mother before him, and her mother before her, and the generations before them who passed on their knowledge, skills and stories, down through the centuries. All these are contained within me and I am hanging on to the threads of their lives. It is sacred, life-sustaining work, the preparation of food, this bloodline. I am part of something much bigger than myself.

I think of my own mother and father, of our kitchen table. My father coming through the door at the end of a long day at work practically shouting, "What's for dinner? What's for pud?" My mother at the stove, stirring jam, or gravy, or making shepherd's pie. The memories crop up out of nowhere. Most often though, the memories are of my grandfather, suddenly there with me, pouring cognac into a snifter, or peeling an apple with a paring knife. I think of his reverence for food, his ability to love, his devotion to kin—those of us lucky enough to call ourselves family and friends. The fluke of it all, this holy trinity of food, love, kinship.

At my desk, even when I sit down to write other things, it is the food stories that keep cropping up. Food, the vehicle for sustenance and nourishment, for connection, for emotional and spiritual needs. For belonging. And for love. I've come to see food stories as the real stories of our lives.

Food is at once practical, necessary, tangible, historical, medicinal, ceremonial, theatrical, cultural, secular, spiritual and religious. It is a huge part of our journey, our history, our home, and the story of ourselves and our ancestors. You only have to look at the storylines of Indigenous peoples to know that food and spirituality are so interwoven they are virtually inseparable. Everything comes from the Earth and we, in turn, are its appointed caretakers. We owe our existence to these two simple facts. There is a reassuring certainty, too. One meal follows the other, just as day follows night. For over fifty-five million years, humankind has roamed the planet in search of food and water. We are hard-wired to think about our next meal, the need encoded in our DNA. Our need for food predates everything—fire, ordered civilization, any kind of organized religion.

Age 6: The Sunday school teacher has written a question on the blackboard that we have all dutifully copied into our little ruled notebooks. "What is the real meaning of Easter?" Below the question, pencilled in fat grey lead in unsteady letters, I have written:

"The Easter bunny brings us Chocolit eggs."

The words are mostly erased but still showing. The page is scrunched with my attempts to rub out the words. Over them, below them, around them, I have written new words, copied again from the blackboard, in awkward shaky writing, "Christ died on the cross to save us from our sins." This is as foreign to me as the new country I live in.

I am stunned when an older boy reads his answer and says that Easter was when Christ, who had been nailed to the cross, died, was buried, then rose again. I feel a little sick. Partly because of the concept. Partly because he says the word *Christ*, a word I am not clear we should say aloud. Mostly though, because I am so far wrong. Taking the eraser out of my pencil case, I start rubbing out my answer. The boy has drawn a picture of Christ on the cross. I have drawn a shaky little rabbit with huge ears, a lot of circular-looking flowers on stick stems, and a scattering of brightly coloured eggs.

I am that stranger in a strange place, belonging nowhere, but especially not in Sunday school. I cling to my books, my memories, and to my grandfather's visits to Canada and mine back to England. The years pass. I beg not to go back to Sunday school. I barter to stay home and wash dishes and peel potatoes for Sunday dinner.

Only now do I see that I got the answer right—that naturally, a child would think Easter was about chocolate eggs. Eggs: the universal symbol of fertility and rebirth—the essence of the message of Easter.

Our first real lessons are so often about love and food. My grandfather could never have known that those hours he spent with me in the kitchen would become my most treasured memories, that they would shape everything about my life, that I would return to those memories again and again, finding solace and connection. That I would write from all he introduced me to—those memories, that life-affirming love.

· · ·

Age 40: My father is dying in a great hurry, fighting his third round of cancer, each bout unrelated. At seventy-two, he is much too fit to die. Tall, lean, fiercely intelligent, unstoppable. Ravenous for more of everything—food, belonging, the meaning of life. We all expect him to continue climbing mountains and spend his summers tearing around France in a Citroën. Surely he has at least another decade. But he does not.

His last days are spent in hospital, seventy minutes' drive from our cottage on Georgian Bay. My mother and I drive to see him each morning and leave again at night, making the trek along dark roads under the dark night sky to our beds and the respite of sleep. Days slide into each other, the outside world becomes irrelevant. In the hospital, time and air and words linger, interrupted by brief, sporadic appearances from cleaners, nurses, doctors and palliative care staff. How odd, I think, to die here in this place, finding mercy among so many strangers.

My father faces his death bravely and entirely without complaint. He spends his awake time traversing backwards through his life. Mostly, when he talks, he talks about travel and food, though technically he has stopped eating, existing merely on the memory of food. He is recalling meals in France, or on mountain-climbing expeditions, and on various special occasions throughout his life. Finally, toward the very end, he is remembering the food he'd once eaten at boarding school.

"Spotted dick," he says suddenly, very clearly. It was always his favourite dessert—a steamed pudding spotted with raisins and served with custard. Then, "Jam roly-poly," another favourite. "Steak and kidney pie." He is grinning like a schoolboy, eyes full of mirth. "Treacle pudding, fish and chips, mushy peas, finnan haddie, bubble and squeak, toad-in-the-hole. Custard tart." It is the most he has said in days. He is making a list of all his old favourites, his joy filling the room. We are all grinning. It seems impossible to be this happy when his death is imminent. I am crying and smiling all at once. It hurts so much I cannot bear it.

My father dies that night.

.   .   .

Food memories, so deeply embedded in our psyche, are often our first and last memories of life. Evolution plays a role here, ensuring that the hippocampus is primed to form memories about what is essential for survival. We tend to remember food more clearly when it's associated with emotion, good and bad, and abundance or deprivation. We eat with our minds as much as with our stomachs.

.   .   .

Late morning, Mum and I awake to brilliant sunshine and an empty fridge. We have been living on hospital sandwiches and paper cups of coffee and tea. Out of the blue, the neighbour, Helen, is at the door, asking us over for an early dinner. She has organized a small mountain of hamburgers, sausages, buns, pickles and salads, and plenty of wine, a beautiful German coffee cake and strong black coffee. "Bring everyone," she says. "You will need to eat."

The rest of the family arrive and we traipse next door to find Helen's husband, Horst, manning the barbecue in the sunshine, mopping rivers of sweat from his brow with a worn-out towel. In a thick German accent, he tells stories of my father until we laugh, cry, laugh again. "Spotted dick! *Mein Gott*!" he cries, gasping with laughter. "Only the English …" his voice trails off drowned in laughter, his Buddha belly shaking, his shirt gaping.

We eat with surprising gusto. Beyond us is the deep blue of Georgian Bay. In the garden, a hummingbird darts between flowers and above us lies the endless, cloudless, June sky. My father would have loved this late afternoon party, the big red umbrella on the old stone patio—the family, the neighbours, the platters of food—this moment cut from time. This sharing of food. So paramount, so imprinted. So much bigger than ourselves—a deeply spiritual, universal and primal bonding experience.

It is just exactly as M.F.K. Fisher wrote in *The Gastronomical Me*: "There is a communion of more than our bodies when bread is broken and wine is drunk."

A Great Silence

K.D. MILLER

I'm making a mask.

First I paint the face glossy black. It's a delicious thing to do, spreading the wet paint over the dry surface, working it into the corners of the eyes, the curves of the lips, the grooves of the nostrils. Finding a spot I've missed and attacking it with the tip of my brush. Next I cut sheets of coloured paper into different shapes to glue onto the black. I have no plan. No vision. My hands just take over. They know what to do. Red *must* slash across yellow. Blue *has* to overpower red. It's a language of colour. A poetry of shape. I feel very powerful, and very young.

.   .   .

I'm four years old, in my grandmother's house for some family gathering. She has given me a needle, some thread and a bag full of scraps of cloth. I set forth—yes, it does feel like being on a quest—to make the biggest, longest, greatest THING ever made. I join scrap after scrap together with huge single stitches, and the thing I am making gets longer and stranger and more magnificent by the minute.

Then one of my big-girl cousins spots it and takes it and holds it up. "Hey everybody," she calls to the room full of family. My thing dangles from her fingertips, frayed and twirling and already coming apart. "Look what this little lady's been up to."

I guess that was my first experience of the critics. One minute, I was powerful and big. The next, not so much. What I learned from it, though, was that I must put my trust in the other experience—that of being on a quest. In choosing each fabric scrap and stitching it to another of my choice, I was on a journey. I was getting somewhere. And once there, I was going to discover something. I didn't know exactly what, only that it would be better and more necessary than anything else I could discover by any other means.

In *A Short History of Myth*, Karen Armstrong writes, "There are moments when we all, in one way or another, have to go to a place that we have never seen, and do what we have never done before. Myth is about the unknown; it is about that for which initially we have no words. Myth therefore looks into the heart of a great silence."

. . .

Long before I started making it, before I even went into an art store to look for the materials I needed, my mask had a name, and a story. Hecate. Goddess of the Dark Moon. The Wise Witch who shadows Persephone once she's been to Hades and back.

I came across Hecate for the first time in the book *Goddesses in Everywoman*, by Jean Shinoda Bolen, MD. It's an old paperback that a friend picked up in a second-hand book store, then passed on to me. It looks and feels as if it's been read and reread, tossed into purses, tucked under pillows. It's travelled a fair distance, too. I found a bookmark inside advertising a bookstore in Bedford, New Hampshire. There's a phone number printed on the yellowing cardboard that I'm oddly tempted to call.

I had trouble with this book at first. I actually judged it by its cover, which is an unfortunate shade of pink, and by its copyright date, which is 1984. I had my doubts about the subject matter, too. In her practice as a Jungian analyst, Jean Shinoda Bolen culled the Greek myths for goddess archetypes that would be meaningful to women at various stages in their lives. Here we go again, I thought. I was remembering far too many social gatherings in the seventies and eighties where people went on at length about their astrological sign or their Myers-Briggs score or whatever. Instant, rubber-stamped identities, achieved by announcing "I'm a Scorpio," or "I'm an introverted extrovert," or "I was born in the Year of the Gnu." And now here was this shocking-pink book offering me a whole new set of rubber stamps in the form of the Greek goddesses.

Once I got past the cover and my own prejudices, however, I was pleas-antly surprised. Reading *Goddesses in Everywoman* has been an exercise in self-recognition. *Selves* recognition, more like. Bolen is careful to point out that no one archetype will apply to any woman throughout her life. And I do seem to have gone through a few goddesses over the years. In high school and university, I was in thrall to Athena. My priorities were intellectual growth and academic achievement. Then, for my master's, I travelled far from home to study directing, which at the time was very much a male preserve. Without realizing it, I was following the example of Artemis, the huntress. In love and in art, I have honoured Aphrodite. I even put in a twelve-year stint at the shrine of Hera, the wife.

Right now, though, it's all about Hecate. She's not a major goddess, but I'm very taken with one of her titles—the Crone at the Crossroads. I can relate to that. At time of writing, I'm less than three months away from retirement. I've spent thirty-eight years—more than half my life—as an employee. My weekdays have been shaped by the job, my free time squeezed into the narrow margin ringing nine to five. As my final Friday approaches, I feel a mix of eagerness and fear. The upside is easy to account for. I look forward to the small changes—not having to pack a lunch, spending as long as I like with the paper in the morning—as much as to the big ones, like having more time to travel and take courses and write.

So what am I afraid of? Again, little things. The retirement party, which, to judge from overheard whispers, is going to be quite the do. Much as I hate that sort of thing, I'll show up and be gracious and try to remember that these events are not really for the benefit of the one leaving, but for those left behind.

Ah. Yes. The people I will be saying goodbye to. People I have worked with for years. Decades, in some cases.

What are colleagues, exactly? Though they qualify as neither family nor friends, I have spent more time with them than I have with any of those. We are part of each others' lives, have shaped each others' existence and will occupy each others' memory. Will I get through my last day in their company dry-eyed? Will they? And why is that so important? Why do I yearn to slip out the door without a word or gesture of farewell?

Because retiring is kind of like dying. In order for a radically new life to begin, the old one must end. That's what's scaring me. All that freedom all of a sudden. Seemingly endless opportunity. The emptiness that I may or may not successfully fill. The new structure for my day that I will create. Or not. The new colleagues I will cultivate. Or not. How likely is solitude to tip into loneliness? Liberty to engender boredom?

I think I'm cocking an ear to the great silence. Time to go on a new quest. Venture into the unknown. Make what is wordless into a story. The prospect fills me with equal parts terror and joy.

. . .

The Crone at the Crossroads. Hecate.

I make her mask in stages, over several days. One afternoon all I do is spray clear fixative onto her patched and painted face, holding my breath, keeping an eye on the skull-and-crossbones warning on the can. When I'm done, her colours glow. The black is glossy again. I spend another day sorting yarn for her hair and tying it in bunches. Black, grey and white. The past, the present and the future. The next morning I attach three old pairs of glasses—one on her nose, one on her forehead and one dangling on a string—to represent Hecate's ability to see in three directions at once. Through the glasses perched on her nose, two commemorative pins that I got from my workplace for twenty and twenty-five years' service glow like the eyes of a cat. Finally I hang two broken watches on either side of her face where they dangle like earrings. And all the while, I anticipate the moment when I will look her square in the face and say, "So what am I supposed to *do*?" I don't really expect an answer from the great silence. But it's been fun framing the question.

I've always had a thing about masks. I can't help believing that they're alive and aware, that they have no real need for our eyes to peer through them in order to see.

Masks have power. To put on a mask is to be both disguised and revealed. Looking at yourself in a mirror through the eyes of a mask can be disorienting. You are a stranger, yet strangely familiar. The mask delights in revealing your flip side. If you have two left feet, the mask might invite you to dance. If you are tongue-tied, it might turn you into a stand-up comic. If you are the life of the party, it might render you shy and introverted.

Writing fiction, for me, is very like putting on a mask. "How exposed you are," a woman in a book club once said to me. I had just finished going through my second book of stories for the group, relating the incidents from my past that had given rise to each one. Her comment surprised me. Exposed? I felt quite safe and comfortable in her living room, curled up on a sofa with a glass of wine. But she was right. Putting on the mask of fiction disguises me to the point that I can strip naked. For good writing demands both. Merely stripping naked would be self-indulgent. But disguising myself beyond recognition, using the mask as something to hide behind, would be dishonest.

The mask of Hecate is both me and not me. Familiar and strange. She is mounted at a crossroads of sorts in my apartment, a spot where hallways branch off in the direction of the living room, the study, the door to outside. Her gold medallion eyes gleam in the light from the windows. Whenever I walk by, her yarn hair stirs with the breeze of my passing.

Sometimes when I glance up at her from my book, she startles me with her strangeness. The dramatic colouring, the long hair hanging down, give her an exotic appearance, as if she might be a shaman enacting sacred rituals. I can hardly believe that I was the one who made her. Other times when I glance up she looks hokey and homemade, with those bits of familiar stuff stuck here and there, and the edges of the coloured paper inexpertly glued down. I'm four years old again, in my grandmother's house. *Look what this little lady's been up to.*

Either way, Hecate herself is silent and still. She is angled in such a way that she appears to be pondering a question that has just been put to her.

· · ·

I grew up in a house where everybody was always making something. One of my mother's oil pastel sketches is framed and hanging in my living room. I remember my father building a boat in the basement and managing to get it up the stairs, out the door and onto a lake, where it actually floated. My brother whittled things out of wood and did beadwork. I still use a beaded bookmark he made for me when he was twelve. It was natural and normal to make things, or so I thought until I got to school and discovered that some children would stare blankly at a piece of art paper, then ask the teacher to tell them what they should draw.

Permission never came into it in my house. The desire within, coupled with the materials at hand, were all that was needed. And materials were always at hand. Paints, coloured pencils, sketch pads, cardboard and glue were staples, right up there with bread and milk and toilet paper. (A few years ago I was over-joyed to hear that in the North American toy market, the top seller continues to be the humble box of crayons.)

Even now, as a writer, I love the tools of my trade. I can never resist going into a stationery store, just to look at the stacks of paper and neat bound blank books and racks of pens. And recently, when shopping for materials for my mask, I rediscovered the joy of art supply stores. The clean new paintbrush-es—I just had to run those bristles across my thumb. I didn't dare pick up any of the tubes of oil paint, arranged by colour and glowing like jewels. I knew that I wouldn't be able to resist squeezing them to feel the soft, living pigment inside. I was almost drunk on the smell of the place—wet clay, turpentine, fresh-cut wood—by the time I staggered out with the papier mâché form that would become the face of Hecate.

The actual making of her sobered me up fast enough. My landlord was installing a new heating system, so workmen were coming and going in my apartment. I'd just be engrossed in one of the tricky parts, like gluing the first pair of glasses to the bridge of her nose, when somebody would knock on the door or call to me—*Lady? We move big plant? Yes?* I wanted to scream, *Throw the freaking plant off the balcony if you want to! Just leave us alone!* We were on a journey together, damn it. We were getting somewhere. And once there, we would discover something better and more necessary than anything else we could ever discover by any other means.

It was still at times a rough trip. Even once the workmen were gone, I kept bumping up against my own inexperience, learning my craft the hard way. Discovering, for example, that I should have left the glasses off the nose until after I'd punched holes to thread the yarn through.

But now she's done. My first mask. And yes, I am already thinking about making another one. Dame Julian of Norwich, perhaps. I've always been fond of Dame Julian. Who couldn't be fond of someone who wrote, "All will be well, and all will be well, and all manner of things will be well"?

Is that what the great silence is whispering? I have a feeling the Crone at the Crossroads is smiling.

Writing from the Inside

ZARQA NAWAZ

"Zarqa, we need you to do an interview with Glenn Beck." Helicia worked for publicity at CBC.

Glenn Beck, Glenn Beck, Glenn Beck. His name sounded like Glenn Miller. I thought of someone happy and congenial, someone associated with big bands, fireplaces, big crinoline skirts, and 1950s' dancing.

"Sure, I'll do it," I said. I was excited. It was 2007. I had just been asked to do my first media interview about *Little Mosque* and I wanted it to be with someone enthusiastic about the show.

Then Al Rae, one of our writers, looked Glenn Beck up online.

"He's pretty right wing, and a show about goofy Muslims living in the Midwest isn't going to be up his alley."

I hadn't done media interviews about *Little Mosque*. The CBC felt it was unwise to give too many interviews early on. But we were getting more attention than expected. Every major media outlet in the world, from CNN to Al Jazeera, was calling.

"Remember the Danish cartoons," cautioned Al. "People are wondering if something similar will happen here." A newspaper in Denmark, the *Jyllands-Posten*, had published cartoons about the Prophet Muhammad that certain Muslims felt were blasphemous. There were riots in Muslim countries. The same Danish newspaper three years earlier had rejected cartoons of Jesus from another cartoonist. The editor's email had said, "I don't think *Jyllands-Posten*'s readers will enjoy the drawings. As a matter of fact, I think that they will provoke an outcry. Therefore, I will not use them."

There was a sense in the Muslim population in Europe of a double standard when it came to things considered sacred. But I wasn't making fun of Islam with this television series, so surely this was different.

Even so, I started to get nervous. I took a shortcut to the interview through the downtown core and wound up at the Toronto Eaton Centre, the largest mall in Canada. The lights, the handbags, the jewellery put me in a materialistic coma and soothed my jagged nerves. When I caught sight of myself in the mirror of the makeup department, I saw I looked freaked out.

"Can I help you?" The makeup woman watched me watch myself. She had pink hair and nails the size of talons.

"I'm doing a CNN interview in an hour," I said. "How do I look?"

"Like crap."

"I'm worried Glenn Beck's going to ask me if Muslims are going to flip cars and set the CBC on fire."

"Why would Muslims do that?"

"I created a television show about the Muslim community," I replied. "It's a comedy set in a mosque."

"Oh," she said. "That sounds like fun."

It was a fun show, but the situation in Europe still haunted me. I reminded myself that the history of Muslims in Europe versus their experience in North America was very different. Many Muslims in Europe were brought in as temporary low-wage workers from surrounding Muslim countries to help rebuild Europe after the Second World War. In Germany, temporary workers brought in from Turkey were never given citizenship and they were kept in living quarters outside the main city. People stayed, and remained marginalized in ghettos for generations, their children unable to integrate, or even to go to university. As of 2010, there were 4.8 million Muslims living in Germany; a fraction have German citizenship. The Muslim populations ended up with high unemployment rates and low education rates compared to the general population.

Canada also had discriminatory practices when it came to immigration. The country was at times "xenophobic and saw itself as an 'Anglo-British outpost of British civility,'" according to immigration historian Harold Troper in a February 2013 article in the *Star*. Then came the 1970s and, at least when it came to Muslims, policies changed. Multiculturalism became the ethos of the day.

"Educated Muslim immigrants were actually sought after and recruited," I told the makeup artist.

"Because Immigration Canada loves Muslims?"

"No, Revenue Canada loves Muslims. Or any kind of immigrant, really. Employed immigrants create a tax base. But in order for the tax base to work, the immigrants have to be integrated, educated and working."

"So you're here because of taxes?"

"Yep, my dad was an engineer in England when Canada recruited him with the offer of fast-tracked citizenship and family reunification, which England was no longer offering. He knew he'd have a better life for his family, so he left."

"Is your father glad he came to Canada instead of Europe?"

"For sure."

What would my life be like if I lived in Europe, I wondered? Many European countries ban high school girls from wearing hijab. In France, separation of state and religion was the official reason, but it was unevenly applied. For example, a Muslim mother came to a school to help with the Christmas play and was told she couldn't participate because of her hijab. Even young girls who don't wear hijab are sometimes removed from class for wearing maxi dresses, which are seen as "too modest" and thus too Muslim. Muslims view these laws and unofficial sanctions as discriminatory. They make Muslims feel unwelcome and misunderstood. At fourteen, I decided to wear hijab when I started high school. My teachers felt it was a little odd, but I was never reprimanded. I wonder what I would have done or felt if I had been told I couldn't continue my education with hijab. The Taliban don't like women getting an education because they fear Western indoctrination. Strangely, the Taliban and French secularists, groups who would never consider themselves aligned on any issue, had both ended up denying Muslim females a right to education, thanks to an irrational fear of a foreign cultural influence.

"Why didn't Canada care about hijab?" The makeup artist's question broke my reverie.

"Canada couldn't care less if you wore a basket of fruit on your head. They just wanted us to get educated, get jobs and pay—"

"Taxes." She nodded. "Yeah, but people still get sensitive about religion and comedy. Especially Muslims."

"True," I said. "But it's too late now."

"It's never too late to look good. TV washes you out so we'll have to add extra colour to make you pop."

"You know how to do that?"

"Of course. I'm a trained makeup artist."

"Where did you train?"

"On the Internet. There were all these tutorials I watched, then I volunteered on real people."

"Like models for fashion runway shows?"

"Birthday parties," she said. "I used to make kids into lions and tigers and stuff like that and then I graduated to the makeup counter." I tried not to think about the lions. I was wearing a turquoise velvet hijab. She took out some turquoise eye shadow.

"That's pretty bright." I flinched.

"We'll tone it down with some silver and gold," she said with confidence, pulling out her makeup brushes.

"Do you have a large clientele?" My eyes were starting to look bigger and bigger thanks to layers of eye shadow and mascara.

"Drag queens love me," she purred.

Half an hour later she was done. I looked like a cross between a parrot and a hooker.

"It's waterproof," she said happily. Had she read my mind? "Here's some special makeup remover. Be careful. It can strip furniture."

I bought some beige eye shadow from the counter as a thank you, then left. As I headed for the studio, I noticed I was attracting a lot of attention.

"Excuse me," I asked one man. "Do you know where the CNN studio is?"

"In there." He pointed. "Are they doing a special on Muslim drag queens?"

I ignored him and walked into the studio, which was located in an underground concrete bunker. One tiny room and one camera guy.

"We're waiting for a female Muslim television show creator," he said. "Our segment on clowns is tomorrow."

"Actually, I'm the show creator, my name is Zarqa Nawaz."

The cameraman recovered quickly. "This interview is gonna be a double ender," he said.

"What's that?" I asked.

"I put a microphone in your ear," he said. "You hear Glenn but you don't see him."

I listened to Glenn finish his interview with another guest. When it was my turn, he started with questions about the show. Then he got down to it.

"So are you concerned? Because some Muslims don't have a real sense of humour. I mean, is this a show that the Taliban would watch?"

I wondered if the Taliban had cable in their caves.

"This is a show that I think North Americans will watch and the world will watch, because it's a very funny show."

"Okay, I understand, I haven't seen an episode—everything I've heard about the show, it's funny, and I appreciate the attitude that you have. But I would like to—I mean, come on. There are people in Dearborn, Michigan, that do not have a sense of humour. Are you afraid at all about those who interpret the Quran and Islam as a licence to kill?"

It was a loaded question. I said the only thing that came to my mind.

"No, I mean, we make fun of everyone. This is a show that is no-holds-barred. We make fun of Muslims, we make fun of non-Muslims, we make fun of extremists, we make fun of the secular, we make fun of the right wing."

He was unhappy with my answer.

"Wait a minute, wait a minute, wait a minute. Right, I know that, but so do political cartoonists, and those people don't seem to get that kind of humour."

He wasn't going to let it go.

"But the thing is, I'm Muslim, right? So I understand my community, and I understand the sensitivity. So when you're from the inside writing about your own community, it's different, right? It's a different thing when you're from the inside."

"I'd beg to differ with you on that one."

The interview continued for what seemed like an eternity. Just blinking felt like my eyelids were lifting weights. When the segment was over, I felt like a bowl of Jell-O. Years later I would reflect back on this conversation when watching white people threatening to kill black protesters at Donald Trump rallies and, in many instances, outright violence breaking out. Acting with hostility against people who don't hold your world view is universal across all communities, including secular ones.

"You did good," said my cameraman. "Except next time don't wear so much makeup."

"Oh, my makeup person told me that analog TV washes people out."

"This isn't analog, it's HD and people are gonna see every pore," he said.

"How ridiculous do I look?"

"Well," he said, appraising me. "Don't stand too long under lampposts or some men might get the wrong idea."

I ran back to the CBC. Anton, the head of comedy, saw me in the hallway.

"What happened to you?" He was staring at my face.

"Nothing," I said, running to the washroom. "I was volunteering at a kid's birthday party. Their clown cancelled."

Face washed, I joined the cast and crew at a local swimming pool. We were about to shoot an episode about Fatima, a conservative Nigerian Muslim woman (played by the wonderful Arlene Duncan), who refused to wear a conventional bathing suit in the coed pool. Resa McConaghy, our costume designer, had ordered a burkini online from Jordan for Fatima to wear.

The next day we were shooting in the sets built in the Dufferin Gate Productions studios in Etobicoke. I walked around the prayer hall of the mosque set.

"It actually faces northeast," I told Al. "I think I'll pray here."

"It's a Muslim miracle," said Al. We were shooting a scene of an episode that dealt with a fight between the men and women and the barrier in the mosque—the exact same subject that had started me down the long road to making a television series.

In 2005, the National Film Board of Canada asked me to submit a topic for a documentary. Patriarchy in mosque culture was something I wanted to discuss, so I went ahead and made a film that examined the subject. I look back now and see that the freedom I had, practising my faith in Canada, also gave me the freedom to criticize the cultural practices of the people who practised my faith. *Me and the Mosque* tackled the issue of women praying behind barriers and up in balconies. Making *Little Mosque on the Prairie* was an extension of my beliefs as a feminist who wanted to work for equality between the sexes in faith-based spaces. By not being demonized by my wider community, it became easier to "wash dirty laundry" in public, without fearing there would be repercussions to the community itself.

Three months later, I watched the pilot of the show with my parents in their home in Oakville.

"What did you think?" I asked my mother.

"I think you should be home with your children," she said, knitting a sweater.

"No, I mean the show. What do you think about the show?"

"I thought the hijabs were very pretty. Where did you get them?"

When the phone rang a few hours later, my father handed it to me. A reporter was on the line.

"The ratings came in for the first episode," he said.

I had been waiting for this. A lot of Canadian shows failed because, unlike American broadcasters, Canadian broadcasters lacked advertising budgets in the millions of dollars. Even so, American media obsession about the show fuelled incredible press, and gave us the edge we needed.

"What were they?"

"Two-point-one million."

"Is that terrible?" I asked. I had no idea what that figure meant. "Like, was the CBC hoping for twenty million? Did we fail?"

"Put it this way, the last time CBC had ratings that high was when *Anne of Avonlea* aired."

"When was that?"

"Twenty years ago."

"So that's good, right?"

"It's very good," said the reporter. "Most shows made by the CBC have failed until now. *Little Mosque* has breathed new life into the network. Think of it this way, it's like PBS discovered the CSI franchise."

"I don't think anyone saw this coming," I said.

"A religious comedy show about Muslims worshipping in a broken-down mosque, within a broken-down church, living in a tiny town in the Canadian Midwest," said the reporter. "No, it doesn't really scream ratings success. Congratulations."

"Thanks," I said. Was he kidding? I couldn't tell.

"So you're a daughter of immigrants, huh?"

"Yeah, my parents grew up in Pakistan, emigrated to England, where I was born, and then moved to Canada."

"So I guess it is worth having immigrants after all. Your show must hire a lot of people."

"Probably over a hundred," was my guess.

"Who will all be paying taxes . . ."

"For sure," I said, "just like me."

"Do you know how much money you'll be making?"

"Are you working for Revenue Canada?"

The reporter hung up.

I saw Anton at a press junket the next day.

"Congratulations," I said. "You must be very pleased."

"It's a good feeling to have a successful show," he said. "People heard cheering in the hallways of the CBC."

"So why'd you pick this show to make?"

"I'm the son of Italian immigrants," he said. "I understand the story of a new community in a new country. Plus, Muslims and Islam were in the zeitgeist. This show managed to capture it at the right moment."

. . .

It's now 2016 and *Little Mosque on the Prairie* has been off the air for two years, after airing ninety-one episodes. What I had realized over the years was that in a stroke of fate—or luck—I was living in a place where I was free to be a practising Muslim and, instead of becoming radicalized or more conservative, I had the freedom to criticize and call attention to the failings of the community when it came to issues such as gender equity. I had been able to make a documentary about patriarchy in mosque culture. I had the support of a national cultural institution, the CBC, which allowed me to express the stories of my life in a television show, where I continued to question the cultural practices of my community but in a place of safety.

It took me years to realize how rare my life was. It took me years to realize the opportunities I had been able to take advantage of. It all boiled down to mutual accommodation and respect.

Recently, I heard the story of two brothers who didn't want to shake their teacher's hand in Switzerland because, in their understanding of modesty, touching a member of the opposite sex was inappropriate. The government is now reviewing their father's refugee claim, threatening to fine the family $5,000 and putting their naturalization process on hold. I had been like those two boys at one time. But everyone has their journey to faith and belonging. Mine was not interrupted by violence or anger or laws that made me feel like I did not belong. Canada may well be one of the few places in the world that value diversity and revel in the strength it brings. I don't think *Little Mosque on the Prairie* would have existed in any other country on Earth, because someone like me wouldn't have had the will, stamina and courage to make it. These attributes would have been snuffed out of me long ago.

Canada is a great example to the world when it comes to integrating peoples with varied belief systems who want to work for social justice in a national setting.

Canada gave me a sense of belonging. And with belonging comes contribution and civic engagement.

Even if I look like I'm the CEO of the World Clown Association.

Ceremony

CHRISTINE POUNTNEY

I was curious about how much less fear I had going into this ceremony than I'd had in the past. I was bringing with me the intention to feel my self-love and my confidence. That's what I was asking for, and a body tune-up. Niranjan was to my left and Jo to my right. Across the room was Soulla and her cousin, Costas, and Kerri and Glenda. Don was just left of Niranjan and beside him, Nadia. It was a good group, half experienced, half first-timers. I had organized the retreat, but I didn't feel overly responsible. My dog, Raffle, was there, lying on the sheepskin rug in the centre of the room. I had my usual immoderate number of talismans: the long brown pinfeather of an eagle; the magnificent wing of a young turkey vulture I found dead on the side of the road in Connecticut and preserved by burying it in a box of salt; my crow feather fan I made from another bird hit by a car, that one in Newfoundland; and a second crow wing that Sheryl gave me after my naming ceremony down in Kentucky. I had my goose and flicker fan, made from wings I found on the shores of Lake Huron, bound together—in true Ojibway style, according to a wry friend from Curve Lake reserve—with black hockey tape. I had three little bottles of *agua de flor-ida*, a jagged smoky quartz given to me by a friend, and a water-smooth ovoid girasol crystal from Madagascar that I bought at a horse farm and in which I can sometimes see, in the semi-translucent jagged plates within, the curved, languid shape of a thin man, reminiscent of the figures painted by El Greco, wearing a flat-brimmed hat tilted forward on his head, playing the mandolin. I had a grizzly bear claw that my sister-out-law, Kathleen, brought back from the Arctic, still with a coarse tuft of red-brown hair; a flat bead of Peruvian turquoise; a fluffy, sandy-coloured rabbit's paw from a rabbit Michael's dad snared one winter in Corner Brook; and an alabaster frog that I found at a market in Cuzco—on the same trip I cured my thyroid by getting, in ceremony, the toad that sat heavily on my throat, to croak. I had my son's baby shoes, the leather moccasins he learned to walk in, with the ghost-trace of his little foot polished onto the bottom of the soles, so distinctly you can see each tiny toe in descending order. I had a ceramic goblet for burning sage, a plastic zip-lock bag full of sage, my abalone shell, and rattle and drum. I had a cone of mapacho Carole brought me from the Amazon, and several mapacho cigarettes. I had my pipe in its bag and, between Jo and me, a lighter. I was wearing the yellow embroidered dress that Claudia gave me years ago, which I have worn in so many ceremonies, as well as the Cowichan sweater my mom knit for me and which has a thunderbird in full wingspan across the back.

How could I not fare well, with all this companionship?

Or would I sink under the weight of my own superstition?

The space I'd rented from friends was perfect. In the country, on a lake. There was snow. We'd pushed all the furniture back and the fire in the wood stove had died down and it was warm and fairly dark. Through the angled front wall of windows, as if we were sitting in the deep glass hull of a ship, small lights reflected off the lake from houses on the other side. Dark shapes of leafless birch, some cedar and fir, stood out against a gloomy winter sky that was overcast, yellowish grey and mauve.

Don lit his pipe, took a puff and whistled smoke into his bottle of ayahuasca, then started handing out doses. People would come forward and kneel, solemnly receive the shot glass with both hands, bow their head and pause, then knock it back, give Don a little nod of gratitude, crawl back to their mat, or sleeping bag, and settle in with a noisy rustling of nylon. My senses took in the rustling as it made its slow progress around the now-dark room, unconsciously calculating space, distance and proximity. Jo was the last one before me, and his beanbag gave a sound like waves coming ashore a pebble beach as he shuffled to free himself with several collapsing attempts. When it was my turn, I remembered to welcome the medicine into my body, to show respect and appreciation to the spirit of the plant and to offer my body as a hospitable host.

Small rituals to assist in the success of a relationship exist in the spirit world just as much as, if not more than, in the material world. Protocol is your protection. Only the spirits willing to invade you ignore these laws of boundary and permission. They will molest you without any consideration. It is the conscientious ones that wait patiently for an invitation, and will not interfere until you ask them. Which means that they will not help you, until you give them licence. Ask and ye shall receive. Don't ask, and you might receive what you never intended to give permission to in the first place. I have experienced this time and time again. People want benevolent assistance, but they forget to ask. Their spirit helpers are right there, waiting to lavish them with blessings, and people forget to invite them in. This may be an argument merely in favour of intention, but I like this more interactive explanation of it. The spirit world peopled with characters.

So I addressed her in my mind. You are welcome here, Grandma. Thank you. I welcome you as a friend and as a teacher, a mentor and a goddess.

I returned to my place and waited. I had never welcomed the spirit of ayahuasca as a goddess before—my tendency toward irreverence and cynicism makes it hard for me to seriously acknowledge the presence of any gods at all, even though I crave their presence—but it seemed right, as if I had remembered an important ingredient. And I did it genuinely, spontaneously. I could feel my trepidation and my willingness, both.

The medicine came on soon enough, not too strong, but strong enough that I felt transported, away from the recognizable into something at once unknown but also deeply familiar. There were no visuals, but the sounds grew so distinct. I felt an energetic surge, as in a kind of liquefying of the muscles. Things grew more vibratory, pulsatory and rhythmic. Don was shaking his chacapa, a bundle of dried leaves, and it sounded like the earliest, most primitive instrument. He started to sing and I felt the sound weave the medicine through me, beginning to affect my insides, reconfigure me. I felt aroused and breathless. Oh, how I long for what scares me most. How drawn I am to mysticism and foreign states of consciousness. How bendy reality can become, and history, and time, like a straight arrow pulled back upon itself to make a circle. We partake of this consensual reality, but we have access to so many more, if only we could loosen the bonds of what it is we think we know, and therefore believe.

And yet, this ceremony (my sixteenth) seemed to want to take a gentle course. It felt sort of subtle, not super overwhelming. I had been asking for this, too. Hoping not to go to a place that was too dark or terrifying. For a long time, my thoughts seemed to paw and double back on that fine line between avoiding and choosing, between suppressing fear and taking control. I'd feel my fear rise up, the potential to have some frightening experience, and I'd say, No, not going

CHRISTINE POUNTNEY

there tonight. And think: Love. Love. Love. Love. But was I avoiding some instructive experience down the scary path? Or was I choosing to create something different from what I might have otherwise slid toward, or been drawn to simply out of fear, or habit, negativity or boundarylessness—that cynicism.

Maya Angelou said that cynicism in the young is a tragedy, because you go from knowing nothing to believing in nothing. Both knowing and belief shape who we are, but our knowing is empirical. It can change. It changes every time we make a mistake, or learn something new. But our beliefs are what determine what we allow ourselves to know in the first place—what we can see and hear and feel. They are far more deterministic than our knowing. They are the invisible forces that limit us or give us our freedom, cloud our eyes with cataracts or peel them off.

To know something, we must perceive it, but we perceive what we believe. Beliefs are generative. They come before and determine the limits of our perception. They are self-prophetic. They create the conditions that they predict, and are therefore reconfirmed. If you believe the world is hostile, you will be on the defensive, reading attack into everything. The world, by your belief, will feel hostile. There is no room for it to feel otherwise. Our beliefs precede us, like a fog bank or a barge that we push ahead of us, or walk behind, and follow through all our lives. Someone might extend an apple, but through the fog bank it looks like a grenade. Maturation is the process by which we become conscious of our perceptual barge, question it and take responsibility for our beliefs.

Many things can bring about this inquiry—sickness, crisis, tragedy, near-death or an ordeal. This is something Indigenous cultures seem to know so well. It is the purpose of the coming-of-age ceremony.

At some point, you start to realize that your parents are not gods, that your home is not the world, and you start to understand that there are other ways of living and being, and that you actually have the power to choose, and indeed must. This is the frightening call of autonomy. You go from the predeterminism of youth (your life consisting of what gets thrown at you, regardless of what you want) to the free will of adulthood (where you get to make choices). This is the giant existential leap into self-responsibility that we all need to take in life. It's called growing up—what Indigenous people sometimes refer to as becoming a human being. And it gets missed in our Western capitalist society, because we are so dreadfully afraid of responsibility, a kind of unavoidable finiteness.

No more buying power. To be responsible means you cannot escape. That you are a limited body, in a limited time and place, and this is akin to accepting the limited and solitary nature of your life, in other words, your death. Avoiding responsibility is the by-product of a fear of death.

And this is the point at which we start to self-medicate. Or, as Gordon Neufeld—an insightful teacher of child psychology, particularly of adolescence—says: we avoid the void. In other words, swing our waning attachments away from our parents, with whom we are experiencing a natural alienation, at the crux of our adolescence, and attach to our peers. Which is like getting on board a ship captained by no one who's ever been to sea. It's like having a spoiled and terrified teenager in the White House. It is like William Golding's *Lord of the Flies*.

So we miss this important milestone. At the very moment our elders could be making room for our emotional reluctance and assisting us into adulthood. Because how often are we, as parents, too busy to stop and commemorate the moment our own beloved children slip out of our hands and into their own? We fail to support them in their terror.

Which is why the ordeal of a coming-of-age ceremony makes so much sense. It enacts the metaphor. At the moment when you have to cross through that very lonely, terrifying void—the metaphorical dark forest—you actually get sent out into the very real dark forest, without food or water, all alone, with instructions not to sleep at night, but to stay awake and stare into the darkness. It is so wise to match this painful internal process with an equally painful external one. It dignifies our pain and terror to acknowledge that there is no way around it. It assists the one who must suffer to say: Yes, this is going to be difficult, and you have to be brave. But this ceremony is going to reveal that you already have the innate strength and courage for the task at hand. And it requires of the people who love that youngster to suffer too, to make a choice to suffer, to worry and be afraid for them, too. There is an implicit understanding of the paradox, that confronting your aloneness is the best antidote to loneliness. Before conscious union comes conscious separation. Before freedom, risk. Before love, courage. You cannot have paradise regained without paradise lost. Nobody regains paradise by accident. To regain paradise is a conscious act.

And every time I do ayahuasca, I am reminded of this challenge. Take the reins, if you can. Or not. Either way, you will learn something about how you are standing currently in your own consciousness.

CHRISTINE POUNTNEY

But, in this very moment, I felt I had no idea how to trust my beliefs; I didn't even know what they were.

If I let my thoughts go dark, the world would rear up frightening. If I let them be light, the world would be exultant. And I felt this wasn't good enough. I needed more certainty. I wanted to know objectively what the nature of the world was. I didn't want to get it wrong. I wanted it to be shown to me, but all that was being shown was that I could create it either way. I was looking not into myself but to what was outside of me for confirmation of where I should go, what I should do. Like I always had. Reaching outward to fill my emptiness, instead of looking into the emptiness and staying with it—that void I, too, have avoided. I skipped that step, years ago, self-medicated, attached to my peers, gave up control, stayed adolescent.

Because there is something in me that resists the relativism of my own judgment and self-sufficiency, or the power of it, I'm not sure which. There is a kind of profound insecurity in the feeling that the world is only the sum of what I make it. Am I that responsible? That powerful? And if so, can I accept the ways I have failed to stand in that power, as well? Do I really want that power? Would it be exhausting? I would have no one to blame. Could it be there are no standards or limits outside the ones I have imposed on myself? I could be less critical of myself, if I chose. There would be no constant rating of success or failure—no guilt—outside the degree of gentleness I held for myself. There would be no reality that did not already emanate from my centre. Nothing to submit to, in order to be right. I could go beyond good and evil. So why don't I embrace this? Why do I hold myself hostage in this awkward place of uncertainty, of doubt and half-crippledness?

I eddied in these emotional waters for a while, drawing no definitive conclusions.

Ayahuasca has always been so refreshing, in part, because it has defied my expectations so wildly. It makes me feel like I'm bursting the bonds of my own restrictive subjectivity and learning new, unprecedented things. But right now, in this mercifully gentle ceremonial space of still having a choice in the matter, I felt unsure of myself. I didn't know what to do. Was it braver to go into the fear, or deny it entry? Was it wise to refuse the darkness, or escape it? I know how addicted I can be to my own suffering, how attached I am to the concept of hard work, that maybe the challenge for me lies in allowing myself to feel my sufficiency and my safety, over and over again, regardless of uncertainty, only without effort, with a cosmic ease. Why am I so suspicious of joy? Of light and pleasure and painlessness? Of humour and unapologetic silliness? I say I want it, and yet I feel to choose it is less valid, less authentic than its darker twin. I am used to the weight of its darker twin. The lightness of having nothing to feel guilty about feels almost too weightless, reckless. I might float away, or faint. I don't know what would happen. I would not be in control. I might be mocked, and I would have no recourse to vengeance. If I was hurt, I would not be able to hurt back. I would not be carrying any weapons. I'd be defenceless.

At this point, inspired by something mercifully un-egoic, I crawled forward to pet Raffle where she lay, in the shrunken centre of the room. There was a sudden collective restless stirring among the group, as if we'd all just called ourselves back from such far-flung mental distances as we'd zoomed off to. Her beautiful fur. Soft as rabbit, black and tan and white. The incredible wild markings on her face, and her ears like damp cardboard cones covered in velvet. I felt so much love for her. She is such a smart, intuitive dog. So intelligent in her gaze. I stroked her and suddenly understood that if I stayed with her, I would observe her death. The medicine would take me down that road. As with all things, she too must pass. That relentless teaching: that always, in the presence of love, you must have the willingness to let it go. We are so inclined to be possessive in love, so the medicine reminds us to feel our love and to feel our helplessness, not as pathetic, but as wisdom, as stoicism. That great acceptance. Ayahuasca is stoicism training: hard lessons for the heart. Feel your love, then feel the loss. Let your heart break. Then try to feel your love again. Trust that your heart is made for this work. That it is designed to break and repair itself. Then, it is doing its job. That's what it's made for. To metabolize beauty and pain, to build up and break down, to digest, the way sunlight is digested by a leaf, to form energy through photosynthesis, and release waste as carbon dioxide. To absorb and to release. To pulsate. This is the part that is not about you, or what you get out of it. But rather, the force of life at work through you. See if you can still love from this place. It's scary. Watch what you most love turn to dust in your hands, and rejoice that there was life at all to love. And that you did. You loved.

I noticed that her breath was slackening, the rise and fall of her body slowing down, that she was beginning to sink into herself. If I lingered much longer,

I would see her fur subside over the contours of her skeleton like a falling tablecloth. Her black lip would curl back into a snarl and spread like burning plastic to reveal her teeth and gums. Accelerated decomposition would occur and, finally, her white bones would be laid bare. I knew this before it happened, and, once again, chose not to allow what might occur. I didn't want to use her in this way—for my edification. It felt invasive, sacrificial. I didn't want her to suffer for my needing the lesson of perceiving her death.

There was also the deep stab of imminent sorrow at losing her, and a new thought came to mind. What if, while I still have the chance, I have a responsibility to keep her alive? To uplift her. I wanted to honour Raffle's trust in me, the part of her life I hold in perceiving her. I had the impression that her life force, to some degree, is amplified or reduced by my perception of it, and I wanted to leave her unmolested by my experiments. I wanted to let her stay fluffy and warm and black and tan and white, with her puppy paws curled at the wrists, sleeping peacefully and breathing through the moist black rubber ball of her nose. So I left her alone. I'm gonna leave you now, I whispered. I don't really wanna watch this. And backed off to my mat, and chose the work of love. I chose to create rainbows of love instead. I was going to choose the manner of my life, and the manner of my dying, and it was not going to be fearful and dark. I had that option. I have that choice. And I was exercising it.

John Pierrakos, in his book *Core Energetics*, wrote: "Energy follows thought." I know this to be absolutely true. A few years ago, a friend's dog died and I had just done ayahuasca and I wrote him this email, which flowed out of me like a fully formed poem:

For now you will feel only loss. Then try to imagine that there is no difference between the visible and the invisible. He's still there. Always was, always will be, because he's you. You created him. He's in a leaf now. A crow. The clouds. He's in the soles of your feet. He taught you how to walk in the woods. You taught yourself. But the hand craves warm fur. I understand that too. And those traits that seem separate from you. His personality. Though I think you created that as well. By being willing to perceive it. You created the gap in the fence for him to leap through.

A Real Woman

HEIDI REIMER

The words on my screen are shocking, mortifying, incongruous. They are my words, written fifteen years and another self ago. A casual self-googling has unearthed them, in an essay called "A Real Woman," published pre-Internet in a magazine when I was eighteen years old. Now, unbeknownst to me, the essay has gone viral.

"A Real Woman," I discover as I click link after link, has been posted and reposted. It is on blogs, websites, discussion forums. It's being debated, defended, derided. One post has 340 comments. Another features a PDF download with colourful bubbles around each of my points. People are printing it, hanging it above desks, recommending it to friends.

I am appalled.

A real woman, say the words on my screen attached to my name, *does not compete for equality with men or chafe at God's design for male and female, but delights in her calling to complement man's role.*

A real woman, argues the me I used to be, *respects and submits to her father's authority, preparing herself to exercise the Biblical role in her relationship with her future husband.*

A real woman, say I, *portrays chastity, modesty and reverence in her manner, and wears the ornament of a gentle and quiet spirit, which is her true beauty.*

"How on earth," asks a friend who knows me only as the person I am now, "did you get from being *that* Heidi Reimer to being this one?"

· · ·

At age thirteen, my bible for how to be a woman—aside from the actual Bible—was a book called *The Way Home: Beyond Feminism, Back to Reality*. The author was once not only a feminist but a radical feminist (in my thirteen-year-old imagination I saw a wild-haired woman dancing braless, screaming, on a burning car in the street) until she relinquished her career and accepted her true place at home—submitting to her husband, trusting God to plan her family, home-schooling the unlimited children He had blessed her with.

My own mother home-schooled her six children. Other families we knew had ten or twelve. Men were reversing vasectomies. Women were leaving careers. Girls (me) were filling hope chests with tablecloths and dinnerware to prepare for our callings as wives and mothers and keepers at home. The movement, known as Christian Patriarchy or Quiverfull, was inspired by a psalm that compares children to arrows in a warrior's quiver—"blessed is the man whose quiver is full of them"—and by several verses in the Apostle Paul's letter to Titus instructing that older women should "teach the young women to be sober, to love their husbands, to love their children, to be discreet, chaste, keepers at home, good, obedient to their own husbands, that the word of God be not blasphemed" (Titus 2:3–5). The very word of God depended on women's obedience and home-keeping, and I did not see how a woman could be aligned with God's will if she embraced any other path.

This was 1990.

I believed, with increasing fervour as I entered my mid-teens, in dressing modestly (voluminous dresses, no pants, no bare shoulders to tempt a Christian brother), in women's submission to men's God-ordained authority (father while unmarried, husband after marriage) and in preserving my purity for my future husband, to whom my body rightfully belonged. I was saving my first kiss for my wedding day.

What the feminists didn't understand: women were equal in *value* to men, but their role was different. Submission meant taking one's part in the play so that all the parts, functioning together, could create the intended whole. There was synthesis here, and liberation, male head and female body, husband loving wife as Christ loved church, wife serving husband as church served Christ. Man as leader, woman as helpmate.

Feminism had duped women, luring their hearts from the home with illusions of freedom, entrapping them in selfish ambition that would never satisfy. Feminism had destroyed marriages and families. It was, in no small part, responsible for the social and moral collapse of the Western world.

. . .

I'm rattled for hours after discovering "A Real Woman." My partner, Richard, pours me wine and dismisses the fundamentalists in the 340 comments. They're crazy and repressive. They just want to keep women down.

But "A Real Woman" has disturbed the wound at the core of me. The authorities stir in my head.

I could be wrong. What if I used to be right, and now I'm wrong?

I am a woman who has fallen out of line.

. . .

On the morning of my nineteenth birthday, I bushwhacked alone across the Crown land surrounding my family's home. Tucked into the journal in my hand was a vow.

By a trickle of creek I spoke my vow out loud:

> I, Heidi Reimer, make a vow to You, my God, that I will from this time forth live in singleness to You. I will serve You without distraction and give myself to You to fulfill Your purpose for me. I will be single to You, set apart to You, and make You my number one desire.

From my right hand I removed the silver ring my mother had given me at menarche—symbol of the purity I was saving for my husband—and transferred it onto the ring finger of my left hand. I was taken. I belonged to God.

The calling I felt was intense. God had created me for a purpose: to spread His word and inspire other young women toward godly womanhood through my writing.

I had always believed wife-and-motherhood were also part of my life's mission, but now I entertained the possibility that God could be calling me to singlehood. Among the mothers and homemakers who comprised the entirety of my concept of womanhood, there were no women who exemplified what I wanted to be. No women whose lives were not devoured by the mundane necessities of day-to-day existence. No women free to pursue a life of the mind.

My spiritual and literary mentors were male. The nearest female models I could find were spinster novelists and missionaries from other centuries.

·   ·   ·

At twenty I studied at Fairwood Bible Institute, a tiny Bible college (student population: twenty) in an aging white mansion at the foot of a mountain in New Hampshire. The men (they were called men) drove the tractors and led the prayer meetings, and the girls (they were called girls) cooked the meals and mopped the floors. In the girls' dorm, despite the rule that no student would experience or show or act on a preference for a member of the opposite sex—we were here to focus on our relationship with God, one of the stipulations that had drawn me to the school in the first place—my new friends were obsessing over their "prefs," choosing wedding dresses and baby names, pining for the time when their real lives as wives of godly men could begin.

Tentatively, in whispered midnight confidences, in half-serious jokes over the industrial kitchen sinks, I suggested that our focus on marriage prevented purposeful living in the present and created unhealthy dependence on an as-yet theoretical man. What if a godly husband never came along? Could we not learn to be single and satisfied? Could we not serve God in roles other than wife and mother?

I became known as the Feminist of Fairwood for my insistence that women could be fulfilled without marriage or children. This word *feminist* was audacious, risky, a hyperbolic moniker exaggerated for its comedy as applied to me, chaste wearer of voluminous dresses, author of Biblical instructions on Real Womanhood.

It was a joke—of course Heidi Reimer was not a feminist—but I was an editor of the Bible school yearbook, so it wasn't hard for me to slip it onto the nickname page: *Heidi Reimer, the Feminist of Fairwood.*

Because, secretly, I was pleased with my reputation as outlandishly independent.

·   ·   ·

After Bible school I flew to Northern California to apprentice for one year with a bestselling Christian novelist. He made me feel seen and understood as an aspiring writer and an introspective person. He too knew the lonely set-apartness of being called to a vocation, of holding standards so high that no one wants to be up there with you.

"Never give up, Heidilein," he said again and again. "You're called to raise a standard in your writing, not to appeal to the base desires mainstream audiences want titillated. You stand for purity, virtue, truth. Never cave to a market that wants palatable Christianity, that prefers an easy God."

I was deeply moved by his example, humbled that he'd chosen me as his protege. Fearful that I wasn't worthy.

I yearned to make him proud.

. . .

The me I have become calls my journey awakening, self-discovery, liberation.

The me I used to be calls it rebellion, selfishness, sin.

I have received letters. I have been sat down for talks. *Be careful. Don't let the world seduce you. You are not your own authority. Beware. Come back.*

My writing has not made the bestselling Christian novelist proud.

. . .

Restless and longing for a bigger life, at twenty-three I set off for three months to discover the world. Turkey, Romania, Hungary, Italy, France: the first half on my own, the second with my best friend, one of the few from Bible school who wasn't already getting married, who had non-domestic life goals. We both wanted to write books.

In a deserted hostel in Cinque Terre, Italy, Anna and I found a quarter bottle of red wine in the fridge, left by the previous guests. "We're in Italy!" we cried—daring, bold—and, "It's practically required!" Then, "Don't get drunk!" she squawked as I poured the wine into water glasses. We sipped it, cold. It was terrible. But we were no longer alcohol virgins, and when a group of Italian businessmen offered us Chardonnay from a trailside café (cultural experience!), when the backpackers at the next hostel pooled bottles of Italian wine along with fresh pasta, pesto and anchovies for late-night communal dinners (international relations!), we did not demur.

For travel practicality I'd compromised my standards with a pair of baggy cargo pants in place of my usual long skirts, but my sleeved shirts felt out of place in the Mediterranean sun, so Anna and I took turns wearing the two sleeveless tops she'd packed. I was self-conscious about my farmer's tan. I had not bared my shoulders since I was a child, not even for swimming.

By the end of my travels, giddy and astonished in a dressing room mirror, I was contemplating a black spaghetti-strap dress in a Luxembourg City boutique: above the knee, two inches of daring sheer fabric at the hem, a purple starburst mandala on the skirt.

Look at svelte, long-limbed, *sexy* me!

Look at me liberated from folds of fabric!

Look at me with a body.

I danced in the dress that night with a boy from Vancouver who held me close while energy pulsed between us. We'd been playing with this energy since we met, two countries ago, as I tortured him with impossible push-pull signals. I'm not available; you're hot; you're not my future husband; I like this feeling; I belong to God; please take me! Finally, "You can't kiss me on the lips," I said, and promptly discovered there were more intimate body parts to be kissed once the lips were declared off limits. I had never even thought to guard against those.

When my father picked me up at the Sudbury Greyhound depot after my flight from Paris to Toronto and my five-hour bus ride from Toronto to home, he circled the parking lot twice. He did not recognize the tanned girl in tank top and hiking boots on the curb beside her backpack.

·   ·   ·

In the beginning, I meant only to discard the outward form of my faith. I still read the Bible and prayed, I still believed in God, but a god who was bigger than the legalism I'd thought necessary.

But once I began to let it go, the legalism proved to have been the mortar that held the whole brick edifice together. Cracks appeared.

There was crumbling.

There was a lot of crumbling.

.   .   .

I was unbearably discontented after travelling. I did not fit into the life of my old self.

I went to a scripture conference in Toronto for a weekend and stayed in a youth hostel in a Victorian house in Kensington Market. Monday morning, on my way home to Northern Ontario, I thought, What for? I turned around and went back to the hostel. I lived and worked there for four months, a site of adventure and transience, of anything goes. I was the resident female, adored and unattainable. The two Aussie boys I worked with both tried to scale the fortress walls.

"You can't kiss me on the lips," I said, and they too found other places.

.   .   .

What was there, once there was no longer "Jesus, Lover of My Soul"? Once there was no longer me set apart to fulfill God's plan, every experience infused with purpose?

Emptiness. Chaos.

Without the grounding of my faith I felt adrift. My centre was gone. I longed for God, and then I longed to long for God.

I remember my emergence from religion as liberating and triumphant, but my journals are full of "Please find me, God, please be in me."

They're full of "I've never felt so lost in my life."

.   .   .

Anna and I, aged twenty-four, were offered a six-month house-sit in the highest town in the West Virginia mountains. Off we went to live together and write books. What we mostly did: learned to dance without inhibition, discovered skinny-dipping, drank beer, turned down a lot of pot, kayaked whitewater and jammed at informal gatherings where everyone played five instruments and we sang our church-choir harmonies. We made friends with women who didn't wear bras, who summered in teepees they'd built themselves and had sex and abortions and small businesses and nerve. We marvelled at their autonomy, at female lives lived outside the rules, lives messier than ours but unabashedly their own.

At one end of the general-store-turned-mountain-music-café where we made sandwiches and served drinks, the owner kept her woman-centric library. We flipped through *Succulent Wild Woman: Dancing with Your Wonder-Full Self*; *The Feminine Face of God: The Unfolding of the Sacred in Women*; and *The Dance of the Dissident Daughter: A Woman's Journey from Christian Tradition to the Sacred Feminine*.

Our curiosity morphed to mind-blown wonder. Was it really possible to be this free, this unrestrained, this juicy as a woman? Was it really possible to claim a spirituality with a female centre?

For the first time I was furious at the absence of divinity that looked like me. How could I worship where I was so excluded? How had I not noticed that I was?

At a retreat I joined hands in a circle with other women and sang a familiar Christian song with Father God changed to Mother God, He pronouns turned to She. My whole body responded with visceral longing.

"Holy" and "her" in the same sentence was the most revolutionary thing I'd ever heard.

One thought swept through me as I stood in that circle, tears streaming down my face. How dare they have kept this from me? How dare they have told me that God was a man?

The idea of a Mother God, the gut punch of understanding that I as a female person could be as sacred and valuable as any male, spoke to a part of me that was parched, starved, unconscious.

I felt it unmistakably: I have been lied to all my life.

I could not sing for weeping.

.   .   .

This is the wound at the core of me: I am female.

I am female. God, source of life and goodness, wielder of power, is male. His spokespeople and thinkers and leaders are male. I am peripheral, and lacking, and other.

I am almost not even there.

.   .   .

I was twenty-five when the man to whom I would surrender my long-held virginity claimed me. I felt powerless. Despite the occasional dalliance, I was still unskilled at handling worldly men. (And they, flummoxed by me: "Do you deny yourself *all* pleasure?" he asked, and, "*Why?*")

As though cramming for exams, I furtively skimmed sex-ed websites.

I felt resigned. I was hardly pure anymore, so what was I holding out for? And I was bred in the belief that men had the power. He wanted what he wanted. What could I do?

Later, he was rumoured to be bragging that he "took a virgin."

Rage surged through me when I learned this—rage like I had never known, originating deep inside my body. Even in that moment I was aware of it as the rage of all the women who ever have raged. It burned. It purified. I felt connected to a sisterhood that extended around the globe and through the ages: women who had lived and laboured and shaped themselves under men's expectations, women subsumed beneath entitlement and possession.

In that rage, I felt righteous and freed. I was done with belonging to men.

The jolt of knowledge came in an instant, a whoosh like kindling igniting all at once: my body did not belong to a future husband. My body did not belong to the predators who circled now that I was released from my baggy dresses and my scruples.

My body belonged to me.

.   .   .

It took me a long time to use the word *feminist*. By the time I was ready to try it on for real, it felt earned. I was amazed at the ambivalence of the other female students in my Introduction to Women's Studies course, raised on the expectation that they could be who they wanted, attending university at eighteen and not, like me, at twenty-eight—because for them at eighteen, higher education was not a corrupting pursuit, unnecessary for a woman whose husband would support her.

"I wouldn't call myself a *feminist*," my classmates said. And, "Being female isn't a big part of who I am."

I identified more with women born in the 1920s, '30s and '40s, women with no birthright of equality, forced to fight their way out of a prescribed life. Women for whom femaleness was the essence around which they had no choice but to be shaped.

In my women's studies class I wrote out the word, charged with all the forbidden power I'd imagined at thirteen and played with at twenty: *I am a feminist.*

.   .   .

This year I'm thirty-four. I'm rattled for hours after reading "A Real Woman." Richard pours me wine. He spurns the notion that I should fold myself under him, a rib from his side. He thinks the fundamentalists in the 340 comments are repressive, crazy.

"Don't forget, being a servant is not bad—Jesus Himself said that He came to serve, not to be served."

"If everyone were a man, ambitious and energetic, just imagine how chaotic the world would be! God knew that Adam needed someone to complete him. He created us because they need us."

I don't think the fundamentalists in the 340 comments are crazy. Reading their arguments is like slipping back into a mother tongue. Jarring at first, but very soon familiar. I recognize this language. I understand these people.

It scares me that I understand them, still.

And that's the wound, right there: the fact that always, a submerged part of me believes it possible that trusting my authority, pursuing my goals, making my choices, thinking my thoughts, owning my body, is wrong.

Because I'm a woman.

The Kabbalist in the Kitchen

SIGAL SAMUEL

Normally, when a daughter hears that her father has just had a heart attack, she does not think to herself: "Well, at least this will give us a good opportunity to study Kabbalah." But that's exactly what runs through my head when I get the call from my grandmother in midsummer, after she assures me that he will be okay but will need time to recuperate.

I'm scared, of course, terrified about what will happen to my dad. But I also remember that he has been telling me repeatedly over the past few months—almost every time we talked on the phone—how nice it would be if we could have three months together to study Jewish mystical texts. He kept saying that three months was all I needed to master them. And he desperately wanted to pass that mastery on to me.

So I tell my bosses in my New York newsroom that I need three months in Montreal, pack a dozen sundresses into one suitcase, get on a plane and move back into my childhood home. That first week, I visit my dad in the hospital every day. Then he comes home and I watch over him closely, dispensing fifteen different medications. When I'm not his nurse, I'm his student, studying Kabbalah with him each night.

My tongue trips over the ancient Hebrew and Aramaic words that I haven't encountered in years. I'm surprised at how happy I am to meet them again, these strange sounds like old friends I'd left behind on a playground. I know that over the coming months I will renew and deepen my friendship with them. What I do not yet know is that I will spend an equal amount of time in the kitchen with my grandmother, smearing my hands with cumin and turmeric, learning how to cook.

Here's another thing I don't yet know: both of these things together will force me to confront my own self-directed Orientalism, my own internalized racism.

. . .

I was never very interested in cooking; it paled in comparison to reading. Growing up, whenever my grandmother forced me to stir, chop, et cetera, I would whine inwardly: I could be reading a book right now! And, as soon as my father called me to his study, I would drop the ladle, knife, etc., and go do just that.

These were the two models I grew up with, one offered up by each of the two people who raised me. I could either be like my grandmother, cooking in the kitchen, or I could be like her son, my dad, reading in the study. I chose the latter every chance I got, and not just because I preferred words to foods. My dad's whole atmosphere was saturated with qualities that appealed to me, though I couldn't name them, while the atmosphere around my grandmother seemed distasteful, even shameful, again for ineffable reasons.

It's only now, in my early thirties, that I can name these ineffables. I picture a scorecard with him on one side, her on the other. In his column: intellectualism, maleness, Westernness, "whiteness." In hers: superstitiousness, femaleness, Easternness, brownness.

I put "whiteness" in scare quotes because no one in my Jewish family is actually white. My grandmother was born in Mumbai back when India still had a thriving Jewish population. Her ancestors, Iraqi merchants, had come from Baghdad in the late 1700s to ply their trade. So, whether you think of her as Indian or Iraqi (she thinks of herself as neither: "Just Jewish!"), her brownness is indisputable. To this day, she continues to cook for me the foods she grew up eating: curry and dal, aloo ghobi and bujiah, bamya and keema and imtabaq and mahasha. I'm pretty sure she has no idea what the hell kugel is.

And yet her son, my dad, who was born in Montreal and happens to be very pale (maybe it's all that time he spends cooped up in the study), insists that he is white and that I am, too. When I went on my first trip to India in 2015, he worried aloud about me, "a white girl travelling alone." I now think his identification with whiteness is deeply flawed, even though it's shared by many Baghdadi Jews born in North America, and even though child me had no problem with it. Child me saw him as the ultimate white intellectual, a sort of philosopher-king whose empire—though it consisted only of a single book-lined room—seemed vast and majestic and infinitely worth inhabiting. A professor at Concordia University, he studied and taught Kabbalah as an academic pursuit, through the lens of modern critical scholarship.

Meanwhile, over in the kitchen, my grandmother practised Kabbalah as an unconscious superstition, through the lens of culinary rituals.

Case in point: A few years ago, I went home for a Passover Seder with my dad and my grandmother. I watched her take the Seder plate's egg and peel it with neurotic carefulness, making sure to capture every tiny bit of eggshell in a napkin. When I asked why she was being so insanely precise about it, she shrugged. "I don't know," she said, "it's just something my grandmother did, and I learned to handle food from her, so I do it, too." My dad smiled across the table and said, "I know why she does it—it's a Kabbalistic ritual."

He explained that her way of handling an egg was rooted in the mystical idea of the Shattering of the Vessels. According to the Kabbalists, when the light of the divine poured down into the Tree of Life's ten vessels—the ten godly qualities that gave rise to all of creation—the force of its holiness shattered them. Bits of the broken vessels went tumbling into darkness, and that was the beginning of evil. My grandmother is careful not to let a single shard of shell escape because of a fear of letting evil into the world.

I sat in silence, savouring the idea of a mystical tradition that is passed down, albeit unwittingly, from grandmother to granddaughter. Growing up in the Orthodox world, I was taught to see male text study as the ultimate means through which Jewish tradition is created and preserved. I loved the thought of it being transmitted matrilineally—not through men who had their heads bent over books, but through the hands of women working in the kitchen.

This was my first clue that the model I'd grown up with was wrong. I'd always associated the Kabbalah practised by my dad with intellectualism, while deeming the Kabbalah practised by my grandmother superstition—but why? It was becoming increasingly clear to me that assumptions about gender and race had intersected to make my ("white," Western, academic) dad seem like a scholar, while making my (non-white, Eastern, less-educated) grandmother seem silly and irrational, even though both were working off the same body of mystical ideas.

Now, I wondered: Can I carve out my own relationship to these ideas, so that I can express them not just in the men's way (through scholarly studies) or the women's way (through culinary rituals), but both or neither?

.   .   .

My father and I are learning about the moon. The ancient rabbis of the Talmud developed a myth to explain why it says on the first page of the Bible, "God created the two big lights," only to then say, "the big light and the small light." Which is it? Are they both big, or is one big and one small? Originally, the rabbis explain, the sun and moon enjoyed equal status. But then …

> The moon said to God: "Master of the Universe, is it possible for two kings to wear one crown?!" God said to her: "Go then and diminish yourself." She said to God: "Master of the Universe, because I have suggested to you that which is proper, I should diminish myself?!" God said to her: "Go and you will rule by day and by night." She said to him: "But of what use is a candle in broad daylight?" He said: "Go and the People of Israel shall measure by you the days and the years." She said: "But it is impossible to do without the sun for the reckoning of the seasons." He said: "Go and the righteous will be named after you, as it is written, 'Jacob the Small,' 'Samuel the Small,' 'David the Small.'" On seeing that the moon would not be appeased, God said: "Bring an atonement sacrifice for me, because I diminished the moon."

That last line amazes me. At the end of the story, God admits wrongdoing. It was a mistake to tell the moon to shrink herself. But God's decree, once issued, can't be retracted, and so He has no choice but to enter into a negotiation with the moon. He offers her three appeasements. She rejects each of them in turn. Now God Himself is in need of atonement, of forgiveness.

Novelist that I am, I point out to my father that the most dramatic moment in the story is a moment of silence: In the dialogue between moon and God, there's one point when the moon doesn't reply at all. After God's third offer, she remains haughtily silent. I picture her like a woman with arms crossed, one eyebrow raised, as if to say, "Seriously? That's the best you got? That doesn't even merit a response." God crumbles under this withering glare and says the equivalent of "You're right, it's my fault, I screwed up."

My father praises this observation. He's not used to parsing rabbinic texts in this literary way; maybe that's why he didn't notice the moon's silence. Or maybe it's because he's just a few days out of the hospital. He's sitting on the couch in grey sweatpants and a white T-shirt, ripped at the neck. He's weak. But he seems happy.

I'm happy, too, although there is a part of me that feels the moon's pain. Away from my work and my New York life, I'm not shining so bright these days. I'm wearing the same raggedy pink sundress I wore most days in the hospital; it's pilling and, let's be real, it stinks slightly. Studying Kabbalah in the middle of a workday instead of running around a newsroom brainstorming story ideas and batting about headlines and feeling the instant gratification that comes with seeing something I've written published and read online, I begin to feel, for the first time, how my life has become slower, smaller, less shiny.

.   .   .

While my father naps (during those first few weeks, he sleeps most of the day), I take cooking lessons from my grandmother. He loves her style of cooking. And I want to make sure there's plenty for him to eat.

I start small, with the simplest of Indian dishes: dal. The ingredients are familiar: red lentils, garlic, green pepper. The seasonings are familiar, too, though my grandmother uses the Hindi names for them: turmeric is *haldi*, cumin is *zeera*, cilantro is *cotmear*. Despite these simple staples, we run into trouble when I try to get my grandmother to dictate the recipe to me. She doesn't use measurements when cooking, so when I ask her "How much?" she invariably makes some vague approximating gesture with her hands, or says, "Don't ask me how much—just put a lot!"

Under her guidance, I wash two cups of lentils and put them in a pot with hot water, *haldi* and black pepper. Cover, simmer, stir. My grandmother tells me that when it gets thick enough, I should rub it into a paste. "How do

SIGAL SAMUEL

I know when it's thick enough?" I ask, and this earns me a sigh of frustration. I'm instructed to add to the paste "a lot" of hot water, then grab a frying pan.

Here's where the tricky part comes in. I line the pan with oil and add two teaspoons of cumin. My grandmother's one clear instruction—"Don't over-fry the *zeera*!"—is the one thing I mess up. I take my eyes off the pan for just a second, to jot down this step in the journal where I'm recording the recipe, and when I turn back the *zeera* is black. Ruined. I'm tempted to use it anyway, but my grandmother's face registers this as blasphemy. I dump the cumin in the trash and start over.

This time I attend to the *zeera* properly, taking it off the fire the second it turns golden. And when I add it into the pot with the lentils, it creates a satisfying sizzle and a pungent smell. The scent is one I recognize immediately: It used to hit me in the face the instant I got home from school on Friday afternoons. I hated it, so Old World, so embarrassing, so unlike any smell in any of my white friends' houses.

Now I look into the pot and my mouth waters. I think to myself: Hey, I made that, and it looks just right! Even as pride bubbles up inside me, I feel a sudden wave of pity for child me, the girl who was convinced there was something deeply wrong with this dish.

. . .

Now that we've read the rabbinic story of the moon, my dad says we're ready to see how the Kabbalists interpret it centuries later. He opens a copy of the Zohar, which says that the moon complained about her status because she didn't want to share the spotlight with the sun; she would rather be "head of the foxes" than "tail of the lion," would rather rule over the lower spiritual worlds with complete power than have only quasi dominion over the highest worlds. The Kabbalists mock her for this immature view and for being demoted as a result.

Then my dad opens a different volume of the Zohar, and I'm surprised to find a second interpretation that turns the first one on its head. Here the Kabbalists offer a much more positive reading. Clearly, they're not afraid to take imaginative leaps or to contradict themselves, even if it seems a bit ridiculous.

This time they tell us that originally the moon and the sun were stuck together, conjoined, a single unit. The moon couldn't actually illuminate anything this way, because her "face" was hidden, stuck as it was to the bright sun. That's why she told God the situation was untenable. She felt purposeless, pointless.

As they explain this, the Kabbalists weave in quotes from the erotic Song of Songs, emphasizing the loving nature of the conversation between the moon and God. "I understand your position," says God. "And you, the fairest among women, since you correctly recognized that the world cannot be led by two identical powers, diminish yourself and go with the flock; be queen and lead justly the whole of the mundane world. I accept your advice: detach yourself from the sun, reduce yourself from your primordial state, embark on your independent quest and lead the world."

According to this interpretation, the moon's demotion isn't a punishment at all. Since it's what allows her to gleam her brightest, it's actually her best possible promotion! Now she may be in a less shiny place, may be only "head of the foxes," but at least she serves a truly meaningful purpose.

This text lands in me like a punch to the gut. I think to myself: Maybe I'm in a less shiny position now. But here, my light can actually do something meaningful. It can illuminate something. Someone.

. . .

Chitarney, a word I've never heard spoken anywhere but in my grandmother's kitchen, is how the Baghdadi Jews of India refer to their chicken curry. It involves cooking a dozen chicken drumsticks in a giant pot with onions, tomatoes, potatoes, tamarind, ginger, garlic, cumin, coriander, curry powder and garam masala. As the Hindi name suggests, Indian Jews borrowed the recipe from their Hindu neighbours, but they introduced a few modifications to make it kosher: instead of cream they use coconut milk (that way there's no mixing meat and dairy) and instead of clarified butter, or ghee, they use oil.

Under my grandmother's watchful eye, I chop the onions, tomatoes and potatoes, and put them in the pot along with ginger and garlic. Then I add in the chicken legs, turning them over and over. After a few minutes of this I think they've browned enough, and I go to move on to the next step of the recipe, but my grandmother stops my hand. Not yet.

"But they look brown to me," I say. "How can you tell when they're ready?"

"Just watch," she says. "This is how you learn."

I pull up a stool and sit by the stove, huddled over the pot, stirring occasionally, watching intently for something I don't yet know how to identify.

After an eternity, my grandmother indicates it's time. By what mystical, invisible-to-the-eye measure has she determined this? I have no idea. I just take note of the current colour in the pot.

Next she takes a cube of dark brown tamarind and puts a chunk of it into a sieve, which she places over the pot. As she pours hot water over the tamarind, its juices leak over the chicken legs. "This will give it the acidic flavour," she says. When I ask her most dreaded question—"How much?"—she says, "Just sprinkle and taste, sprinkle and taste. You have to find your own balance. Trust your taste buds. You have to taste constantly."

Then it's time to add the garam masala, a sweet blend of cardamom, cinnamon and cloves. As my grandmother sprinkles it in, she offers to pack some up so I can take it back to New York. I decline, envisioning the spice bottle breaking open in my suitcase, smelling up all my clothes. She smiles, maybe a bit sadly. "You know, when we first came to Canada, and I was having a hard time, sick with the flu every winter, my granny was so sweet. She would come cook for me. Once, she even gave me a bit of her garam masala, from her own personal mix. She put a finger to her lips, like she was saying, Shhh, I don't want any of your siblings to know I'm favouring you."

This spice, I realize, was once a prized possession passed down from grandmother to granddaughter, so important that it had the power to inspire jealousy. Each teaspoon of it like a handful of precious gems. A treasure that I have unthinkingly rejected.

. . .

The next Kabbalist my dad and I study is a man who confuses the hell out of me. His real name was Yosef Hayyim, but he became known as the Ben Ish Hai because that was the title of his most popular book. The picture of him on the first page shows a sage with a big dark beard, bushy dark eyebrows— and a turban. This probably shouldn't come as a surprise; after all, he lived in nineteenth-century Baghdad. But I'm used to associating turbans with the superstitious Orient, and I've heard that the Ben Ish Hai was an intellectual and a legal scholar. In my head, these things don't mix.

My dad, however, says that this mix is exactly what the Ben Ish Hai was all about. His famous book blends Jewish law and mysticism; the combination is his signature style.

So what does this Iraqi sage have to say about the moon? One thing is clear: he doesn't view her "complaint" as a negative thing; it ends up benefitting the entire cosmos.

> If you're wondering why the moon complained only to be diminished as a result, know that this was no coincidence. Rather, it was divine intervention: God put it in her heart to complain this way, so that she would be diminished as a result. This was for the good of all the celestial worlds, because by descending she linked the bottom of one world to the top of the next world, creating a chain that allowed the divine light to flow down into all the worlds.

In other words: God tricked the moon into complaining.

When I read this, it pisses me off. I blurt to my dad: "If God needed someone to make themself smaller for the good of everyone else, then why did He have to trick the moon—why couldn't He just ask her to volunteer for the job?"

As soon as these words fly out of my mouth, I realize: *I* was asked to volunteer, asked to come to Montreal. But I didn't come. During all those early-summer phone calls, I wasn't listening to the subtle undercurrents in what my dad was telling me. To get me over here, it took a heart attack. I, too, had to have my hand forced. I, too, had to be "tricked."

I don't say any of this aloud to my dad. I'm embarrassed by the lack of attentiveness I'd shown. To escape my own shame, I walk to our home office and photocopy the Ben Ish Hai page. I tell my dad that I'll read the rest on the bus, that I'm late going over to my friends' place, that I'd promised to cook them dal for dinner. This is true, but really I just can't face him right now.

As I run to catch the bus, I look down at my hands. In one fist, I'm clutching the Ben Ish Hai page. In the other, I'm carrying a zip-lock bag filled with cumin. I look up at the sky and there's the moon, waxing.

. . .

SIGAL SAMUEL

Mahasha is the ultimate Baghdadi Jewish dish. It's such an old classic that I feel sure it's what the Ben Ish Hai used to eat on Shabbat and holidays back in Iraq.

The twelve-step recipe involves hollowing out tomatoes, onions and bell peppers, then stuffing their skins with a mixture of rice and raw meat. For this dish, my grandmother pulls out her most gigantic pot. She instructs me to pack in the stuffed vegetables as tight as possible—peppers in the middle, tomatoes and onions in a ring around them. I try to squish them in snugly, but they're oil coated and the stuffing keeps sliding out onto my fingers. Then she tells me to make a mixture of lemon juice, hot water, sugar and salt; again, as to proportions, her only advice is to "keep adding until it tastes good." Eventually, I pour the mixture into the pot, bathing all the vegetables.

My grandmother nudges me out of the way for the next step, because this one needs expert hands and my amateur hour isn't going to cut it. She takes a dinner plate and places it, upside down, over all the vegetables in the pot. Then she takes her giant brass mortar and pestle and places those on top of the plate, to weigh everything down. The lemon juice mixture oozes up over the plate's lip. In my naïveté, I point this out as a matter for concern. She laughs and turns up the heat, causing the juice to ooze and bubble even more violently, as if to say: Child, please. I know what I'm doing!

After the liquid evaporates, she lifts the plate and pokes a fork into the peppers, tasting the rice to see if it's soft. It is, so she covers the whole pot again and puts it in the oven.

Then we wait. For three hours.

Every so often, she has me open the oven, lift the lid off the pot, and check to see whether the top is browned yet. It isn't. When I show signs of impatience, she shrugs her shoulders. "That's how it is with this kind of cooking—you have to pamper it!"

. . .

Many weeks pass this way. As I flit between my dad's study and my grandmother's kitchen, my journal starts to reflect the strange confluence of lessons. One page is filled with a Kabbalistic diagram. The next page contains the recipe for mahasha. On some spreads, a Kabbalah lesson bleeds right over into a cooking lesson. And in the corner of each page, nestled beside the date, is a little picture I've drawn of the moon as it currently appears in the sky: crescent, gibbous, waxing, waning.

Then again, maybe it's not so strange that these two practices—cooking and Kabbalah—are coalescing in me. I'm starting to realize that cooking, the way my grandmother does it, is a spiritual practice. It forces me to get slow and small. It takes forever and it's not glamorous. It stinks up the whole kitchen; it makes *me* stink. It privileges imagination over reason, improvisation over strict rules. It encourages me to make myself a bit ridiculous. It demands that I attend to the smallest details, read meaning in the subtlest of shifts. The transformation, when it comes, happens in private, under the lid.

And as unlikely as it sounds, there is some transformation happening here. I'm healing my relationship to cooking through Kabbalah, as I come to understand that the faculties promoted by mystical study—attentiveness, intuition, a sense of play—are surprisingly similar to the ones Baghdadi cooking unlocks. At the same time, I'm healing my relationship to Kabbalah through cooking. After all, to be able to fully grasp and respect someone like the Ben Ish Hai, I had to first decolonize the part of my mind that sneered at him for smelling of turmeric and cumin, for wearing a turban, for coming from the "wrong" part of the world, for being dark—for being, in short, like me.

At my request, my father and I have moved our Kabbalah lessons into the kitchen. I read the ancient texts aloud, and in between sentences I spoon yellow rice into my mouth, the smell of the spices swirling between our books and bodies. The false divide that separated his world from my grandmother's is slowly crumbling inside me. Through both their practices, maybe I'm also starting to heal my relationship to myself.

Zion's Children

SUSAN SCOTT

News of the vision came on the eve of my high school graduation. All along there had been visions—it was enthralling, the boy's likeness to young Joseph Smith—but this vision was different. The prophet Elijah had appeared, told the boy that he and I should marry. We were "meant to be" is what was said.

We related best, the boy and I, through long hand written letters, which I burned so my mother wouldn't find them, but this one I jammed beneath the pillow. *Thus saith Elijah* … so this was a proposal? The message read like a script for a Book of Mormon pageant. I dared not question the pronouncement—questioning would show a lack of faith. But if this were meant to be, why did I feel numb? This was not the fairy-tale ending I'd envisioned.

I mean, running off together I could picture.

Hitchhiking for Jesus I could picture.

What I could not picture was being someone's wife.

.   .   .

I had fallen for the boy at church camp the summer that I turned sixteen, all lonely and hormonal, and he, in Mom's words, "on the prowl."

"Forget about that boy," she said, rifling through no-name jeans at Kmart. I had wanted Levi's, but that was not to be. This was August, on the heels of camp. Here we go, I thought. There was always some informant, some nosy cook or counsellor who reported back to Mom.

"What boy?" I feigned indifference.

"Don't play dumb with me. You know I mean that long-haired kook. I don't like the look of him, he looks like he does drugs."

"He does not do drugs," I muttered, but not so as she'd hear it. You could not talk back and expect to be left standing.

"You are not to see him, that's my point. He's an instigator." *Instigator* being the former store detective's word for the long-haired-slash-suspicious.

"You know his dad's an elder," I murmured. Descended from the missionary who had baptized Dad's people in the 1890s—another thrilling detail I kept to myself. Mom disliked mention of her in-laws' spiritual advancement.

"I don't care if he's the queen of Sheba. I wouldn't trust that boy as far as I could throw him." She went on to tell him so herself, at the Labour Day potluck at church, after he'd hitchhiked some forty miles to see me. She hauled him off to the nursery, planted a fist in his face. Told him to leave and not look back.

That sealed the attraction. I needed rescuing, and he was game to play the prince.

And a fair prince he was. Wispy blond hair brushed his collarbone. Wire-rimmed glasses and flannel shirts gave him the air of a working intellectual, someone who knew his way around a tool box. A cross whittled out of some soft wood swung from a leather thong looped about his neck. He was restless, the kind of youth who picks up a guitar—our own Stephen Stills was the buzz at camp. A hint of arrogance made him seem precocious. *Principled*, he'd say, not put off by the establishment or overbearing mothers. "Unjust rules were meant to be broken," he wrote after being roughed up in the nursery.

I believed that, absolutely, and for two years we met in secret in the bush behind my dull suburban high school, where he'd woo me with yogurt or granola (I had never tasted either) along with news about the great wide world. "I just felt you needed this," he'd say, and out of his backpack would tumble some cassette (Dylan, mostly) and high-minded reads to set me on the path to liberation: Thoreau and Emerson, Rilke, Castaneda, *Rolling Stone*. Whatever rules Mom laid down for my "own good" could not compete with the high romance of cutting class to walk and talk and kiss in the little woodlot, exchanging ardent letters. I sighed a lot, and he consoled. "You're not meant to live this way," he'd say. On that score he was right. The more phone calls Mom made to the principal, the more she broke into my diary, the greater my righteous indignation.

At the end of my senior year and low point in my behaviour, she finally called in Dad, who weighed in with a solemn "Listen to your mother." I tossed my long dark horsetail hair and smirked.

"That's it," Mom snapped. "I've had it, girl. I'm sending you to a psychologist."

"Good," I piped. Finally, an adult who might listen.

Sadly, the offer was rescinded. So there I was, about to graduate and face the heartbreaking choice of *to marry or to burn* and while the call to wed depressed me, it just felt wrong to doubt the vision. Visions were a first-class nod from the Holy Ghost, a sign of spiritual elevation. I was lucky just to have a boyfriend, let alone someone so evolved. To my discerning teenage brain, a wet dream misremembered trumped the still, small voice of common sense.

And, there was fear—fear so rank I could smell it. Fear of making my way in the world alone. A sullen, bookish girl was fit for what exactly? I had touched a boy, the sap was flowing. Dear God, I prayed, please send a sign.

I got my sign, sans Jesus or the prophets, when the long-faced Rapunzel made her presence felt. Night after sleepless night I tossed on my narrow bed, the spectre hovering by the window, toying with her ropy hair.

The sky in these reveries was starless. This starless state I finally saw as mine. Deception had bought a little breathing space but at a cost. I had lost the moral high ground. I had lost all clarity of thought. The horizon that had lit up briefly with the hope of counterculture freedom had gone dark.

"Sister," the sad Rapunzel shook her ghostly locks. Hers was a voice I recognized, the voice I took to heart.

· · ·

Think: When have you betrayed yourself, denied what your gut said was crazy foolish? Think: What did you tell yourself to make it all okay?

I told myself that what I felt didn't matter.

What mattered was what was meant to be.

· · ·

I turned eighteen right out of high school and by September the boy and I had fled, backpack and guitar in tow, to see our camp directors, Mike and Dar, in the commune they were founding in the tender hills of western North Carolina. The winsome Dar, mother of three, doubled as a nurse; her husband, Mike, a social worker, served as a church elder. Our plan, such as it was, was for Mike to marry the boy and me, out there, on the land. Come winter we'd be home again, awaiting another revelation.

Was the plan God-given? I assumed it was.

We hopped the bus heading south, saying we would visit Mike and Dar. Not a word about eloping. Or Elijah.

The old vw van made the wheezy climb up Piney Mountain. Dar reached back and squeezed my hand. "What a blessing you could join us," she said. We lurched along the steep farm road that emptied into fields, when all at once Mike killed the engine and we tumbled out into the fragrant southern night, into moonlight pooling in a clearing ringed by whistling softwoods. I spied a chicken coop and outhouse on either side of some two-storey shed. A tobacco barn, it turns out. And home. "Welcome to our humble cabin." Dar undid the latch to a stiff pine door that swung open onto darkness. Inside was a table, stove and dry sink. "Make yourself at home." She nudged us up the stairs, toward the wood stove, pullout couch and rocker. A rustic ladder led to the little loft where the family slept. This room too was dark, save for moonlight stealing through a small square pane.

Homesteading in tobacco country meant no neighbours within shouting distance. No water, power or insulation. Just coons and fox and possum, which spooked the family dog, a big old yellow mutt named Cry Baby. She scuttled underfoot while we unpacked the van and Mike carried dozing children off to bed. "You know," Dar said, shushing the dog, "we're building our own cabin using what we can reclaim from an old abandoned factory." Cry Baby settled once her mistress lit the oil lamp. A weak light bloomed in the musty kitchen. Dar cocked her head. "We sure could use your help."

"Of course," I enthused, "that's why we're here." Could the false note be detected?

"You're not afraid of vultures, are you? They skulk about the place, but they're curious is all."

"So this is not your land?"

"No," she said. "It's a ways from here, you'll see."

What I saw that autumn was grit married to imagination. There were homey touches, sure—Dar's merry cross-stitch brightening the barn board; waking up to fresh-baked bread. But these were the exceptions, up there with bacon and Velveeta sandwiches, or cornmeal griddle cakes lathered with peach jam. Weekly showers at the high school were a highlight, thanks to a laconic shop teacher by the name of Wes who smuggled us into the locker rooms on Friday nights. The kids—ages three, five and seven—bathed old-school in a washtub in the kitchen.

"It's like camping," their lanky dad would say. How long could they live in a tobacco barn? Again, the boyish grin. "No more than a few years we hope."

Hope was the watchword for this back-to-the-land living that charmed, inspired—unless you were put off by poverty and dirt, or bloody fox raids that enraged the hens, wings flapping in a mad show of indignation at the loss of another of their sisters.

I wish I could look back at that time on Piney Mountain and see myself wrangling chicken wire or kneading dough at daybreak, anything that would ease the many burdens of our hosts. What I see is a spectre ambling the slopes, contemplating turns of phrase—how Thoreau might have eulogized the brazen kudzu, the pokeweed's bloody juices purpling the fingers—a pastime that distracted me from dreary chores like writing home to say *Dear Mom and Dad, Just so you know, I'm getting married.* For the life of me I could not speak up, could not bring myself to say the simple truth, that I was shutting down. The depression that had dogged my sorry youth had not lifted, it had only deepened. Right after my birthday, I had left in defiance for Niagara Falls, where, in a twist of fate, the boy's family took me in. News soon came that Mom had sold my bed, and that was that: I was launched, a dark Rapunzel, free to seize her independence, or to follow the fair prince, and since the latter had been foretold by an erstwhile prophet, I fell into the age-old habit of following a man. Following had led me here, to sloping fields I would wander in a pre-nuptial haze, girl from the north country, long hair "all down her breast," clueless what to do with my so-called life.

Dar, to her credit, tried to reach me. In return, I was maddeningly evasive. "What will you do when you go back to Canada?" (Sorry, I have no idea.) "What's your heart telling you to do?" (Ditto.) "Did you want to buy a veil?" (Hmm, would it go with the granny gown scrunched up in my backpack?) In truth, I couldn't breathe when I thought about the wedding. But that was normal, right? Eloping casts a kind of spell. Travel casts another. I explained this was my first trip south, first sighting of hickory and hornbeam, my first encounter with rhododendron-covered rocks and spillways. Magnolias were new to me. Sassafras was new. So was the sweet, sweet smell of dried tobacco. I guess I'm kind of lost, I laughed. That much was true. The one thing I could admit—that I was smitten by the fog-wiped, painterly, impoverished and enchanted.

.   .   .

I came to at the wedding in November, deep in R.J. Reynolds's tobacco country, on a thirty-acre parcel of spindly pine and oak brush that went by the name of Zion's Depot.

You will not find that name on any map. Mike and Dar and the others who had bought the land in common had coined the phrase, which, at the time, did not suggest fanatics or an armoured compound. Not to other like-minded souls flocking to North Carolina, hoping for cheap land to buy and settle. In that sense, other than Cry Baby in her festive red bandana, all eight wedding guests were simply older seasoned versions of ourselves—dreamers, seekers, ersatz saints in the latter days of a hopeful era.

I'd first heard about the Zion's Depot vision at that fateful church camp the summer that I turned sixteen, before news of it seeped north across the border and alarmed members of our sleepy congregation—people like my mother, who saw camp as a training ground for braless hippies.

"All this talk about a commune," Mom clucked as she presided over sizzling onions. "That Mike's an instigator."

"Mom, read the Bible. Followers of Jesus held their goods in common." I was preachy and obnoxious and I didn't care. What I cared about was fleeing death-by-suburb.

"Don't get smart with me. Communes are for you-know-what."

I rolled my eyes, but not so as she'd notice. "Look, Mike's an elder. He's doing what he thinks is right. Besides, you've never even met him." I had just met Mike and the moon-faced Dar myself at the most amazing youth camp ever. Their van alone was proof that Jesus freaks could still be cool.

"I don't go in for kooks." Mom smirked. Cold potatoes hit the fry pan. "All this vision talk is nonsense." The onions coiled and hissed.

Her attitude, as always, was unspeakably depressing. I thought of Emerson. *To be great is to be misunderstood.*

"Girl," Mom shook her head. "If you go in for all that vision talk, you really are deluded."

Deluded? Wow, I thought, look who's talking.

Living on the land, as I'd understood from all my reading—as I'd pictured it before setting foot in hard-scrabble Appalachia—would be hard, yes. It should be a test of character, a way to purify the heart. But would you fail at this ennobling life if it were meant to be? No. Clearly Mike and Dar had been led to this death-wed mythic landscape for a reason.

And me? Why was I standing toe to toe with a groom I hardly spoke to under a twisty leafless oak on such a damn cold day?

.   .   .

You will not find Rapunzel in the scriptures, but she's there just the same—wherever there is push-pull over woman. Eve was one such woman, and what was said to Eve? "I will greatly multiply thy sorrow."

God didn't speak to me directly. He didn't have to. Shame drove home the message that I was a failure. *Girl, you are such a disappointment.*

My family never spoke of the elopement. One aunt didn't speak to me for twenty years, she was so put off by my counterculture nonsense.

The in-laws took another tack. "What about a ring?" My mother-in-law would offer up a plain gold band—a family heirloom I moodily declined. (Wedding rings are so conventional.) "Did you two take any pictures?" (Oh no, we'd never pose for pictures.) Our sole memento, the Stokes County marriage certificate with its quaint cameo of two clasped hands, aroused plenty of suspicion, as did the fact that I soon took back my maiden name. That was a real head shaker. Even so, people made an effort to adapt to our playing man and wife. My home church would even throw a shower, which I swore up and down I didn't want, but the women I had known since childhood insisted on the age-old rite of passage. I walked into the old church hall to be met by every piece of Tupperware known to humankind.

"Well, what did you expect?" Mom sighed, battle weary. "They asked me what you needed and I told them."

Mom and I made up in other ways as well, most times without a fight. All fights now were inside the marriage. He grew sullen, I grew loud. It was an adjustment.

There were moments, though. On the bitter cold December morning we arrived back in Niagara Falls, when my new father-in-law met our Greyhound bus with "Welcome home, children, how about some breakfast?" (our first hot meal in days) and we used the diner's pay phone to call about an ad for an apartment in a storied nineteenth-century mansion up on Lundy's Lane—a place we took sight unseen, because it was a *sign*—I was flooded with a fleeting sense of promise. Starting out in a big old funky place filled with drug-dealing misfits could inspire just the pluck we'd need, to emulate our heroes in the Carolina outback.

Sure enough, hardship worked its magic—distracted us from the fact that two kids fresh out of high school could not find work. Finally, when winter fell full force inside and out, when the unheated apartment grew so cold over-night our clothes would stiffen like cadavers, we finally got inventive—tossed jeans and socks and mitts in the oven in the mornings, long enough to toast them and get us up and out the door: he, to the unemployment office and me, to the in-laws before plodding to the library, where I'd look up universities and maybe stew about applying, or plunder cookbooks, scouting recipes for Mormon bread.

Time passed and winter deepened. Niagara Falls is an icy haze in winter, and with the bitter damp comes an eerie pall that tricks the senses. Friends staying overnight complained of a presence in the living room where they'd camped out on the floor. A big old house like this has ghosts, they murmured over breakfast. No, no ghosts, I countered.

Haunted, though, is exactly how I felt.

Each night my spouse took to laying down his fair guitar, then lacing up his boots and saying, "Don't wait up, I'm headed to the Falls." Some nights it was the Rapids, or the Whirlpool, wild places that had been ours not so long ago.

Hour after hour, stiffening on the mattress on the hard cold floor, staring at the frosted window, toying with my hair, I'd wonder *Where the hell was this Elijah?* If the Almighty had something grand in store, now would be the time to show it.

Sad to say, no figures made their presence felt.

What was felt was a towering sense of loss.

Loss filled the awkward silence in an awkward marriage, a union in which neither one of us could bring ourselves to say the simple truth—that we were neither favoured nor appointed. Nor were we pioneering. We were simply keeping time. This preordained joining of a boy and girl—this, *this* was conforming. We had conformed to someone else's vision of how to live our lives. We had fallen for the powerful, alluring—what was not yet love.

Then suddenly it's morning, and once again there we are, hopping about a frigid kitchen, pulling on our roasted socks and jeans, and, well, there's a kind of joy in that—joy in pushing back against the odds of failing, for the odds are overwhelming that you will.

For now, all you can do is bundle up and go your separate ways: he, to look for work, and you, to the holy precincts of the book stacks by way of the in-laws, where maybe, just maybe, you will set aside your sorrow long enough to lend a hand, or do the unexpected. Admit to your affection for the great wide world.

Bad Jew, Good Jew

AYELET TSABARI

A few months after my father died, my brother and I were playing by the row of jagged cypress trees at the end of our street. I was ten. He was thirteen. I have a picture of us standing at that very spot, and though I know it was taken a year or two earlier, whenever I think of that conversation I envision us as captured in that film: barefoot in T-shirts and shorts, mischief in our eyes, long, skinny limbs dirtied from play, and our heads hallowed by the dying light of a summer sunset.

At some point in the conversation I announced, "God is dead." My brother eyed me curiously, eagerly. "Or if he's not dead," I went on, "then he's an asshole." A large grin spread on my brother's lips.

Yes, I was angry and grieving, but I wasn't being glib. I'd arrived at that Nietzschean conclusion after serious contemplation. If we were born in His image, I reckoned, then God, too, must be mortal. Perhaps his work on earth was done. How else could you explain wars? The Holocaust? How else could you explain Him taking our dad away from us? My father was only forty-four when he died and a father of six, the youngest only two. He was a righteous man—a philanthropist, a synagogue-goer, a Tsaddik, some people even called him after his passing. When I asked the adults around me, they said God wanted him near; He always takes the good ones. As though God was a selfish, entitled child who did whatever he pleased with no concern for others.

As soon as I uttered those damning words, I looked up, half expecting to be hit by lightning, but the sky was calm and cloudless. At that moment, I had the unholy equivalent of an epiphany. No one was listening. God didn't exist. The world was an unsafe, hopeless place. Bad things were happening to good people, and there was no one to stop it, no one to protect us. We were on our own, without guidance. Orphans.

It was the moment I became an atheist.

... .

When Gabrielle and I walk toward the Reform synagogue for a Yom Kippur service, Bloor Street is thronged with happy Torontonians, grateful for the unseasonal balmy weather. Patios are teeming with people clinking glasses and laughing; storefronts and restaurants glow with bright, flickering lights. The city feels festive, joyful. It is not supposed to be joyful. It is Yom Kippur, literally a "Day of Atonement," the holiest and most solemn day in the Jewish calendar. In Israel, even secular Jews often observe a "lighter" form of this holiday, fasting and unplugging from technology, while others use the day to meditate and reflect on the passing year. In very religious circles, even laughing is frowned upon. Knowing that Gabrielle is fasting, I'm surprised to see her answering the phone, and later in the synagogue, the rabbi—a curly-haired woman with a hint of an American accent—makes a joke and the room swells with laughter. I look around stunned. Don't these people know they are supposed to be repenting?

Of course, for me as a secular child growing up in Israel, Yom Kippur was less about atoning and more about riding bikes. In fact, it was one of my favourite holidays, and not because of the chance to be absolved of all our sins. Yom Kippur offered an altered reality, a break from ordinary life as we knew it, an escape. Everything was shut down on Yom Kippur. National TV and radio weren't broadcasting. There was no music blasting from cars, no TVs echoing or telephones ringing from neighbours' homes. The world was quieter, serene, dreamlike. Doors were left open and friends and relatives often visited, quietly chatting in the dim light of whatever lamps were left on for the duration of the fast—even turning on light switches was forbidden. But most importantly, for twenty-five hours there were no vehicles on the streets, a chance for us children to take over the adult territory with our bikes and our skateboards and our running feet, while the traffic lights kept changing, painting the pavement in bright, glittery colours.

Later, as rebellious young adults, we often gathered at someone's home in Tel Aviv with a stack of movies and way too much food, as if we might starve without access to grocery stores and take-away. In the morning, we went to the beach, swam and lay in the sun with the rest of the heathens. Still, when the first car whirred down the street at sundown, marking the end of the day, I was saddened.

I try telling all this to Gabrielle on the way to synagogue, but I get the sense that she doesn't quite get it, having a hard time reconciling her experience of the holiday with mine. When I first met Gabrielle, I hadn't pegged her as a synagogue-goer. I saw a hip, feminist, queer filmmaker and thought I knew her. But Gabrielle grew up in Montreal going to synagogues, surrounded by Orthodox families who were welcoming and warm, while I grew up in Israel, where secular Jews are a majority and where Orthodox people keep mostly to themselves. As a young adult in the vibrant city of sin that is Tel Aviv, I hung out in circles where going to synagogue on Friday night (rather than, say, clubbing) might have raised eyebrows. A country of polar extremes, Israel didn't offer much in between.

But at least in Israel I didn't have to commemorate the Jewish holidays. During the High Holidays, just like in Canada during Christmastime, the holiday spirit was everywhere.

In Canada, I have to make an effort.

Which is why I'm in synagogue on Yom Kippur. Because I want my three-year-old daughter to have a Jewish identity. Because I'm searching for new ways to celebrate Jewish holidays, to create traditions that fit my ideology and my lifestyle and my mixed family. On Rosh Hashanah, for example, I found the blessings online and changed the wording so they were less about our enemies trying to annihilate us and more about peace and renewal. On Passover, I presented my guests with an alternative Seder plate, which included—alongside traditional items—an orange as a gesture of solidarity with LGBTQ and other marginalized members of the community, olives as a call for peace in the Middle East, free-trade dark chocolate to acknowledge the slavery that still takes place in our world and an artichoke as a symbol for mixed families like my own.

When I tell people I don't practise Judaism, "I'm naturally good at it," they laugh. It is a joke that works only outside of Israel, because in Israel you don't need to do anything "Jewish" to be Jewish. On occasion, I call myself a bad Jew, which gets a few more laughs. Bad because for the first few years in Canada I'd sometimes let major Jewish holidays pass by without acknowledgement. Because the one time I fashioned a menorah out of a piece of wood and plastic bottle caps, I nearly burnt down the house. Because I fasted only once on Yom Kippur, and even then for the wrong reasons, using the holy day as an excuse for a cleanse. Because, despite growing up in a kosher household like many Israelis, I was now a fan of bacon and shrimp. Because I never, not once, went to synagogue in my eighteen years of living in Canada.

Then again, I hardly ever went to synagogue growing up. Although my father went every Friday evening, and my brothers sometimes joined him, I only went when we celebrated a bar mitzvah or the birth of a baby in the family. Our synagogue was steps from my grandmother's house in Sha'ariya, a Yemeni neighbourhood at the edge of town, where everyone looked somewhat familiar. Built of yellowish stone bricks, a large menorah perched on its roof, our synagogue was small and unassuming, nothing like the big, fancy *shuls* I later saw in North America. I followed my mom and aunts up to the second-floor women's section and stood on my tippytoes to look down over the bannister, watching the kippah-clad men as they bowed and prayed in the Jewish-Yemeni singsong intonation that made Hebrew sound like a foreign language, like music. Despite formulating my feminist world views at an early age, that sexist segregation didn't bother me; already then, I didn't feel a need to participate in the religious ritual. Especially since at the end of the service, my female cousins and I were allowed to slip downstairs and join the boys for the important part: the women throwing celebratory candy from the women's section. We all ran frantically to collect as much as our little hands could muster.

. . .

Gabrielle and I sneak into the synagogue just after Kol Nidrey, which signifies the beginning of the service. I'm disappointed. Kol Nidrey, an Aramaic chant with a solemn, dramatic melody, sets the mood for atoning and reflecting, and frankly, I could use the help. The place is jam-packed with families. Some of the men—and women too, because this is an inclusive, Reform synagogue—have kippahs on their heads and white, embroidered tallitim draped over their shoulders like shawls.

Gabrielle and I sit in the balcony's very last row, from where the rabbi and cantor—both women—appear tiny and faceless. The pew creaks as I lean toward Gabrielle to share her siddur, and we read aloud along with the rest of the congregation. It doesn't take long before I'm fighting waves of cynicism and judgment. I am judging the fact that this is, in fact, a church, dressed up as a synagogue. I find it disorienting and weird, despite the wonderful job they had done covering the crosses with Stars of David. I'm judging these people who are supposed to be "my people"; I think of them as conservatives and conformists. I judge the words we are reciting, the praise of a God I don't believe in, the confessing of a long list of sins, the begging for forgiveness, which feels laden with guilt. How is that productive? We're humans! Shit happens. Besides, shouldn't reflection and repentance be a private thing?

At the same time, as I watch families sitting together, elderly and young, kids shuffling on pews, babies wiggling in mothers' arms, a part of me envies them for giving in to the regularity and commitment of a practice, for having guidelines to follow, for being a part of something bigger than oneself. But even my envy reeks of judgment, stems from my secret belief that they had chosen an easier path: a prepackaged, all-inclusive trip to a resort rather than a backpacking journey through unpaved terrain. Maybe because I became an atheist at such a young age, I find myself viewing religious faith as naive, nearly childish.

This is a day of atonement, our last chance to appeal to God for forgiveness, and what do I do instead of reflecting on my sins? Judge everyone else.

I remind myself that I promised to come into this with an open heart, be present, let myself just experience the service. So, when the rabbi offers us the option to silently say our own prayer ("to God or whatever you may choose to call it"), I practise gratitude and recite affirmations, as I try to do daily. Fleetingly, I wonder, is it really so different?

Then my mind drifts to the grocery list, to the errands I'm supposed to run tomorrow, to the last episode of *Grey's Anatomy*. Resentment begins creeping in. Was this really the best use of my free evening? I could have been writing right now, or catching up on reading. I remember what my sister, who had spent some time living in the US, said: "I get why Jews outside of Israel feel the need to go to synagogue, but still, whenever I went I mostly felt bored." To fight my resistance, I focus on the Hebrew text in front of me, appreciate it for its poetic qualities.

In high school, along with advanced literature, I chose to study advanced Bible for my matriculation exams. This surprised some of my friends who knew me as a diehard atheist. But for me, studying the Bible (in a secular high school, mind you) was a literary exploration rather than a religious one. The

Hebrew Bible fascinated me, the richness of its stories, the complex characters and dramatic situations. I was enamoured with the ancient words imprinted on the flimsy pages, the poetry and music. The Hebrew language is the hand that pulls me into this service. At least I can read the original words in which these prayers were written, know the shape of these letters by heart. Despite the fact that I write in English, my second language, the Hebrew alphabet is etched into my essence, tattooed onto my skin in an invisible ink. The words are where I find my comfort.

My first shiver of excitement comes when the rabbi points us to "Avinu Malkenu." I faked my way through the songs because I didn't know any of them, and the North American accent made the Hebrew words feel displaced, a little bit like me. But this is the one song I know and love. Years ago, on a beach in Thailand, a friend began singing the last verse of "Avinu Malkenu" around the fire and I joined her, and we repeated it, drumming and harmonizing and swaying, and the words—"Our Father, Our King. Be kind and gracious with us"—were humbling, the melody sombre and moving, and though I have chanted Hindu chants before, with local friends in India, experienced the elation brought on by that ritual, the ecstasy felt different, intensely charged and strangely comforting, the words infused with more meaning by virtue of them being sung by my ancestors, chanted by Jews for generations.

In the synagogue, I sing the song loudly and passionately, my voice absorbed by the sound of people singing together, becoming one. There is such power in that unity, in the communal voice and intention.

In this moment, I am one of them. I belong.

At the end of the service, I watch a young woman with a kippah on her long brown hair removing her tallit, folding it carefully and placing it in a hand-sewn bag, and something about the fluidity of her movements, the care and intention she instills in that gesture, radiates harmony and calm. This is a woman with a clear purpose, a woman who knows she belongs. My own Jewishness feels lonesome and untethered. For the first time, I can see why people might choose to go to holiday services despite being atheists. That promise of community and belonging is enticing.

For a moment, I consider it.

The moment doesn't last.

. . .

After the breakfast, I call my mother in Israel. Maybe I'm hoping she can help me understand something about myself, about my failure to find solace in those settings, something about my relationship to Jewishness. We talk about the little synagogue in Sha'ariya that my father used to attend, where my family still celebrates bar mitzvahs and births. "It's very modest," my mother says. "There's no big show. It's not like in the movies from America. Over there it looks like a church! And everyone is coming so dressed up. It feels almost …" she whispers, "Christian."

At my mother's suggestion, I call my uncle, Avi. My uncle has been the synagogue's cantor and its unofficial leader for many years, since the synagogue never had an official rabbi. Avi loves his role. A doctor of education, he is a charismatic, inspiring speaker, and has a beautiful, thundering singing voice. Twice a year he organizes day trips for the congregation, which he guides, because among his many vocations, he was once a licensed tour guide.

Many years ago, my uncle was also a diplomat. He lived in Turkey, Italy and New York. When I ask if he attended synagogue throughout those years abroad, he says, "Of course!" The small synagogue in Turkey had been the most memorable. They sang a Sephardic tune, in Ladino. "It was so beautiful it made me cry." In Brooklyn, they had a Yemeni synagogue, and it was just like home. And once, in Los Angeles, "They had a woman cantor! And men and women sat together and they had music, like in a church. It was so strange I wanted to run away!"

When I mention missing Kol Nidrey, Avi begins singing it in the Yemeni intonation, and something stirs in me. It sounds nothing like the version I'd heard in American movies and surely would have heard in the Toronto synagogue. It is beautiful and singular and it's mine. It reminds me of the sound of men praying in the Yemeni synagogue by my house, the sound that wafted through the wooden blinds into my room every Saturday morning growing up, waking me up, along with the sweet smell of jichnoon, the Yemeni Shabbat bread my mother had baked in the oven all night long.

I realize that what I am looking for cannot be found in a synagogue. A link to my Israeli-Yemeni-secular-Jewish childhood, to my past. Being Jewish for me does not exist in isolation. It can't be taken out of the context of the entire whole that makes me who I am. I am a Yemeni Jew, an Israeli Jew, a secular Jew who doesn't go to synagogue. And the Canadian, Ashkenazi, Reform synagogue didn't suit me because it represents only a small part of my cultural identity.

Like many immigrant parents, I've been searching for ways to maintain my sense of self, the self I'd been before Canada, and pass some of that cultural identity to my child. I want her to have the Yom Kippur of my childhood, to ride bikes through the empty city with the rest of the children, turning an imaginary wheel and stopping at traffic lights, pretending they are cars. I want her to fight with her cousins over the candy from the synagogue's floor. Of course, it is a futile pursuit; it can't be done. All I can give my daughter is a second-hand cultural experience, a watered-down version of my own. And that would be better passed on through visits to my Yemeni neighbourhood in Israel, where the same sounds of prayer might wake her up on Saturdays, and through language, through stories, through words.

Again with the words.

.　.　.

One of the speakers in the Yom Kippur service spoke about feeling spiritually nourished at the synagogue. It made me think. Do we have to find our spiritual nourishment within the traditions we're born into? Shouldn't it be the first place we look? Perhaps, yet I have never felt a presence of the divine in a synagogue. The few times in my life that I felt a sense of godliness was out in the world, alone, often in nature.

But more than anything, nowadays I find it in writing. Writing has been my religion, my spiritual practice, my synagogue. Like any practice, it relies on rituals, meditation, prayer and intention. It requires attentiveness, focus and tremendous faith: faith in yourself, faith in the reader and faith in fiction's power to promote change, to make a difference, however minute. It is in writing that I grasp for the unknowable and the sacred, and search for meaning, for something bigger than myself. It is in writing that I experience the timelessness and self-forgetting that is so often associated with spiritual practices. And in those moments when it works, when the words flow, when everything falls into place, I feel something alight, unnamed, inexplicable. It feels like a revelation.

Out of the Darkness

SANDY WABEGIJIG

Hello darkness, my old friend.

—Paul Simon, "The Sound of Silence"

The darkness was becoming too much of a friend, I could not bear the silence of aloneness. It was like being at sea, lost and drifting. From where I sat in Macon, Georgia, the island in the distance was Atlanta, and that's where I went, straight for Margaritaville—believe me, there's one in every town, and suddenly my world got a whole lot brighter. This was the seventies, after all, and I was in my twenties. Single life was less lonely thanks to barflies, nightly drink specials and some of that good ol' southern music.

In time though, the artificial environment took its toll. I began to suffer flashbacks. Emotional extremes—the happiest I had ever been and the saddest. Haunting reminders of the turmoil I thought I'd left behind left me in pieces. In survival mode, you start rebuilding your life the best you can. Maybe the hurt or pain will go away, you think, if you just move away, if you start over somewhere else. That seemed to be the way to go, but in the back of my mind and in my soul, I knew something wasn't right. I missed the red dirt soil of the country. I missed red roosters crowing. I began to feel empty, the fire was going out. I was feeling sick.

I finally realized what I needed was a different kind of light.

With only a few possessions, I headed north, to the Great Smoky Mountains, where the moon and stars lit up the night sky, the rivers and streams were refreshing, a relief from noisy city streets. The cool mountain air now filled my lungs instead of the stale air of smoke-filled bars. In an area just outside the small town of Murphy, North Carolina, and the Hiwassee River, in the Hanging Dog Mountains, I found an unfinished circular log home. You could walk for miles on trails without seeing anyone. It was quiet and still, with just the birds, their songs, and with nature to keep you company.

One sunny summer afternoon my friend Sharon picked me up and took me on a tour. We travelled old country roads in her old beat-up car until we ended up at the top of a hill in Murphy—an overgrown area, deserted. She knew I'd appreciate the historical significance of this place as Sharon also had old Indian blood in her. Choctaw.

We hadn't walked far from the car when she showed me an old fallen cemetery-style stone almost buried under dead leaves and debris. We brushed the earth off the marker. "Site of Fort Butler," the inscription read, "Commanded by Genl. Winfield Scott during the Round Up of the Cherokee Indians for Removal to Oklahoma in 1837–1838." The "removal," better known as the Trail of Tears, is known in Cherokee as *Nunna daul Isunyi*. The Trail Where They Cried.

My heart sank. I knew this history. I had worked at the Ocmulgee mounds and national park in Macon. I would walk through the museum, study the artifacts and talk to the visiting artists and craftspeople. I had also heard the removal story from the late medicine man, Stanley Smith, a Creek from Oklahoma who was a direct descendant of survivors of the Trail of Tears. He told some sad, gruesome stories. And to think I was standing where Stanley's ancestors would have stood as prisoners 150 years before.

I could feel the sorrow, the loss and grief, standing there on the ground of this tragedy.

I could hear the cries of the children, women and elders as they were brutally forced at gunpoint, corralled into the fort with few possessions.

What was a beautiful and sacred relationship to the land from time immemorial had been taken away from the people in a flash. The rivers of the long people, the songs and ceremonies of the spirits of all beings in this area would no longer be sung and celebrated by the people who once knew them.

The thought resonated deep within me, banished from a deep connection I had made in my life with the land, people and history of Georgia and with my own people's history.

The removal is a very dark part of American history. The Indian Removal Act under President Andrew Jackson was put into effect in the 1830s. The image of seven thousand troops sent into western North Carolina to build six forts to imprison the Cherokee and Creeks fleeing Georgia was chilling. Here I was at the very site of Fort Butler, the largest of the forts and the main collection point of the roundup. I later found out that Creeks from Georgia and some Cherokees had been able to flee into the Hanging Dog Mountains where I was living now. All in all, some three thousand Cherokees were led by gunpoint to Fort Butler. A total of twelve thousand from all the forts were arrested, imprisoned and removed to Oklahoma. It was a massive engagement of military force over Native Americans. And that was just the beginning:

> The long painful journey to the west ended March 26th, 1839, with four-thousand silent graves reaching from the foothills of the Smoky Mountains to what is known as Indian territory in the West. And covetousness on the part of the white race was the cause of all that the Cherokees had to suffer. ... Crimes were committed that were a disgrace to civilization. Men were shot in cold blood, lands were confiscated. Homes were burned and the inhabitants driven out by the gold-hungry brigands.
>
> —Private John G. Burnett[1]

As visions of the sorrow and brutality endured by the Creeks and Cherokees shook me, suppressed memories of my own began to surface.

I began to recall a series of events over several years that explained my mental, emotional and spiritual confusion. So much had happened then I hadn't been able to mourn my losses, including the death of my beloved father, someone I absolutely adored. At the same time, my beautiful romance and marriage had soured into an abusive relationship, followed by divorce and a long custody battle. After all the court proceedings, I said goodbye to the country home we had built on 450 acres. Then there were the deaths of friends and close associates from drug overdoses and a life of recklessness. This time,

....

1   Burnett, a soldier in the American army during the Cherokee Indian Removal (1838–39), gave his personal account on his eightieth birthday.

between 1971 and 1975, we all lived in an environment of alcohol and drugs. Marriages were breaking up. Finally, the music business collapsed, sending everyone in a tailspin. It was not a pretty sight in Macon, Georgia. What had been a utopia of southern music—brothers and sisters united in the idealism of peace and love, flourishing artists and barbecue get-togethers—fell into disarray.

· · ·

After a few months of settling in at Hanging Dog, my friend Doyle introduced me to a traditional knowledge keeper and medicine gatherer, Hawk Littlejohn. Hawk lived in Murphy with his wife, Judy, and their children. Besides picking medicines, he farmed trees and vegetables and kept honeybees on a large piece of land not far from town. Hawk had traditional dwellings called wickiups in the hills, where medical students could live, and learn about the local medicines. The wickiups were constructed of tall saplings that had been driven into the ground, then bent and tied together near the top. The dome-shaped framework was then interwoven with other branches and with cedar. A wikiup was like a large sweat lodge, the womb of Mother Earth.

Hawk and I got to be good friends and I attended sweat lodges he held for men and women. It was a spiritual journey for everyone, lighting the fire from within. What that man lived, everyone could learn from. He showed me where he would go for meditation and prayers in the top room of his house, where he had cedar and sage for smudging. He had another dwelling in the hills where he would go as well. He also offered me one of the wickiups to live in, saying, "As long as I'm here, you will always have a place to stay, if you need it."

Just to know there was a place where there was peace, spiritual protection and an unconditional space was a great blessing. I have never forgotten the importance of always providing a place of safety to those in need.

Eventually, I took Hawk up on his offer.

It was the end of summer when I began my six-month stay. I lived alone in one wickiup, without electricity or running water. There was a fresh stream from the hills that flowed close to the dwelling and I would sit by that stream, bathe in it, take water for drinking, cooking and cleaning. I had an oil lamp and a Coleman stove for light and fire. Windows built into the frame brought me daylight. The window by my bed let me gaze at the moon and stars. I did not read newspapers or watch television. All I had for entertainment was a battery-run boom box I used, to play traditional songs and drum tapes.

I lived without distractions, in the natural world. I learned the power and the truth of the living world that I could only experience alone, in silence.

· · ·

Fall turned into winter, and by early March, I began to think about the significance of spring. I thought about the meaning of the seasons and the wheel of life. Our ceremonies and prayers follow the teachings of the four directions, four stages of life, and recognition of their guardian spirits. To us, the east represents springtime and the birth of all things; the south represents summer and youth; the west, autumn and adulthood; the north, winter and the elderly who are beginning their journey back to the Creator.

My thoughts centred on the beginning of the circle—the springtime, birth, rebirth.

I began to appreciate more than ever my Odawa and Ojibway blood, my family, and teachers and elders in traditional ways. The gifts I was given to guide me to a path of strength. Instinctively, I knew I should fast. I contacted my elder, Dan Pine, great-grandson of Shingwakonse, a highly regarded Ojibway Chief and Midewiwin medicine man who had led the Ojibways in a time of great turmoil. Dan was a true elder and visionary who was also a medicine man who had gifts and visions from the Creator to cure many illnesses. I told Dan about the fast. I asked him to be my protector, to pray for me while I was fasting. His daughter sent a letter with instructions from Dan. One was to smudge morning, noon and night. Dan said he would pray for me every day.

I began my fast during the spring equinox, saying goodbye to the winter of my life.

The purpose of the fast was to review my life from birth onward, and to seek guidance and direction for the future. I wanted to take full responsibility for my actions, seek restitution and forgiveness for any hurt I might have caused along the way. I prayed to the Creator, to make known my intentions and to ask for help from my spiritual guides and helpers. I prayed to the eagle for clarity of vision so I could see clearly what I needed to take responsibility for in my past and resolve what I needed to, so I could leave the past behind and move forward.

I prayed for guidance and instruction.

The first three days without food, and with only water, were a total cleansing of my physical body in preparation for entering the spiritual world. The best way I can describe this is with a teaching of Fools Crow, a ceremonial chief of the Teton Sioux, who spoke of becoming "hollow bones." The metaphor describes chiefs, medicine people and other great teachers who are able to channel wisdom and power through them, to help others. The power makes us what we should be, then flows through us and out to others. All excess baggage in us must be cleared to become a hollow bone.

On the fourth day, I felt light and very close to all around me. Everything started to get clearer. I decided to continue after the fourth day, and for the next three days I also went without water.

Following Dan's instructions, I smudged myself three times a day and stayed close to the wickiup. At night, I noticed that the light in the oil lamp was growing clearer and clearer, as if a veil were being lifted with the passing of each day. I also noticed that I was being flooded with messages from my natural surroundings, as if every living entity in nature was telling me something. Even the moon outside my window was growing clearer and clearer, until I finally saw it as a pure, living, breathing being.

On the seventh day, I received a ten-year life plan in answer to my prayers.

The plan was very simple. The first thing was to go home to Canada. I asked if it was Toronto and was told yes. I was reluctant to accept this answer as I thought it would be culture shock, going back to a city after living in the country. I was afraid I would get lost again. I would want to go out and enjoy the music, bars and so on. I was told that it would be all right, that I could handle it. The second thing was to get a job, any job, immediately once I got there. The third direction was to go back to school and finish my education. The fourth was to volunteer in my community.

On the morning of the eighth day, I said my prayers of gratitude and told the spirits and helpers that I was going to break my fast.

I went to the local gas station restaurant that served excellent home cooking, where I met my friend, Doyle, for breakfast. I said my prayers over the food, to tell the Creator and guides that I was ending my fast, and I asked for a sign, to let me know that what I had experienced was real, that the instructions were real.

I was about to take a mouthful of my oatmeal cereal when a shadow passed. Doyle said, "Did you see that?"

"No," I said. "I had my head down, but I saw something pass by the window."

The look on his face was priceless. "That was a huge bald eagle! I never saw one around here before. And it came this close to the window!" He was in shock.

"Really?" I said, and kept on eating. There it was, I had received my answer.

Twenty Pages and a Razor Blade

BETSY WARLAND

I sent a copy of my first book, *A Gathering Instinct*, to my parents in 1981. I also mailed a copy to my brother, who visited my parents soon after. When the topic of my book arose, our mother indicated that she was upset about a suite of poems in the book regarding the breakdown of my marriage. She then showed my brother her solution. She'd removed those first twenty pages with a razor blade. Needless to say, I never mentioned my subsequent books to my parents.

After writing the above, I suddenly felt an urgency to clean the bathroom. This could merit analysis but I will resist. During that activity I recognized what needed to be said next.

I've previously told this "anecdote" in two of my books.

The above rendition, however, differs.

In those two books, our mother threatens to do her razor blade delete and my brother dissuades her from doing so.

Recently, he corrected me.

"She did cut those twenty pages out."

. . .

Over the decades of writing twelve books, teaching, mentoring and editing writers, I have come to believe that we are given certain stories to write: that regardless of genre or length, these stories seek us out. Entrust themselves to us. Utterly depend on us to tell them to our utmost ability. Not infrequently, these narratives that grab us by the collar are not ones we would choose. At all. They are too difficult, too demanding.

"The story tyrannizes us until we understand it."
                                        —*Oscar of Between*

So, we turn away from them, often for years. Make up a bunch of excuses, but the stories keep arising. Haunt. Wait. When we finally surrender to them, our surrender is a sacred act. These are the narratives that offer profound insights about respect, compassion, endurance, morality, craft, veracity's complexities and humility.

Writing is my spiritual teacher, as are nature, my Buddhist practice and my son. The spiritual insights and understandings that infuse me most are the ones that haven't intentionality: the ones that don't manifest with predetermined outcome in mind. Their often surprising, vibrant, moment-to-moment ways of existing provoke my entire attention. This is when transmission occurs.

Transmission? I am surprised by my use of that term. I've never used it before yet I think it may be the most accurate word. Recognition is perhaps another. Why? For me, spiritual insight transpires as something I sense or "knew" in some other time and we've finally met again. Wholly met. When I teach creative writing and work one on one with writers it is much the same: the deeper our trust and presence with the writing, the more acute our recognition is of what that narrative is seeking to transmit.

As in daily life, we often misunderstand what our narrative, or another's, is about. Consequently, we perceive and tell it in a manner that confuses its meaning, undermines its power.

Every narrative knows what it is about. Exists before we write the first words. Sound strange? Not really. How else are we (or an astute reader, mentor or editor) able to sense where we've gone off course? Even if there's an outline, plot, lived experience underpinning it (seemingly flawless GPS!) this floundering, loss of momentum and resonance still happens. It's then that the narrative itself must regain our attention, alert us about our misguided assumptions, avoidances, oversimplifications. Otherwise, the very narrative itself loses interest. Resists. Frustrates us like a horse refuses to move forward no matter how hard we jab it with our heels. Words may be accumulating on the page or screen but there's little life in them. To move forward, we must surrender to what each narrative is really about (its "pre-existence"). In turn, it guides us about its specific voice, narrative position, form and content.

I am reminded of a couple of narrative misunderstandings I had as a child. I held these misunderstandings for years until I matured and recognized that they didn't make sense. Here they are.

TRESPASSERS WILL BE PERSECUTED

This sign, posted on farmers' fences, actually said "PROSECUTED."

Having no notion of prosecuted, for years I read it as "persecuted," which was far more threatening, to say the least.

The other happened on a Sunday when our congregation stood up and recited the Nicene Creed. To my young ears (unfamiliar with archaic English), the passage "from thence He shall come to judge the quick and the dead" sounded like "then Nancy will come to judge the quick and the dead." I said this for several years. I must admit, each time I recited "Nancy will come," I felt a thrilling zing. At least there was one significant woman in Christianity. Mary, in Lutheran orthodoxy, was sidelined, barely a postscript.

Then I became friends with a Nancy. She lived across the road but despite our proximity, the fact that both families were farmers, we never met. I could hear the voices of Nancy and her sisters playing outside but had no notion of what they even looked like. Why? They were Catholic. We were Lutheran. Thus, we lived in utter ignorance of each other. Until. Until a new school was built in our nearby town and all the one-room schools closed. Suddenly Nancy and I found ourselves in the same classroom. Despite the taboo, we became fast friends. It was then that I began to puzzle about exactly who "Nancy" was in the creed. Certainly she wasn't the Nancy I now knew. One Sunday, as the congregation sat down after reciting the creed, I whispered to my mother: "*Who is* Nancy?" She had no idea what I was talking about. We sorted it out later.

In writing, every single word is an important signal: one key word can get us off track, as my childhood anecdotes illustrate. This is why deep listening is crucial. In this attentiveness, and absence of assumptions, transmission happens. The narrative in all its idiosyncratic nuances, power, surprise takes up residence on the page. Inhabits us. Touches our readers.

． ． ．

A vexing aspect in all of this is voice. A frequent adage, "Find your voice," suggests that you've had it and in a moment of absent-mindedness misplaced it. For years, when I was teaching, I consistently encountered women writers who were flattening their voices on the page. The expressive, engaging quality of each one's distinct voice was almost absent. I decided to take on this conundrum and designed a course, Vox: Out of the Box.

I suspected that this flattening out was indicative of an uneasiness we have about occupying the public voice. Perhaps it's not far-fetched to consider that it may also be the lingering residue of an "Eve complex." Her eagerness for knowledge and the consequences of that.

It's still far more common in men's daily experience to occupy the public voice than it is for women. We're afraid of what may happen to us if we do. Also, afraid of hurting others, even though there is no intention of doing so. Protection (of self and others) is our first instinct, not projection (in the public arena) of our narratives and ideas.

Even the voice of the much-consulted and revered oracle at Delphi only emitted from a small portal in stone.

The problem when it comes to writing is that when the voice on the page is restricted or camouflaged, so is the narrative.

One exercise we did in the course was to meet in pairs. First one told her partner the story of the narrative she'd written. (How satisfying to look around the room and see so much animation in body language and voice expressiveness.) After this verbal account, the partner read back to the writer two pages of her written version, and then compared the two versions. The partner pinpointed where the narrative was muted, even monotone, on the page, as well as where important aspects of the oral version were missing from the written version. Without exception, there were crucial absences, muffled cues and unnecessary explanations. The following week, when they each read their revised two pages, the difference was palpable, even stunning. What's left out, or obscured, is often what's most needed. In this short passage from my book *Oscar of Between: A Memoir of Identity and Ideas*, Oscar considers this.

Part 20
Montreal, Vancouver, Iowa, Edmonton 2012

Among the array of topics, they always discuss their work. Oscar observes that her manuscript keeps returning to violence. Cheryl asks what her thinking is about this. Oscar grasps at a couple of reasons but says she is taking her time in articulating why.

Cheryl, who has been making numerous bodies of work over the past fourteen years comprised of frame grabs from surveillance Web cams and home cams remarks that all our systems rely on various forms of aggressive control, threat and underlying violence.

Oscar: "And none of this will change if women remain silent."

One strategy I use, from time to time, to strengthen my resolve is the generative force in etymology. These three words below are a mantra I return to again and again:

"*story*, Greek, history, wisdom,"
"*narrative*, Latin, knowing,"
"*write*, German, to tear, scratch."

For the *story's* wisdom to release its *narrative* knowing we must *write* its tear and scratch.

As a young woman, I grew seedlings for a university's experimental flower garden. To enable propagation in seeds with hard shells, I had to scarify each seed (scratch or cut a line through its shell to its germ). The wide array of women writers I've had the honour to work with have inevitably been writing narratives barely present in, and not infrequently completely absent from, books. These are the very narratives that our world is so in need of.

Repression of, or refusal to recognize, the sacredness of our deeply held stories is the greatest violence we can inflict on ourselves, on one another: is our greatest crime.

This is my plea: tear, scratch.

Saved by a Red-Winged Blackbird

JULIA ZARANKIN

I hadn't expected to find birds instead of God. I had moved back to Toronto, at a crossroads in my career; I had just moved in with the man I would later marry, but I didn't know that then, and the concept of movers suddenly uniting my belongings with his terrified me. We had decided against merging bookshelves because we believed that my poetry books and realist novels couldn't amicably coexist with his tomes of fantasy and sci-fi. The day the movers introduced my upright piano into the equation, I had a slight anxiety attack, a fear of permanence catalyzed by the piano. How would I ever be able to run away—if need be, and in my experience, the need always arose, usually around the three-year mark, if not earlier—now? I scrutinized various scenarios, but it wasn't until I imagined myself limping around Toronto with a piano strapped to my back, planning a potential escape route from a relationship that had not yet been assailed by its first argument, that I paused.

I needed some perspective. A way of seeing the world that extended beyond my own mind. A rabbi's voice had once helped me through the darkest days of dissertation-writing anxiety—she sang wordless melodies, niguns, every Friday evening at Reform services on campus, and I felt at home there—and I wanted to replicate the experience. And so, I tried one synagogue and then another. I bounced from Reform (where I loved the songs) to Reconstructionist (where I could relate to the message) to Conservative (where the tradition felt soothing), and no matter what the denomination, I still left services with images of hauling my piano out the door at the first sign of trouble. It might have been for lack of vocabulary or sheer restlessness, but nothing soothed me and I began to worry that I might be searching for something I knew not how to name.

.   .   .

Having grown up entirely indoors, I suddenly clung to the idea that all the answers lay in the outdoors. I remembered the cycling group I had met in Missouri—the Sleasy's, short for *slow and easy*—and the feeling I had of forgetting myself on our arduous ascents. And they weren't exactly mountain peaks. The time I mastered a rolling hill on my own without the help of colleagues pushing me along, I felt I could tackle anything. Once, while cycling, a sunset interrupted my colleague's interminable monologue about tomato harvesting. At the sight of a burning red patch over an empty field, I ignored Brenda's endless stream of summer tomato talk. I barely had time to inhale and the intensity of the scarlet sunset began to bleed out horizontally, invading the sky hovering above the field. Suddenly, unexpected respite.

I began auditioning hobbies—anything to increase my patience and hopefully acquire a greater sense of being in the moment without actually having to do yoga. The idea of finding another cycling group would require repairing my bike, in which I didn't want to invest. Cycling held too many memories of a failed life, a job left behind, a landscape I found alienating. I thought of joining a hiking group, but the meeting times were inconvenient.

In the midst of my silent piano-trekking frenzy, which I hadn't shared with my partner for fear (would he think me insane?), I bought a memoir about birdwatching at a second-hand bookstore, all for a sentence I'd read on the back cover. "Couples who bird together, stay together."

I had no idea what it meant, but I couldn't get it out of my mind. The author argued that birdwatching had changed her life and had not only given her a new, more empathetic understanding of love, but also helped her reassess her place in the world.

I wasn't convinced. The proposition that spending hours in the field with people clad in khaki multi-pocketed vests and Tilley hats could bring one to a higher truth of some sort sounded borderline delusional. And yet I kept returning to the thought. At this point I was ready to latch on to anything that would steer me away from self-sabotaging thoughts of a relationship that was doomed simply on account of its goodness.

About a year later, I googled "bird watching Toronto class beginner life change desperate" and then removed the last three words from the equation. I didn't want the stakes that high from the get-go.

I settled on a group deep in the west end of Toronto run by someone named Brete, and after a series of emails, decided to meet up with his group one Saturday, mid-April.

First wrinkle: a 6:00 a.m. start time. I hadn't been awake that early since marching-band practice days in university. Second wrinkle: I lacked the gear. Third, and perhaps most severe wrinkle: my birding lexicon was limited to pigeons and, in a pinch, owls.

The group turned out to be friendly, greeting me with incessant chatter about optics—spotting scopes and binoculars—including price and quality comparisons.

I introduced myself, and sheepishly admitted that I was a complete beginner.

"Not to worry—folks in our group have varying degrees of experience. I mean, there isn't a single person here who can ID all the warblers."

"Uh … a warbler?"

"Wow. You weren't kidding when you said beginner."

"Nope."

"Do you have binoculars?"

I shook my head.

"That might be a good place to start," said Brete with a chuckle, which I thought might be code for "Who is this interloper, how did she find me on the Internet and why on earth did I ever email her back when she clearly said she didn't know a thing about birds?"

Once we got into our respective cars, a cavalcade of optics-endowed birders soared down the highway until we reached a park at the foot of Kipling Avenue, where the city collides with Lake Ontario. A kind gentleman draped in a long-lens camera and binoculars, and with a telescope casually resting on his shoulder, let me borrow his spare pair of what he alternately called his bins, binocs or glasses.

The binoculars felt heavy around the neck, and when I raised them to my eyes, they wobbled in my hands. A duck dove as I tried to focus my sights on it and left me staring at the hyperactive early-April waves out on the lake. I didn't know what I was looking at exactly. People shouted out words I couldn't process: Northern shoveller! Red-breasted merganser! American widgeon! Common merganser! Bufflehead!

And then, a delirious scream, "OH MY GOD, I think I got it, horned grebe, over there, next to the pied-billed grebe, you can't miss it, to the right of the dozens, no, hundreds of red-necked grebes out there, oh wait, oh sweet mother of God, is that a western grebe? Julia, are you seeing the grebes? It's not every day you get four species in one place."

My mind bobbed in and out of consciousness amidst this sea of names. I nodded, binoculars pointed at the CN Tower—the only thing I could safely identify on the horizon.

"What's a grebe?"

"Start with the red-necked grebes, can't miss them, there are close to five hundred of them out there. Pick one and focus on it—gorgeous rust-coloured neck, look at that elongated bill, it's a textbook grebe, no doubt about it."

I saw, but I didn't see.

On our way back to the cars, my extremities frozen from standing still by open water in gale-like temperatures, we stopped near a bush and someone called out, "Red-winged blackbird."

I almost didn't look because the thought of lifting my binoculars to my eyes brought with it a wave of slight nausea. But the bird stood still, balancing on a cattail, and I managed the trifecta of raising the binoculars, focusing them and finding the desired object magnified in my field of vision.

"What *is* that?" I gasped, blinded by the unexpected vermilion patches on the blackbird's epaulettes.

The sound it made didn't match the majestic chromatic statement of the glistening black contrasting with the burning red on the bird's lesser coverts. A protracted screechy gurgle, which Sibley's field guide transcribes as "kon-ka-reeeee," sounded primal. A reminder that something of the prehistoric exists within. Descendants of dinosaurs, birds make sounds that force us to venture into prehuman territory, the world before our own, of which we have only bones as record—a world of which paleontology speaks with certainty, but which for us pedestrian non-scientists retains a note of magic. The call of the red-winged blackbird—a trace of the ancient, a shade of creatures that had once been.

Red-winged blackbird. *Agelaius phoeniceus.* The Latin translates to "the gregarious red bird." That gregarious, often screeching black bird with miraculous red markings on its wings etched itself in my mind. I started seeing them everywhere, learned to identify them, pointed them out to anybody who would listen. I had expected the shock of their plumage to grow dull with time—*Oh, just another red-winged blackbird*, I thought I'd say. Instead, each sighting only magnified the intensity of the encounter.

It's the bird that kept drawing me back into the field, transforming me, incrementally, into a *birder*. Into one who *birds*. The acquisition and appropriation of a new verb: *to bird*.

Connoisseurs call it a sparkbird. The sighting that changes everything. The glimpse of colour that alters one's perception of the world, that demarcates past from present, distinguishes before from after.

I kept returning to one and the same thought: If the red-winged blackbird had been there all along and I had never noticed it, what else was I missing?

．　．　．

Incremental changes seeped into my life. I found myself unintentionally immersed in a community, entrenched in a new language where optics-talk, bird species codes and Latin binomials no longer sounded like gibberish. What's more, they started to roll off my tongue. My bookshelves overflowed with bird books—field guides, ornithology primers, biographies of famous birders and even a guide to shorebirds of North America, which I eventually relegated to a lower shelf because even after months of studying the birds still looked identical. I started keeping a list of bird sightings, and the more I could see and name, the more I wanted to see. I watched my hometown of Toronto transform from a concrete web of buildings, which I longed to escape, into an urban wilderness patchwork dotted with thrilling and surprising avian sightings, a haven for migratory birds.

The best thing about looking closely at that red-winged blackbird as he posed and unabashedly belted out his screeching song is that he didn't even

　　　　　　　　　　　　　　　　　　　　　　　　JULIA ZARANKIN

register my presence. He had other business to attend to, namely securing a mate that was partial to his cacophonic song—business that had absolutely nothing to do with me.

What a miraculously liberating epiphany: that I could be a part of something beyond the world of my study, or my apartment, or my anxieties about whether I would or wouldn't one day fight with my husband—of course we would—and whether said potential argument would dismantle the shaky edifice of a life I had been working so hard to construct, and whether I would one day find myself roaming the streets with a piano strapped to my back.

The bird returned to me a sense of perspective and allowed me to simply *be*.

Acknowledgements

This volume would never have come to fruition without the generosity of each of the writers, and without the unflagging support of Carolina Echeverria, Eufemia Fantetti, Ron Grimes, Pam Johnson, Kirsteen MacLeod, Lindy Mechefske, Pamela Mulloy, Alison Pick, Ayelet Tsabari and Betsy Warland. Deep gratitude to each of you. Thank you for believing in this project, and for helping to bring it to fruition.

I would like to thank, in particular, Eve Joseph, K.D. Miller and Christine Pountney. What they set in motion at the 2015 panel on spiritual memoir at the Wild Writers Festival in Waterloo, Ontario, has resulted in this book.

Thank you to Vici Johnstone and her resourceful team at Caitlin Press for their ingenuity, integrity and care. Collections like this would never see the light of day were it not for the willingness of indie presses such as Caitlin to step up and take risks.

Thanks also to the following editors and publishers:

Alison Pick's "Wake Up" appeared in *The New Quarterly*, issue 145, winter 2018.

Carleigh Baker's "In a Canoe, Chasing My Métis Grandmother" appeared in *The New Quarterly*, issue 143, summer 2017.

Dora Dueck's "Mother and Child" appeared in *The New Quarterly*, issue 146, spring 2018.

Meharoona Ghani's "My Uterus Is a Tree" is from the memoir "Letters to Rumi" (unpublished).

Sue Goyette's "Poetent" appeared in *The New Quarterly*, issue 145, winter 2018.

Liz Harmer's "My Flannery" is adapted from a longer version in *The New Quarterly*, issue 137, winter 2016.

Pam Johnson's "Second Chakra" is from the memoir "Magpies" (unpublished).

Amanda Leduc's "The Places in Between" was published on The Toast, November 26, 2014.

Emily McKibbon's "The Seraphim" appeared in *The New Quarterly*, issue 139, summer 2016.

K.D. Miller's "A Great Silence" appeared in *The New Quarterly*, issue 139, summer 2016.

Zarqa Nawaz's "Writing from the Inside" appeared in *The New Quarterly*, issue 140, fall 2016.

Susan Scott's "Zion's Children" is from the memoir "Sainted Dirt" (unpublished), funded in part by a generous grant from the Region of Waterloo Arts Fund.

Julia Zarankin's "Saved by a Red-Winged Blackbird" appeared, in much shorter form, as "Beginner Birdwatcher" in *Orion* magazine, vol. 36, no. 4, winter 2017.

Contributors

JAGTAR KAUR ATWAL left the English Midlands to travel around the world and settle in the wilds of Canada. She now lives in not-so-wild Cambridge, Ontario. You can find her work in *Room, Love Me True* and *The New Quarterly*, on Invisible Publishing's blog and in *Prairie Fire*, as winner of the 2017 creative nonfiction contest. Jagtar enjoys painting as another form of self-expression, where ideas and feelings surface, ready to be challenged and explored.

CARLEIGH BAKER is the author of *Bad Endings* (Anvil Press), which won the City of Vancouver Book Award, was shortlisted for the 2017 Rogers Writers' Trust Fiction Prize, a BC Book Prize and an Indigenous Voices Award. CBC has named Carleigh one of "17 writers to watch."

SHARON BALA is trapped on a rock in the cold North Atlantic. If the spirit moves you, please send mangoes. She still drives that little blue Honda featured in her story in this collection. For a long time, the crucifix was a permanent fixture in the cupholder; it vanished a couple of years ago. Sharon's first novel, *The Boat People*—a CBC Canada Reads finalist—was published in 2018.

DORA DUECK is partner, mother, grandmother, author—of two novels, a collection of short fiction, and stories and essays in various journals. Her novel *This Hidden Thing* was Book of the Year at the 2011 Manitoba Book Awards, and her story "Mask" won the *Malahat Review*'s 2014 novella contest. She currently lives in Tsawwassen, BC, where she writes a weekly blog on aging and is working on a memoir. www.doradueck.com

CAROLINA ECHEVERRIA is a community builder, a storyteller and an artivist whose works are in private collections and exhibited in museums and galleries internationally. As a Canadian who was born in Chile, she now seeks her deepest roots in Indigenous cultures. She is the founder of Native-Immigrant arts collective as well as co-founder and artistic director of the Atelier d'Art Métèque in Montreal, where she fosters active cultural collaboration.

EUFEMIA FANTETTI is a recovering Catholic with the heart of a happy heretic. Missions accomplished: wrote and published several essays and stories, performed stand-up comedy, took a vow of silence at a Buddhist retreat, briefly held peacock pose in yoga class. Her work has appeared in the *Globe and Mail*, *Event Magazine* and *The New Quarterly*. Her next book, *My Father, Fortune-tellers & Me: A Memoir*, will be released by Mother Tongue Publishing in 2019.

MEHAROONA GHANI was eight years old when she wrote her first poem and won a competition. Her work now appears in numerous anthologies. Inspired by music, art, mysticism, spiritual and oral traditions, myths, legends and classic poets like Rumi, she reclaims the space in between, the marginalized and hybrid identities, the hyphen in Canadian-South Asian. She is a graduate of the SFU Writer's Studio and the Vancouver Manuscript Intensive, where she worked with mentors Betsy Warland and Jen Currin. She is working on a book, *Letters to Rumi*.

SUE GOYETTE lives in Halifax and has published six books of poems and a novel. Her latest collection is *Penelope* (Gaspereau Press, 2017). She's been nominated for the 2014 Griffin Poetry Prize and the Governor General's Award and has won the CBC Poetry Prize, the Bliss Carman, Pat Lowther, J.M. Abraham and ReLit poetry awards and the 2015 Lieutenant Governor of Nova Scotia Masterworks Award for *Ocean*. Sue teaches in the Creative Writing Program at Dalhousie University.

LIZ HARMER is the author of the novel *The Amateurs*. Her award-winning writing has been published in *The New Quarterly*, *The Malahat Review*, the *Globe and Mail* and elsewhere. Her unpublished story collection was a finalist for the 2014 Flannery O'Connor Award for Short Fiction. Born and raised in Hamilton, Ontario, she now writes about madness, love, faith and other confusions in Riverside, California.

SHENIZ JANMOHAMED creates land art to leave behind for others to discover. An arts educator with an MFA in creative writing, Sheniz is inspired by language and learning and by collaboration rooted in compassion. The author of two books of poetry, *Bleeding Light* and *Firesmoke*, Sheniz is also the founder of *Questions for Ancestors*, a blog that encourages BIPOC writers and artists across Turtle Island to ask questions of their ancestors, and to listen for the answers.

PAM JOHNSON first entered the world of storytelling with acting in New York and, later, as a member of the Toronto Writers' Salon. A dedicated yoga and chi kung practitioner, the call of her Wild Soul finally took her west. Watch for this expat Calgarian on trails in Kananaskis Country and along coastal shorelines, exploring the intersection between body, breath, creativity and nature. Pam is honoured to be part of this collection.

TAMARA JONG is a Montreal-born, mixed-race writer of Chinese and European ancestry, who now lives in Guelph, Ontario. She has published in *Ricepaper*, *Room*, *The New Quarterly*, *Emerge 18* and *Invisiblog*, the official blog of Invisible Publishing, where she served as a guest editor. Tamara is a graduate of the Writer's Studio and part of the Room Collective.

JÓNÍNA KIRTON is a Red River Métis/Icelandic poet. Born in Portage la Prairie, Manitoba, she currently lives in the unceded territory of the Musqueam, Sḵwx̱wú7mesh and Tsleil-Waututh. She published her first collection of poetry, *page as bone ~ ink as blood*, at sixty. Her second book, *An Honest Woman*, was a finalist in the 2017 Dorothy Livesay Poetry Prize. Her interest in the stories of her Métis and Icelandic ancestors is the common thread throughout much of her writing.

AMANDA LEDUC is the author of the novels *The Miracles of Ordinary Men* and *The Centaur's Wife* (forthcoming). A mediocre violinist (and even more mediocre cellist) who is okay on piano, Amanda lives in Hamilton, Ontario, with a dog who once destroyed a manuscript but hasn't yet damaged the instruments. She still longs for God and slips between the spaces of things—knowing, not-knowing and everywhere in between.

KIRSTEEN MacLEOD is a writer and yoga teacher with a short fuse. Her first fiction collection, *The Animal Game*, was published in 2016. Now she's writing poetry about embodied life and a nonfiction book about the art of retreat, due out in 2020. Kirsteen sees red whenever people opine, "Anger isn't spiritual."

EMILY McKIBBON is a Hamilton-born, Barrie, Ontario–based curator and writer. She's won *The New Quarterly*'s Edna Staebler Personal Essay Contest, was a finalist for a National Magazine Award and was shortlisted for the Constance Rooke Creative Nonfiction Prize at *The Malahat Review*. Her chapbook *Notes on Photographs* was released by Baseline Press in 2016.

LORI McNULTY is a Vancouver-based writer, digital storyteller and world wanderer. Her writing has appeared in *The Fiddlehead*, *The New Quarterly*, PRISM *international*, *Dalhousie Review* and *Descant*. *Life on Mars*, her debut short fiction collection, was shortlisted for the Danuta Gleed Literary Award in 2018. Her nonfiction and fiction have been finalists for CBC Literary Prizes. She is now at work on a novel. Say hello at www.lorimcnulty.ca

LINDY MECHEFSKE is the award-winning author of *Out of Old Ontario Kitchens* (2018) and *Sir John's Table*. She is the food columnist for the *Kingston Whig-Standard* and blogs sporadically about her adventures in the kitchen at lindymechefske.com. Her passions include her family, a large shaggy dog, walking, hiking, eating, baking, cooking, foraging, pilgrimages and all manner of perennial edibles.

K.D. MILLER has published four collections of short stories, a novel and a book of personal essays. Her story collection *All Saints* was nominated for the Rogers Writers' Trust Fiction Prize and named one of the year's best books by the *Globe and Mail*. *Late Breaking*, her newest collection of stories, was published by Biblioasis in 2018.

ZARQA NAWAZ is the creator of the hit TV sitcom *Little Mosque on the Prairie*, which demystified Muslims for millions of people around the world by explaining how practising Muslims live their lives. The author of the best-selling memoir *Laughing All the Way to the Mosque*, about growing up Muslim in

Canada, is a frequent public speaker on Islam and comedy, gender and faith, and diversity in the media.

ALISON PICK is the author of *Strangers with the Same Dream* and *Far to Go*, which was longlisted for the Man Booker Prize. Her memoir *Between Gods* won the Canadian Jewish Book Award, was a finalist for the BC Award for Non-Fiction and a *Globe and Mail* Best Book of 2014. She won the 2002 Bronwen Wallace Award for most promising writer under thirty-five in Canada. In 2018 she celebrated becoming a first-time aunt, to her sister's new daughter, Tabitha Alice.

CHRISTINE POUNTNEY is the author of the critically acclaimed novels *Last Chance Texaco*, *The Best Way You Know How* and *Sweet Jesus*. She has written for the *Guardian*, *New York Times Magazine*, *The Walrus*, *Brick* and NUVO. Christine divides her time between writing, and her private therapy practice in Toronto.

HEIDI REIMER's short stories and essays have appeared in *Chatelaine*, *The New Quarterly*, *Little Fiction* and *Literary Mama*, and in the anthologies *The M Word: Conversations about Motherhood* and *Outcrops: Northeastern Ontario Short Stories*. Her work explores what it is to be female, the conflicting pulls of art and domesticity, and the struggle to break free of what we've been given to create what we yearn for. For news on her debut novel, see www.heidireimer.ca.

SIGAL SAMUEL's writing has appeared in *The Atlantic*, *The Daily Beast*, *The Rumpus*, *BuzzFeed*, *Electric Literature*, *Tablet*, *The Forward* and *The Walrus*, and on NPR, BBC and CBC. Her novel *The Mystics of Mile End*, which was nominated for the International Dublin Literary Award and won the fiction prize at the Canadian Jewish Literary Awards, deals with the intersection of mysticism, madness and mathematics.

AYELET TSABARI was born in Israel to a large family of Yemeni descent. Her first book, *The Best Place on Earth*, won the Sami Rohr Prize for Jewish Literature and was a *New York Times Book Review* Editors' Choice, and has been published internationally. Excerpts from her memoir, *The Art of Leaving*, have won a National Magazine Award, a Western Magazine Award and *The New Quarterly*'s Edna Staebler Award.

SANDY WABEGIJIG is an Odawa woman from Wikwemikong Unceded Territory, Manitoulin Island. She moved to the United States in the late sixties and returned to Canada in the mid-eighties. Her personal life includes a marriage to Dickey Betts of the Allman Brothers Band in the early 1970s. The union produced a daughter, Jessica. Sandy, who is often referred to as Sandy "Bluesky," is writing a memoir about her life in the sixties and seventies.

BETSY WARLAND has authored numerous creative nonfiction, lyric prose and poetry books. Her 2010 book of essays, *Breathing the Page: Reading the Act of Writing*, was a bestseller. Dedicated to supporting writers, Warland is a mentor, consultant and editor. She received the City of Vancouver Mayor's Award for Literary Excellence in 2016. In 2018, Lloyd Burritt's opera *The Art of Camouflage*, based on her memoir, *Oscar of Between* (2016), was given an in-development read-through. www.betsywarland.com

JULIA ZARANKIN is a writer and lecturer to lifelong learners in Toronto. Her writing has appeared in such publications as *The Walrus*, *The New Quarterly*, *Orion*, PRISM, *Threepenny Review*, *Antioch Review* and *Maisonneuve*. An unintentional birder and an aspiring birdsplainer, Julia now knows the whereabouts of most sewage lagoons in Southern Ontario.

Editor

Photo credit: Ron Grimes

SUSAN SCOTT works with artists, activists and scholars to release powerful, transgressive stories that inspire change. A lifelong passion for community-building and healing inform her collaborations, publishing and teaching in communities and classrooms, from life-story writing groups in the Colorado foothills to literature at St. Jerome's University and religion and the arts at Wilfrid Laurier University. Humanitarian arts initiatives she has led or been part of include the award-winning Walkerton Water Stories Project and Native-Immigrant's culture work in Montreal and Chile. She is the editor of *Stories in My Neighbour's Faith: Narratives from World Religions in Canada* and the author of *Temple in a Teapot*, which was launched on a thousand-mile road trip throughout the American West. Her stories and essays appear in books and magazines. Her next book, "Sainted Dirt," is a reckoning with land, language, family and imperfect teaware. Susan directs Write on the French River Creative Writing Retreat and is the nonfiction editor of *The New Quarterly* (TNQ). Email Susan at sscott@tnq.ca.